Sweet Surrender

Sweet Surrender

How Cultural Mandates Shape Christian Marriage

DENNIS HIEBERT

CASCADE *Books* · Eugene, Oregon

SWEET SURRENDER
How Cultural Mandates Shape Christian Marriage

Cascade Books
An Imprint of Wipf and Stock Publishers
199 W. 8th Ave., Suite 3
Eugene, OR 97401

www.wipfandstock.com

isbn 13: 978–1-60608–896-8

Cataloging-in-Publication data:

Hiebert, Dennis.

Sweet surrender : how cultural mandates shape Christian marriage / Dennis Hiebert.

xii + 268 p. ; cm. Includes bibliographical references and index.

isbn 13: 978–1-60608–896-8

1. Marriage—Religious aspects—Christianity. 2. Marriage—Social aspects. I. Title.

BV835 H45 2013

Manufactured in the U.S.A.

To Judy

No one is so terribly deceived as the one who does not suspect it.

—Søren Kierkegaard

About the Cover:
A white picket fence conventionally represents traditional, idyllic domestic life in Western society. Such fences are designed and constructed to add charm, to define boundaries, and to enclose inhabitants. Flawlessly aligned and unblemished, the white picket fence here remains as un-weathered as the blue sky is cloudless. Everything seems timeless, pure, and perfect. Too perfect—contrived, sterile, and suspiciously surreal.

Contents

List of Figures and Tables   viii

Acknowledgments   ix

Forms of Surrender   1

Reading Culture and the Bible   8

Mandate 1 **Mate Selection**   30
Should marital partners select each other?

Mandate 2 **Connectedness**   45
Should marriage be a separate social unit?

Mandate 3 **Calling**   62
Should our marriage be our primary calling in life?

Mandate 4 **Need Fulfillment**   78
Should our spouse be our primary source of personal need fulfillment?

Mandate 5 **Love**   94
Should marital love be romantic?

Mandate 6 **Intimacy**   112
Should the goal of marriage be intimacy?

Mandate 7 **Sex**   132
Should sex be primarily the pursuit of physical pleasure?

Mandate 8 **Conflict**   154
Should conflict in marriage be understood as relational weakness?

Mandate 9 **Dissolution**   174
Should marital dissolution be understood as personal failure?

Mandate 10 **Commitment**   195
Should marriage be a commitment to an institution?

Reclaiming Christian Marriage   211

Bibliography   223

Index   239

Figures and Tables

Figure 1   Sternberg's Triangular Theory of Love

Table 1   The Maltz Hierarchy of Sexual Interaction

Table 2   Balswick and Balswick's Styles of Conflict Management

Table 3   Attributions for Success or Failure

Table 4   Witte's Historical Stages of Marriage

Table 5   Balswick and Balswick's Types of Marital Commitment

Acknowledgments

I REMEMBER WELL THE author who, in his acknowledgments, observed that above all others, he needed to acknowledge himself, without whose help his graduate students could never have written the book. Most honest authors, I surmise, have a profound sense that they do not write alone, that they are merely the synthesizer and scribe whose fingers happen to be the last on the keyboard, and that theirs is simply the name and face at the end of an indeterminately long line of inputs. I cannot possibly acknowledge adequately all whose voice and wisdom are re-presented however inadequately here. I cannot even cop out and say "they know who they are," because they may not. I can only, as I must, name but a few.

I have taught a course in Marriage and Family at Providence University College in Canada for over twenty years, with visiting stops in Russia, Ukraine, Kenya, and other institutions along the way. First acknowledgment must therefore go to the administrators of Providence UC, who have not only granted me the professional opportunity to research, write, and teach, but more specifically granted me my most recent sabbatical leave, during which the skeleton of the following pages first came together. The many students over the years who absorbed the brunt of my pedagogical passions and helped me refine these ideas deserve equal salutation.

Other groups, forums, and conferences, such as the Association of Christians Teaching Sociology, have heard earlier, partial iterations of these ideas, and provided useful feedback. The most informative and formative feedback came from a benevolent and faithful cadre of readers who critiqued earlier drafts of chapters as I completed them. Al Thiessen, Kurt Armstrong, Scott Monsma, Michael Gilmour, Patti Parker, John McNeill, Al Hiebert, Marilyn Neufeld, Chris Summerville, and Jeff Wheeldon all read significant portions of the drafts and offered valuable comments and suggestions, each from their own unique perspective. All have enhanced what in its limitations remains mine.

Acknowledgments

My former student and now friend Jordan Ross exercised his attention to detail in providing invaluable editorial assistance. My colleague and friend Val Hiebert (no relation) served as the primary sounding board for the content as it took form and voice, and her more practical wisdom is woven throughout. She also buttressed my will whenever it wavered, and without her encouragement—no, insistence—that I write this book it may well not have happened.

My wife, Judy, has been the primary enabler of this project, being generous in time and space and support. That is probably true of the spouses of most writers, but doubly so when the topic is marriage. Judy has been my sole, personal, lived experience of marriage, not just the first reader of my thoughts on marriage. Despite initial misgivings about the project, her growing enthusiasm freed and fueled my own. This book is not our story, but it is now part of our story, and I could not be more grateful to her and for her, and for so much more.

PERMISSIONS

Sweet Surrender
Written by: Sarah McLachlan
© Sony/ATV Music Publishing LLC, Tyde Music. All rights administered by Sony/ATV Music Publishing LLC, 8 Music Square West, Nashville, TN 37203. All rights reserved. Used by permission.

"Brilliant Disguise" by Bruce Springsteen. Copyright © 1987 Bruce Springsteen (ASCAP). Reprinted by permission. International copyright secured. All rights reserved.

"Secret Garden" by Bruce Springsteen. Copyright © 1995 Bruce Springsteen (ASCAP). Reprinted by permission. International copyright secured. All rights reserved.

Song ID: 18544
Song Title: More Precious Than Silver
Witer(s): Lynn Deshazo
Label Copy:
Copyright © 1982 Integrity's Hosanna! Music (ASCAP) (adm. at EMICMGPublsihging.com) All rights reserved. Used by permission.
EMI CMG Percent Control: 100%
Song Rate: $40 per song

Forms of Surrender

HOW SWEET IT IS!

Walking into sweet surrender can be a rush. Sometimes the surrender is a day-long anticipation come true, sometimes an urge of the moment that you cannot subdue. When shared with your favorite people, you can justify it as the fostering of friendship. When indulged alone, you can justify it as a reward richly deserved, or dismiss it as a harmless weakness. Either way, you've given in. So you abandon yourself, just for a moment, to the sensual pleasure, the emotional release, the inexplicable comfort. The stress of the day eases away. For a few sweet seconds, nothing else matters. Just this rapturous relief. Just this delicious delight. Just this fleeting feeling. It is inconceivable that such heavenly bliss could be anything but good. Who wouldn't love it? Who wouldn't surrender? It seems so natural, so universal, and, well, just meant to be. It must be one of God's good little gifts to us all. So you take just a few more bites. After all, the mini chocolate éclairs were undoubtedly made especially for you.

CANDY STORES TARGETING CHILDREN do not apologize for the high sugar content of their products, nor do they acknowledge the compelling reasons to resist them. Conversely, dessert specialty shops targeting adults know they must counter the sometimes vague sense of guilt they induce in their salivating customers. More than one such bakery is called Sweet Surrender. The not-so-subtle invitation is to yield to something sweet, and the not-so-subtle implication is that the act of surrender itself is sweet. Indeed, "sweet," in contemporary idiom, has come to mean good in any sense. To good of any kind, we say "Sweet!" The notion of sweet surrender seems then to be oxymoronic, because people do not ordinarily hold out against good. Only evil must surrender to the good. And surrender itself can only be good if the surrender is *to* the good.

But despite its delectable taste, sugar is no unqualified good. Sugar is in the category of drug foods that includes coffee, tea, cocoa, alcohol, and tobacco, foods that deaden hunger pangs and stimulate effort without providing nutrition, and do so cheaply. As any chocoholic will attest, sugar is at least equally psychologically addicting. To be addicted is to need a drug to maintain a sense of well-being and avoid withdrawal symptoms. To become addicted is to lose control, to become preoccupied and obsessed, and to continue despite negative consequences. The personal consequences of current sugar addiction include historically unprecedented rates of mood disorders, tooth decay, obesity, and adult-onset diabetes.

Furthermore, our craving for sugar is not natural, it is cultural. Foods and the tastes they cultivate are one of the primary variants of human cultures, as evidenced by the apprehension occasioned by being served an exotic food. Abstaining from soft drinks for a year and then trying to consume an entire can reveals the unnaturalness of a "sweet tooth." Our extreme collective appetite for sugar has in fact been acquired over time, accelerated by the European colonization of the Americas and by the rise of international capitalism. It turns out that our modern habits of sugar consumption have a very particular history, telling of the political, economic, and social forces that constructed them. Those forces combined to convert a luxury good believed to have health benefits into a commonplace necessity with harmful health consequences. In the process, it contributed greatly to labor exploitation, environmental degradation, and personal deterioration.[1] Our surrender to sugar has been neither sweet nor merely personal. As good and natural as it tastes and feels, sugar is more than a "sweet" physical substance. It is a historical-cultural story begging to be told and critiqued.

SURRENDERING THE BODY

There are other physical forms of sweet surrender. I am writing this in the evening of a day in which I failed to finish running a full marathon. I had already conquered the 26.2-mile course over 10 years ago, when I was 50 years of age. I don't know why I thought I needed to do it again. Today, many others didn't know either. The organizers shut the race down when the heat and humidity index shot from their code green, past yellow and red, directly to white hot in 15 minutes. Sweep buses were sent to clear runners off the course. Despite feeling strong through the first few miles, about two-thirds through the course I fought fiercely for a few miles until my will sweetly surrendered, in deference to my aging body, which had already succumbed

1. Mintz, *Sweetness and Power.*

to the elements. Giving in felt good. It was undoubtedly the right thing to do. I didn't have to kill myself. But it was a death of sorts.

Literal death in old age is not losing everything, it is just letting go of the little we still have left. We have by then been letting go of many things for many years, as I did today. I doubt I'll ever again attempt to replicate the fabled run of the soldier from the Battle of Marathon to Athens to proclaim Greek victory as he collapsed in death. When death is a prolonged passage, Kubler-Ross famously claimed that it goes through stages of denial, anger, bargaining, depression, and acceptance.[2] The last phase is perhaps the ultimate sweet surrender, but only if we construe the stages of death through our religious and cultural lens. Death in Hindu culture, for example, with its notions of reincarnation, will feel and mean something very different. Some would argue that sexual orgasm is the ultimate sweet surrender. The French have a rather androcentric phrase for it: *la petite mort*—the little death. Medieval Europeans believed that a male lost one day of his life for every time he ejaculated. This too is a cultural meaning given to a physical experience. The human experience of physical forms of sweet surrender, be it to our taste buds, our failed endeavors, our sexuality, or even our death, is profoundly shaped by human history and culture.

SURRENDERING THE SELF

Non-physical forms of surrender are often more immediately ambivalent experiences. Surrendering to a person or relationship, instead of a physical want or need, is a more social psychological dynamic, and that much more indeterminate. Surrendering to a life circumstance, or life itself, is often even a spiritual or existential experience. Listening to Sarah McLachlan's "Sweet Surrender" is a bittersweet, melancholy mix of both.[3] We first notice the strong allusions to interpersonal relationships in the lyrics. "You take me in / No questions asked . . . / I only hope / That I won't disappoint you / When I'm down here / On my knees / I miss everything (about you)."[4] But then we watch the music video[5] and fail to find an "other" with whom to be in relationship. There are only dream-like, almost immaterial images of

2. Kubler-Ross, *On Death and Dying*.

3. There may be almost as many different songs entitled "Sweet Surrender" as there are pastry shops. John Denver's lyrics have a markedly different and buoyant mood of living without care, at one with nature.

4. Sarah McLachlan, "Sweet Surrender," *Surfacing* (1998).

5. http://www.metacafe.com/watch/sy-25142306/sarah_mclachlan_sweet_surrender_official_music_video/

the singer and her own corpse fading in and out. The relationship at issue then seems to be only to self, and surrender ultimately to life itself, not in an indulgent manner, but in acquiescence to who one is and what life is. The (post)modern self is constantly in flux; we can die and be reborn socio-psychologically several times within our physical lifetime, living a series of identities. Each new self must acknowledge the past, because we can never entirely escape the haunting multiple senses of self we leave behind. The still twitching corpse in the video, not fully dead, never leaves the singer's side. The meaning of it all is entirely elusive, if not illusive. The existential refrain that both opens and closes the song laments that "It doesn't mean much / It doesn't mean anything at all." In the end, "Sweet, sweet surrender / Is all that I have to give." The twists and turns of life, and our relentlessly morphing sense of self, cannot be managed or resisted. All we can do is give in.

The most common form of non-physical surrender remains that of one person to another. Most Western individualists recoil at the thought. Surrender is understood to be what conquered countries do in war, or what cornered criminals do to police. But interpersonal surrender, our Western social norms tell us, is surely a psychological pathology. Subordination or submission yes, but surrender, never! To *subordinate* is to place oneself or another in a lower position in a hierarchal order. To *submit* is to yield to the legitimate authority of another person. To *surrender* is to give oneself up completely into the power and possession of another. Yet the hierarchical social structures that make subordination and submission appropriate, such as relations between management and labor, or parent and child, tend also to facilitate inappropriate surrender occasionally. Bosses sometimes harass employees, parents sometimes abuse children. Nevertheless, it is not the surrender of one individual to another that is most common and problematic. It is the surrender of one whole category of people to another, regardless of the merits of the individual, that is most troublesome. Class, race, gender, and age are primary categorical forms of social inequality, and surrender predicated on any one of them begs ethical scrutiny.

Surrender is sweet when it feels good and natural. But as sweet as it feels to surrender to sugar, doing so is in fact dangerous, not good. And our craving for sweets is culturally induced, not natural. Other forms of surrender—to self, to other, to society, to life itself—may feel just as sweet, but often prove to be equally unnatural and unhealthy. The act of surrender itself may feel sweet at times, but it is not always good, because that to which we surrender may not be good, or because we may be surrendering to something other than what we think. For Christians to "surrender all to Jesus" is indeed good and sweet, but what if we are actually surrendering to something else? What if we are actually surrendering to culture coming to us in the guise of Christianity? What if we are merely surrendering to cultural conventions instead of the call of God? The two may coincide at times, but we are warned of mindlessly conflating them, and called to the mental effort required to keep them separate. "Do not be conformed to this world, but be transformed by the renewing of your minds, so that you may discern what is the will of God" (Rom 12:2). This is the only sure means and measure of maintaining personal and interpersonal health.

OVERVIEW OF THE BOOK

Traditionally, marriage has been understood as the state of being united to a person of the opposite sex as husband or wife in a consensual and contractual relationship recognized by law.[6] More informally, marriage in Western culture is experienced as the union of sweethearts, the term of endearment revealing much about what and how we think of marriage. Christians in Western culture actively seek to base their thinking about marriage on what they understand the Bible teaches about it. Yet their thinking has already been formed passively by what their culture has led them to believe about marriage. If they cannot effectively distinguish the directives of one source from the other, they are vulnerable and prone to conflating them. The thesis of this book is that many Christians frequently mistake what their culture teaches them about marriage for what the Bible teaches about marriage. Wittingly or unwittingly, many Christians surrender to culture on significant aspects of marriage, and furthermore, take as biblical what is merely cultural. Because this Christian surrender to culture feels so sweet, natural, and healthy, it is rarely questioned or challenged, even when its consequences are anything but healthy. The task of this book is to take up that challenge.

The second chapter overviews the nature of culture. Gender is used as an example of how both culture and the Bible shape Western Christian thinking on a central aspect of marriage, and how culture factors into reading the Bible. Ancient and contemporary mandates of marriage are compared, with Jesus serving as a model for Christian engagement with culture on gender. The body of the book that follows is organized around ten questions on ten different aspects of marriage. Each succeeding chapter identifies a different cultural mandate of marriage, assesses relative Christian concurrence with the mandate, and rethinks the mandate in light of the biblical text. The mandates include how marriage is formed, connected, valued, pursued, characterized, focused, energized, troubled, ended, and

---

6. To include same-sex marriage, "of the opposite sex as husband or wife" is simply deleted.

perceived—virtually every aspect of marriage. The purpose of each chapter is to ascertain whether Christians have surrendered to culture on the particular issue and, if so, whether that surrender has been sweet.

Mandate 1: Mate Selection examines how marital couples are formed. The historical evolution of couple formation from arranged marriages to self-selected marriages is explored, before evaluating current dating and mating practices. *Mandate 2: Connectedness* examines how marriage is connected to its social environment. The ramifications for marriage of the historical shift from the premodern to the modern world are explored, before wrestling with issues of individualism and communalism with regard to marriage. *Mandate 3: Calling* examines how marriage is valued. The historical and cultural development of current "family values" that put "family first" is explored, before evaluating them in light of what Jesus said about marriage and family. *Mandate 4: Need Fulfillment* examines how marriage is pursued. The basic human needs best met by marriage compared to other sources of need fulfillment are explored, before evaluating how realistic and healthy it is to expect spouses to be the primary source of need fulfillment. *Mandate 5: Love* examines how marriage is characterized. The dimensions, components, kinds, and correlates of love are explored, before describing the origins and portrayal of romantic love in popular culture, and questioning its role in Christian marriage.

Mandate 6: Intimacy examines how marriage is focused. Notions of the self and identity that undergird intimacy and the role of communication in intimacy are explored, before assessing the extent to which and the basis on which Christians have made intimacy the goal of marriage. *Mandate 7: Sex* examines how marriage is energized. The history of Christian thought about sex, the formation of personal sexuality, and the rise of the pleasure principle of sex are all explored, before suggesting the meanings that sex can communicate, and how it is best understood biblically. *Mandate 8: Conflict* examines how marriage is troubled. The social sources and dynamics of interpersonal power and conflict are explored, before describing how conflict and its effects are managed in different kinds and stages of marriage. *Mandate 9: Dissolution* examines how marriage is ended. Biblical perspectives of divorce, social causes of divorce, and theoretical explanations for both individual divorce and divorce rates are explored, before reviewing Christian assessments and interventions. *Mandate 10: Commitment* examines how marriage is perceived. Marriage is understood as a social institution, and its evolution through Christian history is traced. The notion of marriage as a covenant is explored, before considering exactly to what it is that a married person is best committed.

The closing section offers some final reflections on Christian embeddedness in culture, and some suggested ways forward for enculturated Christian marriage, without prescribing in any detail how to proceed. The chapters or mandates can be read independently if the reader is only interested in selected topics; there is sufficient analysis in each discussion for it to be understood on its own. Of course, they are best read in sequence, as there is a steady accumulation of concepts and references to previous mandates that enable the fullest comprehension and contemplation of the respective issues. Each chapter includes a less than equal balance of analysis at both the micro, personal level and the macro, societal level. The topics of the chapters progress from the less familiar to the more familiar, so readers should prepare to be challenged early.

Though I am a professor of sociology in a Christian university, I am not writing here primarily to other scholars in a manner intended to advance scholarship on the issues, or engage in academic debates according to academic protocol. I am writing instead to all contemplative Christians interested in rethinking marriage in a manner they likely have not done before, and assuming they have no background in sociology. I write as a white, middle-class, Canadian of Mennonite heritage, though I have never been a member of a Mennonite church. Raised in the evangelical tradition, I have been a Christ-follower, a person of varying depths of Christian faith, my entire life. I came upon sociology only in midlife and, finding it more illuminating than other academic disciplines I had sampled, have devoted my professional life to employing its perspectives in engaging other sojourners. Finally, I write primarily as a man who married a woman at twenty-two years of age, and fully expects one of us one day to bury the other as having been our closest companion through life. What follows is by no means an implicit account of my marriage to Judy, but it is also no doubt informed by it, as well as the marriages of family, friends, and foreigners I have been privileged to observe, listen to, and learn from.

Reading Culture and the Bible

MARRIAGE IS AN INTENSELY personal experience, but it is not an entirely private one. There are powerful social forces that shape Christian marriage relationships, irrespective of what any particular couple may desire for themselves. Indeed, their desires will already be largely a product of those social forces. The two most powerful are culture and the Bible; marriage is both a cultural construct and a biblical construct. On one hand, marriage has been a foundational social unit in almost all human societies, including those with no trace of Christianity in their culture. On the other hand, marriage is also endorsed in the Bible, and because Christians take it as authoritative, they seek to base their marriages on biblical principles, regardless of what their culture may say. Of course, some entire cultures have been shaped by Christianity, as one of the fascinating threads of especially Western history reveals. But influence weaves both ways, and culture is at least as capable of shaping Christianity in return, including Christian concepts of marriage. Many Christians do not recognize the breadth and depth of cultural influence on marriage, and consequently are unknowingly and unintentionally guided more by their culture than their Bible. Of greater concern is that they mistake the cultural for the biblical in the process.

To understand how cultural mandates shape Christian marriage requires a more than cursory comprehension of both culture and the Bible. One way of doing so is to view them both as texts to be read. The Bible is obviously a text in the traditional sense. The academic field of biblical hermeneutics is devoted to examining the words and interpreting the meanings of the biblical text, and biblical scholarship more generally examines the various contexts in which the Bible has been produced, distributed, and received. To read or decode a text is the active process of making sense of it, always only in one social context or another. All texts can be interpreted in a variety of ways and generate a range of meanings. As much as possible, the meaning intended by the author of a text should constrain its interpretation, but authorial intent, being as elusive as it is, cannot control reader reception. Possible interpretations of a text include a dominant reading that is accepted by most readers, negotiated readings that accept only some of what is presented, or alternative readings that oppose the preferred or dominant reading.[1]

How the Bible is read and regarded is shaped by the cultural context in which it is read. For example, assertions of the inerrancy of the Bible were evidence of how "the rationalism of the Enlightenment infected even those who were battling against it."[2] Insistence on the infallibility of the Bible was a reaction to liberal modernism and the Roman Catholic insistence on papal infallibility. In recent years, readings of the Bible have become polarized to the point where one eminent biblical scholar has catalogued the misreadings of the "right" and the misreadings of the "left."[3] One particularly problematic reading of the Bible is biblicism, "a theory about the Bible that emphasizes together its exclusive authority, infallibility, perspicuity, self-sufficiency, internal consistency, self-evident meaning, and universal applicability."[4] At the level of popular culture, such a reading reduces the biblical text to a compendium of doctrines and morals that together comprise a holy how-to handbook or instruction manual for Christian living. Regarding marriage, it leads to books such as *Holding Hands, Holding Hearts: Recovering a Biblical View of Christian Dating*[5] and *God's Blueprint for Building Marital Intimacy.*[6]

Culture is itself a "text" to be "read." In the academic field of semiology, texts are not limited to words or images on a page or screen, but include anything that represents an idea or communicates a message. So while the Bible is a verbal text, coffee, for example, is a nonverbal text. Like the sweet surrender to sugar described earlier, coffee has become engrained in Western culture to where it is far more than a brown liquid drug. It is a text that represents Western popular culture in profound ways.[7] "Going for coffee" can mean many things depending on the context, including not drinking it. It represents a complex and contradictory set of social rituals from relaxation to stimulation, from social engagement to solitude. Like sugar, coffee has a long political and economic history of first colonization and now globalization, of an exploitative divide between the quality of life

1. O'Shaughnessy and Stadler, *Media and Society.*
2. Wright, *Simply Christian*, 183.
3. Wright, *Scripture and the Authority of God.*
4. Smith, *Bible Made Impossible*, viii.
5. Phillips and Phillips, *Holding Hands, Holding Hearts.*
6. Jackson and Turner, *God's Blueprint for Building Marital Intimacy.*
7. O'Brien and Szeman, *Popular Culture.*

of producers in the Global South and consumers in the Global North. In the urbane ambience of pricey Starbucks, the largest coffeehouse company in the world, coffee signifies the creative, sophisticated, educated, middle-class individualism of consumer choice. In the folksy atmosphere of thrifty Tim Horton's, Canada's largest fast food service known for coffee and donuts, coffee signifies the comfortable, ordered, uniform, working-class traditionalism of family values. Starbucks supports free trade, Tim Horton's supports the military. The same simple substance signifies different things.

Coffee and donuts are also a staple of the warm fellowship in church foyers and small groups, and as such represent a melding of Christian and cultural texts. The relationship between texts, the way they interconnect, interweave, and interact with one another, is known as intertextuality.[8] In effect, culture is simply a web of intertexts, the power of which blurs the boundaries between individual texts. So Christian and cultural texts often knowingly borrow and refer to each other, shaping each other in the process. The danger is that one might be entirely lost in the other. Any one text that is known, explicitly or implicitly, by a whole group of people, and functions as an overriding text that informs a society, becomes a social text. *The Encyclopedic Dictionary of Semiotics, Media, and Communication* actually uses "the Christian social text" as an example in its definition of a social text,[9] referring to the bygone era of Christendom. Enhanced literacy enables us to read texts, recognize social texts, and retrace intertextualities sufficiently well to reveal social forces, and to choose our allegiances and course in life. To grasp adequately how cultural mandates shape Christian marriage requires both a biblical and cultural literacy sufficient to read well the texts of both culture and the Bible.

If and when Christians mistake cultural mandates of marriage as biblical mandates, it is precisely because the boundaries of the two texts have become so blurred that they become indistinguishable. To alter the metaphor, it is precisely in contexts where there is no longer tension at territorial boundaries, where there are no border skirmishes, that a sweet surrender occurs quietly. To press the political and military metaphor further, perhaps the relational dynamic is not so much one surrendering to the other as one annexing or colonizing the other. Each implies different levels of force used, relationship established, and identity retained, but it is clearly not a peace treaty of mutual non-interference. There is good evidence to suggest that the influence of culture and the Bible on Christian marriage has not been equal.

8. Watson, Hill, and Watson, *Dictionary of Media and Communication Studies.*

9. Danesi, *Encyclopedic Dictionary of Semiotics, Media, and Communication.*

Before embarking on our examination of specific aspects of marriage, shaped however unequally by both culture and the Bible, it is necessary to illuminate the character of culture, the components of culture, and the various functions those components perform. The question of gender will serve as an instructive case study of how both culture and the Bible are formative of a central aspect of marriage. Gender will also raise further questions of the role of culture in the Bible itself, and the challenge for contemporary readers to distinguish between what is cultural and what is transcultural in the biblical text. An overview of ancient and contemporary mandates of marriage will then demonstrate the historical and cultural diversity of Judeo-Christian marital practices. Jesus will be seen to model a certain engagement with his culture. And we will be led to ponder our cultural and Christian fidelities and infidelities.

MOTHER CULTURE

When we read the biblical text, we are reading through the lens of our own culture about another culture very foreign to ours, seeking to hear the Word of God despite its written form being in the context of that other culture. We dare not equate either our own culture or the culture of the text with the Word of God. The challenge always is to keep them as separate as we can, recognizing that we are seeing through our own cultural lenses, just as the original writers were seeing through theirs. If we are not mindful of this, we inadvertently surrender to one culture or another, losing the possibility of discerning the call of God that transcends cultures. Culture is a collective definition and interpretation of reality that produces a whole way of life, a whole design for living. As the sum total of the heritage of a people, and a system of shared meaning and behavior, it can sound like the call of God because it is so comprehensive and compelling. Though humans alter their physical environment, it is essentially given to them. But they construct their social environment. Culture is created and sustained by human social interaction, and each individual acquires a measure of it through the process of social learning, not through the biological or psychological unfolding of "nature." We may be born of Mother Earth, but we are nurtured by Mother Culture, and in the classic nature-nurture debate, nurture plays a much more powerful role in shaping who we become.

Of special interest here are three particular components of culture. Cultural *knowledge* is what a culture holds to be true about the world, cultural *values* are shared ideas about what is desirable in the world, and cultural *norms* are shared rules of personal conduct in the world.[10] Different cultures have astonishingly different stocks of knowledge, assessments of good, and patterns of behavior—the variety is astounding, and a testament to the creativity that is part of the image of God in humans. Theories, beliefs, customs, and all kinds of collective ideas become unquestioned over time, taken for granted when transmitted in culture. A way of handling a challenge, such as mate selection, becomes *the* way of handling that challenge collectively. Cultural knowledge, values, and norms are usually grounded in what are known as cultural myths, which are not simply falsehoods or untruths in the sense that "myth" is conventionally understood. In effect, they are quite the opposite. Cultural myths are dramatic narratives that convey powerful truths about how those who tell them see the world, whether or not their factuality can be determined. Folk tales, for example, consist of truth-telling stories, even if they are not necessarily true stories; they tell us *what* in the big picture is true, even if the narrative itself is not literally true. As further example, all cultures and religions have some kind of creation myth, some story of how the world began. The Judeo-Christian creation myth is contained in the book of Genesis, which tells us that God originated the world and filled it with meaning and purpose. Whether every detail of the Genesis narrative is historically and scientifically accurate is unclear, unintended, unlikely, and ultimately of significantly lesser importance than that "God did it."[11] The details of whether God created the world in six literal twenty-four-hour days, was the intelligent designer, or used evolution as the method (theistic evolution) is debated among Christians.

Cultural myths perform at least two important social functions. First, pertaining to knowledge, they provide a worldview or way of seeing, even if they are not historically or scientifically true in every concrete detail. They are belief systems that help people understand the nature of the cosmos, the purpose and meaning of life, and the origin and role of evil and suffering. This is clearly evident in the Christian creation myth. Second, pertaining to values and norms, by creating the reality out of which the individual lives, cultural myths facilitate social control, or the control of the individual's thoughts, feelings, and behaviors by the group. In our example, the thematic

10. Other components of culture include our collective symbols (like language), forms of expression (like art), ideologies (a coherent set of interrelated ideas and ideals that explain and justify the prevailing distribution of power, wealth, and privilege), and technologies (methods of using physical resources to pursue values). All of these components are generally non-material culture, except for technology, which is mostly material culture, and often deemed the most powerful component. Postman argues in *Technopoly: The Surrender of Culture to Technology*, that technology has overridden non-material culture in contemporary society.

11. Fischer, *God Did It, But How?*

truths of the Christian creation myth constrain how Christians ought to live, such as our notions of stewardship of the earth. Cultural myths are not just narratives that provide knowledge. They provide values and norms that together become the imperatives by which we live, the mandates that compel human thought and action. A mandate is an authoritative command, and a cultural mandate is what culture directs us to think and do.

This second function of cultural myths as cultural mandates is the sense in which the term has been used in two recent book titles, not coincidentally connected to matters of marriage. The better known is *The Beauty Myth*, in which Naomi Wolf examines how idealized concepts of female beauty function as a demand and judgment on women in Western culture.[12] The site of patriarchal oppression has shifted from the socioeconomic realm to women's own bodies, as they are pressured to conform to impossible standards, and are kept under control by the weight of their own insecurities. The more recent title is *The Purity Myth*, in which Jessica Valenti examines how cultural obsession with virginity hurts women by reducing their moral status and agency to a question of sexual abstinence.[13] Excessive focus on chastity at the expense of virtues such as honesty, kindness, and altruism places a young woman's worth not on her beauty, but on whether she has "lost" her sexual value. In both book titles, "myth" means a cultural imperative or mandate.

Every new person born or brought into a group or society will be taught its cultural myths and mandates. He or she will develop a sense of self according to the conceptions of that society, and acquire the knowledge, values, and motivations required for participation in social life. She or he will internalize the culture of the group, and in effect carry that society around in their head like a monitor. As such, each of us surrenders to our culture long before we are aware of it. In truth, we have no choice, and would suffer meaningless, valueless, and normless lives if we did. The only question is whether we will at some point rise up and question or challenge it.

THE CASE OF GENDER

Perhaps the most common form of categorical interpersonal surrender mandated by culture is that of gender, the subordination of women to men throughout history. When the marital status of wife and husband is added to the general social inequality of the sexes, the term and dynamic of choice has traditionally been submission. But sometimes outright surrender is still urged as the sweetest, most virtuous, and most pragmatic posture a wife can

12. Wolf, *Beauty Myth*.
13. Valenti, *Purity Myth*.

take in relation to her husband. Laura Doyle, in her bestselling *The Surrendered Wife*, explicitly instructs married women never to instruct their husbands in any way, and never to correct, much less criticize, their husbands in any manner. A self-described former shrew and feminist, Doyle tells wives that they are to act as if they respect their husbands, whether they actually do or not, and apologize profusely if they ever roll their eyes. Interestingly, one printing of the book is subtitled *A Practical Guide to Finding Intimacy, Passion, and Peace with a Man*,[14] thereby supposedly pointing out both what women want and what is difficult to achieve. Apparently intimacy does not require the authenticity of self-disclosure, and peace can only be achieved by surrendering. A different printing of the book is subtitled *A Woman's Spiritual Guide to True Intimacy with a Man*.[15] Apparently the surrender of authenticity, dignity, and ultimately a sense of her own self is the spiritual calling for wives. Driven by deep desires for close personal relationship, wives are called to become pragmatically manipulative. Surrender becomes tactical, and holy, made sacred by the relational sweetness it delivers.

Of course, the subordination, submission, or surrender of wives to husbands is as entrenched in human cultures and religions as any interpersonal relational principle could be. Some degree of patriarchy, in which males rule females, is universal; matriarchy has never been documented in human history.[16] The sacred texts of most religions are routinely read in such a way as to require patriarchy, and Christians have certainly been no exception. For example, between founding several international Christian ministry organizations and authoring numerous bestselling books, Bruce Wilkinson produced a video series on Christian marriage entitled *A Biblical Portrait of Marriage*.[17] In explaining "Helper: The Role of the Wife," Wilkinson interprets verses from Genesis to be saying that God intended wives to be helpers, not companions, and that the husband was to define the exact kind of help he needed. He claims that contemporary Western society has moved ever further away from what is taught in the biblical text, to where, in his on-stage physical dramatization of the distance, the Bible is "here" and society is "way over there." The church, he declares, is tucked up tight to society, far from God's call. He then follows with the familiar exhortation to turn away from culture and follow God's blueprint of gender hierarchy in marriage. In explaining "Submitting: The Responsibility of the

14. Doyle, *Surrendered Wife: A Practical Guide*.

15. Doyle, *Surrendered Wife: A Woman's Spiritual Guide*.

16. Some societies have practised matricentricity, the centrality of women in society without necessarily the rule by women of society. See Marilyn French, *Beyond Power*.

17. One of Wilkinson's bestselling books is *The Prayer of Jabez*. The video series is Wilkinson, *Biblical Portrait of Marriage*.

Wife," Wilkinson interprets various New Testament texts to stress that husbands are never told to make their wives submit, but rather, wives are told to submit themselves to their husbands. It is her responsibility to organize herself underneath him, not his to demand it. And Wilkinson is not shy about specifying the terms of a submission that in truth sounds more like surrender. She is to submit with joy, in everything, without a word, in fear, and with a gentle and quiet spirit. She is told that if she gives herself up completely into the power and possession of her husband, she will be sweet in the eyes of her husband, and God.

Pastor/comedian Mark Gungor's video series on Christian marriage, *Laugh Your Way to a Better Marriage*,[18] is a cruder combination of Doyle's manipulative surrender and Wilkinson's sweet surrender. There could hardly be a more blatant Christian legitimation of male power and privilege relative to females. In his hypersexualized and altogether demeaning analysis of marital relations, husbands are only interested in the "happy place" of their wife's anatomy, and would "otherwise have nothing to do with her." They are to remember that their sexual urges are a reminder from God "to be nice to the woman." Men are simple and single-minded sluggards who can only be coaxed off the couch to clean the garage by wives withholding sex from them; otherwise they will do nothing. Yet wives must keep their husbands sexually satisfied to prevent them from going elsewhere "after the second or third refusal," and because "it is very difficult for a sexually frustrated man to worship God." Women are fools to surrender their sexuality to a man before securing the commitment of marriage, and they have essentially no sexual desire of their own within marriage, unless aroused by their husband. What Gungor apparently cannot comprehend is that when a woman's sexuality is reduced to the only means of securing commitment from a man, the only mechanism of coercing a husband to action, or the guilt-ridden obligation to facilitate her husband's spirituality, it is no surprise that she becomes alienated from her own sexuality. It becomes a tactical tool to be used prudently, not a deep dimension of who she is as a person. Such surrender of sexuality becomes bittersweet at best, a humiliating, self-betraying means to an end.

COMPLEMENTARIANS AND EGALITARIANS

So is female subordination, submission, or surrender a case of God's will made manifest in nature, or is it an optional product of human culture? We certainly see extensive evidence of gender hierarchy in all human cultures and history, and in our sacred texts. Did God intend for humans to be unequal based on

18. Gungor, *Laugh Your Way to a Better Marriage*.

their sex, and then set about to create males and females as totally "other" opposites to ensure male privilege and power? Or is gender inequality a social dynamic that humans have created, and enacted, and legitimated to the point where it feels natural, and therefore inevitable? Why are males and females the way they are? Where does their difference come from? What should the social consequence of that difference be? Have we merely received and obeyed our sacred texts and created the culture they prescribe, or have we made sacred what human culture has already produced? That is, have we allowed biblical values to shape our culture, or have we taken cultural values and read them into the Bible, domesticating God's Word in the process? Is the Bible free of cultural elements, speaking to us from beyond human influence? How should we read it? Are traditional gender relations biblical or cultural? What does God really want? Gender surrender can lead to some very big questions about self, and society, and the sacred.

The past few decades have seen evangelicals split into two camps on the question of gender, based primarily on how to read the Bible relative to culture. Those who advocate the clear headship and submission and division of labor of traditional gender roles in marriage, church, and society are represented by the Council of Biblical Manhood and Womanhood.[19] They contend that God created men and women to be equal in value, worth, and dignity, but different in function and role. Men are seen as instrumental heads of the home who naturally lead, while women are seen as expressive hearts of the home who naturally follow. Theirs is a more literal reading of Scripture because they interpret a text without taking its cultural context into account, which then becomes a pretext for applying it in a direct manner. They label themselves as "complementarians," because men and women are seen to complete each other, and though that is true of their view, it conceals the defining characteristic of their view, which is the hierarchy explicit within it. For organizations like Focus on the Family and Promise Keepers, female submission is a sweet and biblical surrender.

Those who advocate for the abolition of predetermined gender roles in marriage, church, and society are represented by Christians for Biblical Equality.[20] They contend that in Christ there is no longer any moral

19. CBMW's main statement of their position is Piper and Grudem, *Recovering Biblical Manhood and Womanhood: A Response to Evangelical Feminism*. Their website is at http://www.cbmw.org/.

20. CBE's main statement of their position is Ronald W. Pierce et al., *Discovering Biblical Equality: Complementarity Without Hierarchy*. This book is clearly designed to counter the 1991 printing of Piper and Grudem's *Recovering Biblical Manhood and Womanhood*; the titles, size, and cover design are almost identical. CBE's website is at http://www.cbeinternational.org/.

or theological justification for permanently granting or denying a person status, privilege, or prerogative solely on the basis of that person's sex ("neither male nor female"), race ("Jew nor Gentile"), or socioeconomic status ("slave nor free") (Gal 3:28). While they view the sexes as different, they advocate shared authority and equal opportunity in marriage, church, and society. Their reading of Scripture takes into account the androcentricity, or male-centeredness, of a text written by and to men and interpreted by and for men,[21] in a patriarchal culture in which allowing for anything else would have been incomprehensible. The Bible is inspired and authoritative for all times and places and peoples, but must be understood as an enculturated text if it is to be interpreted properly. It was, after all, written from a particular cultural location. Like complementarians, they too advocate complementarity, but with equality, not with hierarchy based on sex, and therefore label themselves as "egalitarians," meaning those who hold to the equality of human rights and opportunities in every social dimension, including gender. They maintain that God's kingdom leaves no room for ascribed, comprehensive, permanent authority of one person over another. Any such surrender is anything but sweet.

The middle ground between the two camps is occupied by what Wilcox termed "soft patriarchs," and is characterized by slippage between belief and behavior, a contradiction between gender theology and gender practice.[22] These are Christians who hold to hierarchical principles of male headship and female submission, but nevertheless practice pragmatic egalitarian relations in everyday life. These "iconic new men" are emotionally involved in marriage and parenting, expressing gratitude for their wives and being affectionate with their children, but are not practically involved in the housework still assigned to wives in a traditional gendered division of labor. "[C]onservative Protestantism domesticates men by linking male authority to a demanding ethic of male familial involvement. It offers men a 'patriarchal bargain' that accords men symbolic authority in the home in return for the exercise of greater responsibility for the well-being of their families."[23] Gallagher's data also revealed a careful distinction "between men's responsibility *for* their family and men's taking responsibility *in* their family," and a proclivity to "seeing themselves as responsible for spiritual

---

21. For example, the Tenth Commandment is a list of property owned by men, including wives: "You shall not covet your neighbor's house; you shall not covet your neighbor's wife, or male or female slave, or ox, or donkey, or anything that belongs to your neighbor" (Exod 20:17).

22. Wilcox, *Soft Patriarchs, New Men*.

23. Wilcox quoted in Allen, "Patriarchal Bargain," 43.

leadership, even if they are not doing the job."[24] She concluded that, despite being disregarded in practice, the idea of gender hierarchy persists among evangelicals because it functions as a symbolic boundary of identity. The duplicity is regrettable.

CULTURAL AND TRANSCULTURAL

In all matters concerning the cultural, one of the first tasks of biblical hermeneutics is to ascertain what is cultural and what is transcultural in the text. Cultural aspects of the text are those understood to be limited to the culture of the writer, bound to place and time, and are therefore no longer mandatory. Head covering for women is a simple concrete example. Transcultural aspects of the text are those understood to apply to all cultures as universally normative and timeless, and therefore remain mandatory. Love of God and neighbor is a clear example. To welcome people warmly is a transcultural Christian ethic. To greet them with a holy kiss is a cultural practice, more likely to offend people in North America today, if not lead to charges of sexual harassment. Literally "doing the text" may actually violate the intent of the text.[25] Egalitarians interpret the wife submission texts as cultural, rather than transcultural, partially because it was so functionally pragmatic in the culture of the Bible. Women were generally kept uneducated and therefore could not read or write. They were generally kept socially isolated in homes, and therefore knew nothing about the public realm of society. They were generally kept economically dependent, and therefore needed to attach to a man to survive. And they married much older men, and therefore needed to defer to seniority. These and other factors had already created a gender hierarchy, regardless of what the biblical writers might say. The four wife submission texts[26] say nothing new to the Jewish culture of that day, but express concern to maintain social propriety[27] so as not to mar the reputation and witness of the new Christian church. None of these factors exist in our culture, and female submission is no longer practical. It no longer makes the cultural sense that it did in the culture of the Bible, and may in fact cause

24. Gallagher, *Evangelical Identity and Gendered Family Life*, 104.

25. A. J. Jacobs humorously but poignantly documented his year-long attempt to observe the Bible's 700-odd rules for righteous behaviour in *The Year of Living Biblically*.

26. Eph 5:22; Col 3:18; Titus 2:5; 1 Pet 2:1–6.

27. Paul's instruction to women to be "silent in churches" (1 Cor 14:34–35) is similarly motivated. He did not want public decorum disrupted by uneducated women interrupting teachers and asking naïve questions of clarification that would more properly be answered by their educated husbands later. He was not permanently silencing all women or prohibiting them from teaching/preaching, only the uneducated women of his day.

offense.[28] If Paul called for female submission in order to commend Christianity to the world of his culture, he would call for egalitarianism in ours.

William Webb has outlined one of the more useful guides for sorting out the biblical and the cultural, or more precisely, the cultural in the biblical.[29] He argues that we need to discern the "redemptive spirit and movement" of the text instead of simply taking a static reading of the text, and living out the literal words on the page. Doing so requires discerning four points of reference: 1) the original ancient Near Eastern and Greco-Roman culture, in and to which the text was written, 2) the literal words of the text, frozen in time, 3) the practice of current culture, and 4) the ultimate ethic reflected in the spirit of the text. For example, the cultures of the Bible practiced abusive slavery, the Bible teaches a benevolent slavery, and our biblically informed culture has abolished slavery, so perhaps God's ultimate ethic is no racism whatsoever.[30] By the same logic, the cultures of the Bible practiced a strong patriarchy, the Bible teaches a moderate patriarchy, our biblically informed culture practices a soft patriarchy, so perhaps God's ultimate ethic is egalitarianism. The point is that depictions of social structure in the Bible do not necessarily represent an ultimate biblical ethic. There is no more reason to insist on patriarchy as a social system than there is to insist on monarchy as a political system or slavery as part of an economic system, just because they were social practices and institutions entrenched in the cultures of the Bible. There are many ways in which the biblical text appears sexist, but relative to the cultures of its origin, it was redemptive, and had already begun women's liberation. The overall call of the text is to keep the movement going toward the ultimate ethic to which the text points.

MODERN CULTURE

With a fuller understanding of culture in hand, Wilkinson's claim that the mandates of culture and the Bible regarding gender and marriage are separate and far apart is rather problematic, if not unintelligible. So too is his claim that the church is adhering more to culture than the Bible. In the

---

28. In a project similar to Jacobs's, Rachel Held Evans also dramatized how interpretively the Bible is normally read and how selectively its instructions are normally practiced by following all the Bible's directives for women as precisely as possible for one year. She reported and reflected on her experience in *A Year of Biblical Womanhood: How a Liberated Woman Found Herself Sitting on Her Roof, Covering Her Head, and Calling Her Husband Master.*

29. Webb, *Slaves, Women, and Homosexuals.*

30. The problem with Webb's analysis here is that slavery in ancient Near Eastern and Greco-Roman cultures was not as based on race as modern slavery has been.

context of discussing the role of the wife, Wilkinson is presumably equating the second wave of the women's movement (1960–1995) with contemporary Western culture, and warning Christians of its peril. Wives who hesitate to submit unilaterally to their husbands are supposedly guilty of conforming to the world, instead of Christ. Egalitarian wives and husbands who practice mutual submission are allegedly defying God's will. Wilkinson apparently assumes that 1) there are no cultural elements in the biblical discourse on gender and marriage, that 2) the Bible speaks for itself without fallible human interpretation, that 3) his own reading of the Bible is somehow free from the influence of his own culture, and that 4) God's detailed transcultural design for marital relations is clear and unequivocal. Yet wife submission was perfectly consistent with the ancient Near Eastern culture of the early church. It was Paul's instruction that husbands love their wives that was completely countercultural. Biblical egalitarians today claim their view of gender in marriage is more consistent with God's transcultural intent as revealed in the overarching themes of the biblical text, than is the view of complementarians. Given the presence of the cultural, the countercultural, and the transcultural in the text, there can be no easy dichotomy between culture and the Bible.

If the gender egalitarianism of the later twentieth century represents culture to today's church regarding marriage, as Wilkinson maintains, then abolition represented culture to the nineteenth-century church regarding slavery, and democracy represented culture to the eighteenth-century church regarding politics. It is more than ironic that both the democratic movement and the abolition movement were, like the first wave of the women's movement, led largely by Christians. Democracy arose in modern Christian societies, evidently fostered by Protestant principles of authority and governance. Abolitionists and civil rights advocates from William Wilberforce to Martin Luther King Jr. were driven by Christian convictions about the dignity and image of God in all humans. The first wave of the women's movement (1780–1920) was led by evangelical reformers such as England's Catherine Booth of the Salvation Army, who focused on saving souls. America's Frances Willard of the Women's Christian Temperance Movement focused on alleviating the painful social consequences of alcoholism. Canada's Nellie McClung of the suffragette movement focused on gaining for women the legal status of persons, and the right to vote. The biblical text tells only of monarchs and emperors, even Jesus as King, but we hear no call to adopt similar political structures. It instructs slaves to obey their masters, yet Christians have long understood those texts to be culturally bound. Why then do we insist that the female submission texts are not culturally located as well? Are democracy, abolition, and egalitarianism cultural or Christian? Are they both? They appear nowhere in the biblical text, but given their Christian beginnings, they are at least partially products of Christian convictions.

If gender egalitarianism is anti-Christian because it is not in the plain words of the Bible, supposedly we should then also rush to repent not only for democracy as a form of government, and for the abolition of slavery, but for individualism, capitalism, human rights, and other inventions of modern Western culture not found in Scripture. Yet many fundamental ideas and ideals of Western culture are routinely sacralized or mythologized by Christians, who do indeed (mis)understand them as God's intent for all humans everywhere. God created humans with the ability to create—it is an awesome manifestation of the image of God within us—and culture is the greatest human creation.[31] Products of any particular culture are not automatically congruent or incongruent with God's will; God may even be rather indifferent to some.[32] However, as the history of biblical interpretation reveals, a problem arises when Christian ministers mistake their cultural values, norms, and ideologies as God's universal intent, and then use God's word to preach their culture. They thereby betray their cultural naiveté, do a disservice to their audiences, and speak for God at their own peril. This is nowhere more evident than in popular Christian conceptions of marriage.

ANCIENT MANDATES OF MARRIAGE

Cultural mandates of marriage vary markedly, and Christians have adopted most of them in some place and time or another, convinced they represent God's intent for marriage. Perhaps one of the few they have not adopted is the absence of any idea of marriage whatsoever. In a persuasive example of the power of culture to define reality and normalcy, and in direct challenge to the naturalness and universality of marriage, the Na people of southwestern China have for centuries organized their households and society around sibling units, not marital units. Brother-sister couples are practically inseparable companions for life, a relationship far more meaningful, involved, and permanent than relationships that are merely sexual. The incest taboo is exceptionally strong, and children are born as a result of furtive nighttime visits with non-siblings, to be reared by the mother and her brother, who live together and constitute the primary social unit. "This society makes one thing clear: marriage is not the only way to impose an incest taboo, organize child rearing, pool resources, care for elders, coordinate household

---

31. Crouch, *Culture Making*.
32. The church has long had a notion of "matters of indifference" (*adiaphora*).

production, or pass on property to the next generation."[33] The very idea of marriage itself, it would then appear, is in one sense a cultural mandate, because it does not exist in all cultures.

The peoples of the Bible clearly believed in marriage, but they did not practice it uniformly, nor do we.[34] Marriage in ancient Israel was extremely patriarchal,[35] granting husbands the power of divorce over wives, and of life or death over all family members. The well-known chapter on the godly wife (Prov 31) that depicts her as an industrious, generous, and powerful businesswoman thus seems incongruous, until we understand that she is really a metaphor for wisdom, just as the adulterous woman is a metaphor for folly.[36] The Hebrew language had no term for "bachelor" or "family" as we know it. Instead, the terms of reference were "kin" or "household," which was an open, fluid, collectivistic, multigenerational mini-community. In many ways, including morally, their marriages and families could not be more unlike ours. Abraham's various sexual escapades, for example, were beyond scandalous by today's Christian standards.

> In fact, much of what took place in these families is deplored [today]. The United States and Canada outlaw polygyny, concubinage, slavery, and marriage between siblings or cousins, regarding such unions as incest; . . . omit next-of-kin obligations; decry arranged marriages; discourage marriages between older men and younger women or vice versa; oppose reproduction outside of marriage; dismiss bride-prices; denounce the notion of females belonging to males; . . . and discard having a specific period of mourning—even though all of these were common practices within Old Testament families.[37]

In New Testament times, marriage was neither a legal contract, as in the West today, nor a sacrament, as taught by the Roman Catholic Church. It was rather a tribal affair, arranged through parents, sanctioned by the

33. Coontz, *Marriage, a History*, 33.

34. For fuller discussions of marriages and families in the cultures of the Bible, see Mace and Mace, *Sacred Fire*; Balch and Osiek, *Early Christian Families in Context*; Campell, *Marriage and Family in the Biblical World*; and Hess and Carroll, *Family in the Bible*.

35. Block prefers the term "patricentric," to emphasize both the rights and the responsibilities of the father. Block, "Marriage and Family."

36. In the Wisdom of Solomon, feminine wisdom (*sophia*) slowly gives way to masculine rationality (*logos*).

37. Maugans, *Faith Families Then and Now*, 47–48. In *Flawed Families of the Bible*, Garland and Garland offer a more redemptive reading of selected biblical narratives that is flawed by projecting contemporary relational norms back into the biblical text.

community, and sanctified by God. The family in general remained far more integrated into the community than is our practice today, becoming virtually synonymous with the early house church. The New Testament texts pay surprisingly little attention to marriage, and many passages actually downplay it relative to the primacy of spiritual concerns and relations.[38] Self-discipline and denial regarding marriage had replaced the celebratory view of marriage and family in ancient Israelite culture, as emphasis shifted from building a nation of chosen people through families to building a kingdom of Christian converts through the church. The early church was led by clergy and monks who, though they had never married themselves and regarded married life as an inferior level of Christian living, nevertheless stipulated the standards for marriage. The sexual expression built into marriage was especially problematic, because sexuality was equated with the fall, and even with original sin itself. The net effect was the degradation of marriage and women, who were deemed culpable for all things sexual. Celibacy was held to be the highest spiritual state, and at least one of the early church fathers, Origen (185–254 CE), castrated himself to be free of sexual desire. In perceiving marriage in the early church, extra caution must be taken to distinguish between the ideal and the real, how leaders of the church thought marriages ought to be conducted, and how the ordinary majority of Christians actually lived. History tends to be the story and thoughts of elites, but an accurate social history is not just a history of theology or ethics.

CONTEMPORARY MANDATES OF MARRIAGE

Shifting focus from the past onto the present, but not yet onto our own culture, we observe that marriage among contemporary Christians in other cultures also looks very different than Western Christian marriage. For example, the storied Maasai are mobile cattle-herding pastoralists settled predominantly in Kenya and Tanzania, whose family structure is not all that different from the families of early ancient Israel. They too practice arranged marriages and polygyny, as well as extramarital sexual relations that they do not consider adulterous, though they retain a concept of adultery for specific circumstances. They condone marriage between older men and younger women, value large families, emphasize the tribe, and revere the aged.[39] When they become Christians, not much about marriage changes.

---

38. For example, Luke 18:28–30; Mark 3:33–35; Luke 14:18–20, 26.

39. Like many other cultures, domestic violence is common, but unlike many other cultures, they also practise female circumcision, or genital mutilation, both now

Some slow movement away from polygyny seems more a result of education and modernization than religious conviction. In eastern Africa more generally, there exists no single model of what a Christian marriage and family looks like. "Christians follow the family structures, roles, and values of their own people without a great deal of modification. . . . Rather than fretting over this, we should recognize the combination of family and faith by culture creates any number of possibilities."[40] That diversity, in historical fact, is the summation of Christian marriage across cultures.[41]

Popular Christian conceptions of marriage in North America today were portrayed dramatically in the hit movie *Fireproof*, the low-budget but highest-grossing independent film[42] of 2008. Though critics panned it, Christian ministries like Focus on the Family and FamilyLife raved about its representation of all that our faith and culture holds dear about marriage. Fighting to save his marriage, firefighter Caleb Holt takes a forty-day Love Dare[43] from his father, a series of acts designed to win the heart of his wife Catherine. Enlightened by the realization of the character of God's love through a conversion experience, Caleb[44] eventually succeeds, and though most of the film depicts Caleb and Catherine's unhappiness, the audience is left with the assurance that they will live happily ever after. Alex Kendrick, one of the cowriters/producers, stated flatly that "Our goal is to reinforce God's intention for marriage."[45] Exactly what in the storyline is God's intent is not clear. Presumably it includes that marriages stay intact, but the implication is that it also means couples should marry for love, live alone together, be primary to each other, meet each other's emotional needs, be romantic, seek intimacy, be childless dual wage-earners, and blame themselves or the other if they fail, among many other mandates. Yet the children of Israel, the Christians of the early church, and the Christian Maasai of Tanzania would

---

considered violations of human rights.

40. Maugans, *Faith Families Then and Now*, 104. This account of Maasai marriage and family is drawn from Maugans, 87–104.

41. For example, Omoregbe offers a Christian defense of polygamy, arguing that the Bible nowhere prohibits polygamy, that there is nothing specifically more Christian about monogamy than polygamy, and that imposing monogamy on African cultures is "the result of unconscious (European) cultural bias rather than the call of the gospel." Omoregbe, "Is Polygamy Incompatible with Christianity?," 372.

42. The film grossed over $33 million in theatres, and over $28 million in the first four months of DVD sales.

43. Kendrick and Kendrick's *The Love Dare*, a spin-off forty-day Christian devotional book designed to strengthen marriages, has sold over two million copies and reached the top spot on the *New York Times* bestseller list.

44. The name alludes to the Caleb of Joshua 14: "Give me this mountain."

45. "Featured Filmmaker: Alex Kendrick."

likely be altogether bewildered by these notions of marriage, and astonished to hear them asserted as God's intent. Are these marital values and norms cultural or biblical? If they, by lack of historical and cross-cultural Christian consensus, turn out to be more cultural than biblical, what should our response to our assumptions of Christian marriage be?

WHAT WOULD JESUS DO?

At the risk of being cheeky with a phrase originating in the social gospel movement at the beginning of the twentieth century,[46] and co-opted by conservative Christians at the end of the century, "What would Jesus do?" How would Jesus respond to the Western culture of marriage today? We know he firmly subordinated the marriage of his day in order to bring it into the service of the kingdom; marriage was secondary to kingdom. What would he put right today? Given its centrality to marriage, perhaps returning to the issue of gender is instructive of what Jesus might do with culture. Clearly he was thoroughly immersed in first-century Judaism, and frequently complied with Jewish religion and culture—but not when it came to how Jewish men should act toward women.[47] Jesus would have been taught an extreme gender hierarchy that left women as second-class citizens. They were believed to be by nature too ignorant to be educated or learn. They were kept cloistered in their homes because of their hazardous sexuality, and husbands were discouraged from talking much even with their own wives. A man was commanded by Torah and the scribes never to talk to another woman in public, much less in private, and certainly never to touch a woman other than his wife or mother. A wife's role was to bear and rear children, though to have borne a daughter was disappointing, and raising her was demanding. Because of various menstruation purity laws, a woman was ceremonially unclean and therefore not allowed in the temple or synagogue for approximately half of her adult life.

Yet Jesus deliberately ignored the strongest of social and religious norms regarding gender, daring others to question his integrity in the process. He readily talked with women, both publicly and privately, and often touched them as well, even "loose" and menstruating women, thereby

46. Charles Sheldon's 1896 novel, *In His Steps: What Would Jesus Do?*, is a social gospel tract that ranks as the thirty-ninth bestselling book of all time. He later made his social justice agenda explicit in *In His Steps Today: What Would Jesus Do in Solving the Problems of Present Political, Economic and Social Life?*

47. For a fuller discussion of cultural practices related to gender in ancient Israel and first-century Judaism, see Hurley, *Man and Woman in Biblical Perspective.*

violating cleanliness codes. In his teaching on adultery, and his handling of the woman caught in adultery, he refused to blame women alone, holding men accountable for their own lust and sexual behavior. He also refused to define women in terms of their sexuality, marital status, or childbearing, but treated them as persons called equally with men by God. He included women as postive examples in his stories, even scandalously using a female image of God in the parable of the lost coin. Furthermore, Jesus welcomed women into his travelling party, and developed very close and frank friendships with some. He respected their feistiness, and treated them as intelligent and articulate, teaching them complex understandings of God and salvation, even commissioning the Samaritan woman at the well with his first announcement of being the Messiah. And it was women who were the first witnesses to the resurrection, despite the fact that they would not have been considered legally valid witnesses. Jesus knew exactly what he was doing in all his teaching about and behavior toward women. He could not have been more intentionally countercultural in defying the religiously sanctioned gender oppression of his day, refusing to concede that it was God's intent.[48] Would he equate our current Christian notions of marriage with God's intent?

CULTURAL ADULTERY?

All Christian conceptions of marriage are embedded in culture, and it cannot be otherwise. Paul Hiebert has articulated three foundational dimensions of understanding the nexus of the gospel and culture.[49] First, the gospel remains distinct from all human cultures; no one culture can ever be completely identified with the gospel, or vice versa (gospel *versus* culture). Second, the gospel calls all cultures to change; all cultures fall short of exemplifying complete gospel values (gospel *to* culture). Third, the gospel can only be expressed in human cultural forms; it comes to us contextualized in a particular culture to facilitate understanding and response (gospel *in* culture). As Webb noted, this again is the recognition that the biblical text itself contains much that is culturally specific, and not intended to be transcultural in application. So too, our form of Christianity is shaped by the culture in which we live. Therefore, Christians will always conceptualize marriage within one cultural context or another; the practice of Christian

48. For a fuller discussion of Jesus' interactions with women, see Wahlberg, *Jesus According to a Woman*. I am indebted to my colleague Valerie Hiebert for the research I have summarized in this section.

49. Hiebert, *Anthropological Insights for Missionaries*.

marriage will always be enculturated. The gospel *in* culture means that it cannot be otherwise, yet to proceed without recognizing this is to be vulnerable to making naïve claims in the name of God.

Human culture is the bed of the sacred bond of marriage, and of all other social institutions as well. It is challenge enough for Christians to "keep the marriage bed [sexually] pure" by avoiding adultery (Heb 13:4), but it is impossible to keep the cultural bed of marriage entirely pure, try as we may and are called to do. We cannot keep culture out of marriage. All cultures are as fallen and finite as the individual humans that together socially construct them. Nevertheless, it is crucial that we consciously and constantly attempt to keep at least our Christian conceptions of marriage separate from our cultural conceptions of marriage. We may be bound circumstantially to live within our time in history and our place in culture, but we need not be bound intellectually to our social location. We need not be culturally limited in the questions we ask. We can seek understanding of the essentials of God's Word, beyond its mere cultural imperatives, or our own. Indeed, we must. If we fail to do so, we are at risk of mistaking the cultural for the biblical, and unwittingly surrendering to human social constructions when we think we are obeying God's call. Culture then becomes folly, the adulterous woman of wisdom literature, who leads us into the insidious infidelity of consorting with "the world." After all, as the book of Hosea reveals and Hosea himself experienced, there are diverse non-sexual ways for Christians to be promiscuous Gomers. When sexual relations become metaphorical,[50] as in Hosea, perhaps a Christian subculture that sustains a notion of private emotional adultery should consider adding a notion of public cultural adultery.[51] If we can be emotionally unfaithful to a spouse, perhaps we can be culturally unfaithful to God by adhering to culture more than to God's call.

Not that cultural imperatives of marriage are necessarily wrong or anti-Christian, as, for example, the current cultural ideal of spouses being best friends that feels so intuitively desirable. But when that ideal is presented as the definition and measure of Christian marriage, it renders all God-honoring marriages in which the couples are not best friends to be deficient, or problematic, if not failing. Conflating the biblical and the cultural,

---

50. For example, we speak of emotional adultery when a spouse is more emotionally attached to someone of the other sex than they are to their spouse, we speak of organizational incest when an organization promotes only from within, and we speak of obscene profits when a corporation has been unusually exploitative. The classical sociological theorist Georg Simmel spoke of prostitution as one general form of social interaction that ranged far beyond the specific content—exchanging sex for money—with which the concept began. People are prostituted in diverse non-sexual ways.

51. The term "cultural adultery" was suggested to me by my colleague Valerie Hiebert.

and failing to distinguish between essentially Christian and merely cultural conceptions of marriage, can leave spouses disheartened, marriages pressurized, and society destabilized by divorce. Ideal culture, or that to which people aspire, can undermine real culture, or how they actually live. When real spouses feel they cannot authentically be who they are told they should be, when real couples feel obligations they cannot achieve, and when real society cannot sustain the ideals it demands, then the ideal has actually contributed to personal, interpersonal, and societal dysfunction. Yet Christians often persist in parroting even dysfunctional cultural ideals.[52] Too much of what most Christians are saying is only what our culture is already saying to itself, such as insisting on best-friends marriage, and Christians are only claiming dubious biblical warrant for it.[53]

Two conceptions of marriage are too consensually biblical to be debated here, and a third is too contested. First, despite God's seeming tolerance of polygamy in the Old Testament, and in accordance with its illegality in most Western nations, we will simply avow monogamy and not debate it here. Second, while many Christians are open to same-sex marriage, many more understand it to be contrary to God's intent. Despite it now being legal in an increasing number of political and legal jurisdictions, we will likewise simply disavow it for the purposes of our discussion to follow. Questions about the number and sex of marital partners will not be addressed. Third, having used gender as an example of the intersection of the biblical and the cultural, and having made my own position on the issue clear, we will simply set that fractious debate aside, though the issue of gender will of necessity resurface repeatedly.[54] Our interest is in other notions taught by well-meaning Christians in sermons, seminars, and self-help books that upon examination appear more cultural than biblical. Because Christianity is endemic to Western societies, a historical-cultural analysis of Western society is more instructive for our purposes than a cross-cultural analysis. Looking back on the development of our own society, instead of looking laterally at the current values of

52. On some issues they do not. For example, many Christians are actually saying publicly something other than what our culture is already saying to itself regarding same-sex marriage.

53. Two recent Christian calls for best-friends marriage are Driscoll and Driscoll, *Real Marriage*; and Brennan, *Sacred Unions, Sacred Passions*.

54. In *Marriage at the Crossroads*, Spencer et al. demonstrate how egalitarians and complementarians can engage in fruitful dialog about marriage. Some complementarians are less willing to dialog about gender, or set the issue aside. In *Biblical Foundations for Manhood and Womanhood*, Grudem calls gender a watershed issue. In *God, Marriage, and Family*, Kostenberger overviews the dilution of essential gender differences, together with polygamy, divorce, adultery, homosexuality, and sterility, as violations of God's ideal for marriage.

other contemporary societies, reveals how our cultural mandates of marriage have shaped our Christian conceptions of marriage.

What are some key conceptions of marriage that common Christians mistake as God's intent, when they are merely cultural? Those conceptions include how marriage is formed, connected, valued, pursued, characterized, focused, energized, troubled, ended, and perceived—virtually every aspect of marriage. We must first assess whether it is true that Christians conceive of these aspects of marriage in concert with current Western culture, and then whether those conceptions also harmonize with the biblical text. Just as the historic submission of women to men is not an incontestable good, so too the surrender of Christians to cultural mandates of marriage is at least questionable, and may at times be a form of cultural adultery. Christians have adopted various, often disparate cultural values and norms of marriage throughout history, and so we need to "test everything; hold fast to what is good" (1 Thess 5:21). It is imperative that we let go of what is not explicitly and essentially biblical *as Christian*, even when we may want to retain it as cultural. Simple surrender to culture can prove to be not only misguided and adulterous at times, but unhealthy as well. The first step toward greater individual and collective purity and well-being is to gain cultural awareness. So we must test the cultural mandates of marriage.

Mandate 1

Mate Selection
Should marital partners select each other?

WE BEGIN TESTING THE cultural mandates of marriage, and how they may shape Christian conceptions of marriage, by examining how marriages are formed. As noted in the previous chapter, a culture will include a stock of knowledge about how to handle the challenges of collective life. *A* way of handling a challenge, such as mate selection, will become *the* way of handling that challenge collectively. Our contemporary Western way of handling this challenge is to have a male and female, soon after they have entered adulthood, go through a series of dating rituals before they themselves decide if they will marry each other. This method of couple formation is taken for granted by current Western Christians and non-Christians alike as the natural or even God-ordained method of mate selection. The term "mate selection" is actually somewhat misleading, as it conjures up images of standing in front of an assortment of choices, like at a vending machine, and pondering which one to choose. "Hmm, let me see, I think I'll have that one." In actual practice, the process is more accurately termed "finding a mate," like searching to find a suitable job. Other than fantasy worlds and melodramatic reality television shows, which are much the same thing, few of us are in a position to select from an array of equally appealing and available choices.

Cultural methods of deciding who should marry involve at least two analytically distinct dimensions: who decides which two people should marry, and on what basis. The current Western norm is that the two persons who will marry each other should decide for themselves, and that they should do so for love. Perhaps the easiest distinction between biblical and cultural mandates regarding marriage is that, though the Scriptures insist that spouses love each other, nowhere do the Scriptures stipulate that potential partners should select each other for marriage because they already love each other. Yet to suggest to Christians in Western society today that two people should marry for any reason other than romantic love would be deemed painfully archaic, pathetically unfeeling, and probably laughable. Little could be more offensive to our cultural belief in the virtues of the passions of the heart, and the right to self-determination, or the natural wisdom of employing those passions to guide our self-determination in mate selection. Tragically, little could make it more difficult to stay in such marriages once begun than those same cultural beliefs. Passions empowered by self-determination can then as readily end a marriage, if those passions reverse direction.

We begin by examining how God's originally chosen people formed their marriages. How was mate selection conducted in ancient Israel? What were the social conditions that produced those patterns, and what were the social and private consequences to the individuals involved? Marriage by arrangement of someone other than the couple themselves has persisted throughout most of human and Judeo-Christian history until a relatively recent and sudden shift to the alternate cultural mandate and method of self-selection based on love that now predominates Western culture.[1] How do young people now do for themselves what used to be done for them? How well are they doing it? Do they still date as their parents did? What should Christians be doing? We will find that God is strangely silent on the issue; the biblical text tells stories of mate selection, but never provides specific guidelines for it. So Christians have simply adopted their cultural norms and practices of mate selection. They have simply surrendered to their culture.

ENDOGAMY AND POLYGAMY

In premodern societies, authoritative third parties arranged marriages.[2] Most frequently it was the parents of the couple, usually the fathers, often

---

1. There is a third general method of couple formation that has been practised by various cultures throughout history: marriage by bride capture. Women were sometimes seized as part of the spoils of war, and other times simply forced into marriage. Deuteronomy 21:10–14 outlines a formal procedure for dealing with wives captured in warfare, and Judges 21 gives an account of the kidnapping of young women to serve as the wives of the tribe of Benjamin. It was legal in England until the reign of Henry VII. See Ingoldsby, *Families in Multicultural Perspective*.

2. There are many subtypes of arranged marriages, with differing degrees of involvement allowed to the persons to be married. See Hamon and Ingoldsby, *Mate Selection across Cultures*.

agreeing when their children were small, and sometimes before they were born. When it was not the parents, the matchmaker was usually a kin of some relation, and when not a kin, it was one or more elders in the community with that designated status and role. The young persons to be wed may not have known each other, or not even known of each other, consequently ruling out love between the two as the criterion for selection. The criteria instead included advantageous economic exchange, political alliance, familial connection, temperament suitability, and other such pragmatic considerations. The predominant criteria were external to the couple themselves, placing the interests of the extended families and community ahead of the personal, subjective interests of the couple. Marriage was not for love but for "money," or the community assets the marriage produced and protected. It was not as if people lived without interpersonal preferences and passions, just that they were secondary and easily overruled by the practical and often communal demands of life. As Coontz puts it, "I don't believe that people of the past had more control over their hearts than we do today or that they were incapable of the deep love so many individuals now hope to achieve in marriage. But love in marriage was seen as a bonus, not as a necessity."[3]

Two father-son pairings in the Old Testament are well-known examples of arranged marriages. In his advanced age, Abraham sent his servant back east to Mesopotamia to "take a wife" for his son Isaac from his relatives, instead of from the daughters of the Canaanites. When Rebekah drew water from a well for the servant's camels, unknowingly signifying that she was God's appointed, the servant negotiated with her father Bethuel and brother Laban, who agreed to send her to Canaan to be Isaac's wife. As a footnote to the story, it is mentioned that after she became Isaac's wife he loved her (Gen 24:1–67). Rebekah bore Isaac two sons, Esau and Jacob. After tricking Esau out of his birthright, Jacob fled back to the east and met Rachel, his uncle Laban's daughter, not surprisingly also at a well. Jacob loved Rachel, and agreed to work for Laban for seven years in order to acquire her as his wife. When the time came, Laban gave Jacob his older, less attractive daughter Leah instead, because of the custom of ensuring that the oldest sibling married first. So Jacob worked for Laban another seven years in order to obtain Rachel, his first love. Initially, Leah was fertile, whereas Rachel was not, leading to jealousies and favoritisms. But eventually Jacob fathered twelve sons, who became the twelve tribes of Israel through Leah and Rachel and their respective maids, all while still living in his uncle Laban's household (Gen 29:1—30:24).

3. Coontz, *Marriage, a History*, 19.

The other father-son pairing of note is the monarchs David and Solomon. David married Michal (the daughter of King Saul),[4] Ahinoam, Abigail (the widow of Nabal who had scorned David), Maacah, Haggith, Abital, Eglah, and Bathsheba (to cover up his infamous adulterous affair with her). He sired many children through his wives and concubines (2 Sam 5:13), and had a beautiful maiden care for him and lie in bed with him to keep him warm as he was dying in old age. Solomon, the second son of David and Bathsheba, was chosen by David as his successor to the throne. When Solomon's brother Adonijah, who had been passed over by David, asked to marry one of David's concubines, Solomon immediately ordered Adonijah's death, seeing it as a political threat. As king of Israel, Solomon is notorious for his seven hundred wives and three hundred concubines. He is said to have loved foreign women, who regrettably turned his heart away from God in his old age (1 Kgs 11:1–8), but it is difficult to imagine meaningfully loving that many women in the full sense of the word. Lust for sex, status, and power is a more likely possibility.

These stories exemplify two characteristic features of ancient arranged marriages: endogamy and polygamy. Endogamy is the practice of marrying someone within one's own social group or community. Conversely, exogamy means marrying someone outside of one's group. In short, endogamy is marrying in, exogamy is marrying out. One's social group can be defined in terms of race, ethnicity, nationality, region, religion, education, social class, and so on. Endogamy has been the predominant pattern of marriage throughout history; indeed, without it there would be no concept or categories of race and ethnicity. However, how relatively tightly or loosely endogamy has been defined and practiced has varied greatly. In most Western societies today, it is illegal to marry siblings or first cousins, and we think of those who do as incestuous. Not so in ancient Israel; Sarah was Abraham's sister, and Rachel was Jacob's cousin. Soon the entire nation thought of itself as one large extended kinship group, a "people" that was divided up into twelve "tribes," each comprised of several "clans," in turn consisting of the smallest social units, "households."[5] Arranged marriages ensured that they occurred within the clan; to marry outside the clan was to marry exogamously. The driving forces for arranging marriages were economic and social, such as the exchange of money and land that occurred in marriage, the administration of justice, facilitating the terms of the year of Jubilee, ensuring that married women would not live too far from their family of origin, and inhibiting the introduction of

---

4. For Michal, David doubled Saul's bride price of the foreskins of a hundred Philistines. Michal later protected David from Saul, before coming to despise David for his immodest and undignified behavior in public.

5. Block, "Marriage and Family in Ancient Israel."

foreign elements into the clan community. As such, Jacob's early endogamy set the pattern for building the nation, whereas Solomon's later exogamy began the disintegration of the nation.

A second feature of ancient arranged marriages is that they were associated with polygamous marriages. Polygamy, meaning the plurality of spouses, is comprised of two subcategories: polygyny (*poly* = many, *gyne* = female; simultaneous marriage to more than one wife) and polyandry (many *andros* = males; simultaneous marriage to more than one husband). Polyandry is extremely rare in human history, and therefore it is more accurate to characterize ancient societies as polygynous rather than polygamous. Though the more inclusive category of polygamy became illegal in most Western states by the modern era, polygyny was a common practice in ancient Israel,[6] in keeping with its pronounced patriarchy. Though the power of males to assert their sexual desires was no doubt a contributing factor in polygyny, it was driven primarily by economic and social factors, as endogamy was. Having multiple wives was a means of securing additional childbearing and domestic labor, a measure of greater wealth and higher social status, and a form of political alliance between clans and kingdoms.[7] For example, Solomon formed an alliance with Pharaoh of Egypt by taking his daughter as one of his wives (1 Kgs 3:1). Many of his other wives would have been the result of similar motivations.

Taking monogamy (one husband, one wife) as God's intended ideal (Gen 2:21–25), biblical scholars struggle to explain why God accommodated polygyny in ancient Israel, never expressly forbade it,[8] and never unequivocally prescribed monogamy. One explanation is that it was a functional arrangement for a semi-nomadic, pastoral people with high male mortality rates, though female mortality in childbirth would have been equally high. However, polygynous marriage clearly complicated household life, rousing all sorts of jealousies, frustrations, and competition among wives, and injustices and even violence among children. There is little in these stories from the Hebrew Bible highlighted here about the formation of marriage that we would accept today as godly, yet these were all regarded as great men of

6. When Jacob married the sisters Leah and Rachel, he engaged in what is technically defined as sororal polygyny.

7. Not surprisingly, the Old Testament says nothing of polyandry, though it too is not the outcome of sexual fantasies (or perhaps nightmares for the single wife) as much as the economic conditions of males. When too poor to afford a wife of his own, a man could opt to share a wife with his brother.

8. The only person for whom the multiplication of wives was expressly prohibited was the king (Deut 17:17), presumably to prevent the exact religious infidelities to which Solomon succumbed.

faith, in the lineage of the Messiah, loved and honored by God, enshrined in the Hebrews 11 "Hall of Faith." Though they all struggled mightily with sin in their lives, how their marriages were formed and conducted evidently had little bearing on their status in the eyes of God.

MAKE ME A MATCH

Fast-forwarding through the early church and the Middle Ages, we see a continuation of arranged marriages as the cultural and Christian norm, along with redefined endogamy and waning polygyny. Love remained a secondary consideration, and self-selection just a foolish dream. Marriage continued to be arranged by third parties for social and economic convenience or advantage, and was now a religious sacrament. The conventional marital advice of the day was "They who marry for love shall lead their lives in sorrow," and "He who marries for love has good nights and bad days." The experienced wisdom of elders was held to be superior to the slightly dizzy and usually delusional longings of inexperienced lovers in discerning a good marital match. Third parties could best ensure that the interests of the respective families and community would be best served by a particular marital match. Plus, though love was not necessary for striking a good match, third parties were also better positioned to assess whether a particular match had the potential to develop real love. A well-arranged marriage, it was thought, was superior soil in which to grow *agape* love, freed from the weeds of simply erotic or manic love.

As we shall see more fully later, this historical norm was overturned by the great transformation in marriages in the modern era. By the nineteenth century, spurred by the individualistic ideas of the Enlightenment and the spread of the market economy, individuals gained the freedom to choose or refuse a partner, and therefore tended to marry later and be closer to each other in age. Personal choice of partners based on love replaced arranged marriage as the social ideal.

> For the first time in five thousand years, marriage came to be seen as a private relationship between two individuals rather than one link in a larger system of political and economic alliances. The measure of a successful marriage was no longer how big a financial settlement was involved, how many useful in-laws were acquired, or how many children were produced, but how well a family met the emotional needs of its individual members. Where once marriage had been seen as the fundamental

unit of work and politics, it was now viewed as a place of refuge from work, politics, and community obligation.[9]

The classic 1965 musical *Fiddler on the Roof*, set in a small Jewish village in 1905 Russia, depicts its main character Tevye as caught and confused in this profound transformation. Tevye is a man of "tradition!" who expects to arrange the marriage of his five daughters, and fully intends that those marriages be endogamous, as was his. The three oldest daughters are hoping for a good match—"Matchmaker, matchmaker, make me a match / Find me a find, catch me a catch"—but the childless widow matchmaker has to make a selection without the aid of a dowry because of Tevye's poverty. When Tevye tells his oldest daughter that she will marry a wealthy but elderly butcher, she refuses, insisting on marrying a poor tailor who has been her friend since childhood, and whom she loves. The "new way" is that children will decide partners for themselves. His second daughter selects a student revolutionary for a mate, and informs Tevye that they are not even asking his permission, only his blessing. In trying to justify this pre-eminence of love to his wife, Tevye gently coaxes an admission out of her that she too has come to love him, as he loves her, in the twenty-five years since they met for the first time on their wedding day. However, when the third daughter chooses to marry a Russian soldier, the ethnic and religious exogamy is too much for Tevye; when she elopes, he considers her dead to him.

By the twentieth century, romantic love was solidly entrenched as the criterion *par excellence* by which a man and woman should choose to marry each other. Some still had reservations about its wisdom and sustainability. George Bernard Shaw, for one, quipped that "When two people are under the influence of the most violent, most insane, most delusive, and most transient of passions, they are required to swear that they will remain in that excited, abnormal, and exhausting condition continuously until death do them part."[10] Yet if such love was all that was needed, a new social method was clearly required to facilitate the new values and freedoms of mate selection.

FROM THE FRONT PORCH TO THE BACK SEAT

Despite the attempts of Victorian society to carve out separate social spheres for men and women, by the end of the nineteenth century a system had evolved whereby young men were invited to "call" at the home of a young

9. Coontz, *Marriage, a History*, 146.
10. Quoted in Jacobs, *All You Need Is Love*, 9.

woman. "Calling" still gave the young woman's parents extensive control over whom she saw and how she behaved. In the early twentieth century, fledgling couples began meeting in the public sphere, away from her home, and "dating" had begun—the term referred to a specific time, place, and activity. Because they would be drinking Cokes at a restaurant instead of mother's homemade lemonade, and given the young woman's lesser earnings, if she had any at all, the young man would have to pay. The initiative and responsibility thus rested even more on the male. This new custom of dating spread rapidly, sped along by the invention of the automobile, which brought mobility and privacy; the invention of the telephone, which increased communication; and urbanization, which brought large numbers of young people into proximity with each other, an increase in free time due to technology, a rise of commercial entertainment, and an increasing entrance of women into the public realm.[11]

This method of couple formation reached its zenith in the mid-twentieth century. It consisted of a formally arranged series of meetings governed by distinct gender roles that functioned as preparation for traditional marriage. He would decide, initiate, pay, and be the sexual aggressor; she would wait, respond, receive, and be the sexual controller. There would be a series of predictable stages, beginning with casual dating, or "playing the field," which was random, non-committal, and event centered. This progressed to "seeing each other," indicating romantic interest, whereas the next stage of "going steady" signaled the emergence of commitment and exclusivity. It meant dates were now relationship centered, and that the couple now "had a relationship," providing a new public social status and fostering private intimacy. With increased self-disclosure, emotional attachment, and volitional commitment, they were said to be "serious," meaning courting, which constituted a private agreement to marry that was an informal engagement. The public declaration of intent to marry, an engagement, completed the process.

As cultural phenomena, dating rituals and protocols were constantly in flux. By the end of the twentieth century there was much less formality and façade involved, less advanced planning, more flexibility, and as a result, more honesty. Casual or random dating had all but disappeared, and genuine friendship became the ground of relationship, with dating now seen as the expression of friendship, not the search for it. Young people had previously dated in order to find out if they liked the other person, but now they do not date unless they already know they like the other person. At the same time, there is less restriction on other cross-sex friendship, as the dating relationship has become less exclusive. Young people now "hang out" more in group

---

11. Bailey, *From Front Porch to Back Seat.*

activities, and are less inclined to identify, display, or separate themselves as couples.[12] There is more freedom for females due to increasing gender equality, as couples now share opportunity and responsibility more equally. The days of the exploitative, gendered exchange of money and sex, where he would "pay out" financially and she would "put out" sexually, are fading.

Indeed, the term "dating" is itself increasingly uncomfortable and unacceptable to many young people, though no term has yet been able to supplant it in general parlance. It connotes passé practices of traditional dating that have progressively been rendered obsolete by gender egalitarianism, postmodern informality, sexual hook-ups, and online match-ups. The picture of courtship in the new millennium is of young people on one hand insisting on authentic friendship and searching the Internet for real compatibility, while on the other hand simultaneously "hooking up" in impersonal, uncommitted sexual encounters formerly known as "one-night stands" to avoid relational pain.[13] The mix is incongruous, and uneasy. But in the span of one century, couple formation has evolved from calling on the front porch,[14] to dating in the back seat, to living in the coed dorm, to searching on the Internet. The sheer rapidity of change is the product of multiple cultural and technological factors, but it is also telling of the difficulty in establishing a satisfactory method for potential partners to select their own mates based on love, when they will no longer allow others to select someone for them based on more pragmatic reasons.

THE MODERN MARRIAGE MARKET

When single persons today look for a mate, they often use the same contradictory criteria that matchmakers of yesterday might have. They may evaluate themselves in terms of their status, appearance, abilities, and personality, and look to strike a fair exchange with someone of similar "social goods," much like dowry and bride-price systems conceived of marriage as an exchange of assets. They may look for either general personal similarity or complementarity, or more specifically the combination of similarity in central aspects, such as values, and complementarity in peripheral aspects, such as interests.[15] After all, folk wisdom claims both that "like marries like" and

12. Segell, *Standup Guy*.

13. Levine and Cureton, *When Hope and Fear Collide*.

14. The shift in North American domestic architecture from the convivial front porch to the enclosed backyard deck embodied the concomitant shift in social values over the course of the twentieth century.

15. In *Falling in Love for All the Right Reasons: How to Find Your Soul Mate*, Neil

"opposites attract." They may subconsciously look for a substitute for their parent of the other sex—"he's marrying someone just like his mother"— sometimes perpetuating interpersonal pathologies, such as domination, in the process. Most vulnerably, they may formulate their criteria for choosing while in the process of choosing. By letting the relationship itself determine the criteria, the relationship more often than not selects itself, thereby becoming a self-fulfilling prophecy.

Regardless of their criteria, self-selecting couples will be bedeviled by the inherent courtship dilemma of intimacy versus imaging, which is the desire for mutual self-disclosure countered by mutual impression management. Both partners will be driven to try to get to know the real other ("Whom do I love?") while at the same time trying to present themselves as lovable ("Am I worthy of your love?"). Bruce Springsteen depicts the dilemma well when he sings: "So tell me what I see when I look in your eyes / Is that you baby or just a brilliant disguise . . . / I want to know if it's you I don't trust, cause I damn sure don't trust myself . . . / So when you look at me, you better look hard and look twice / Is that me baby or just a brilliant disguise."[16] The actual goal of imaging or impression management is mutual attraction, not honesty, and it therefore works at cross purposes with intimacy. The problems and pitfalls of contemporary courtship are not insignificant.

Even those couples who negotiate these challenges successfully may succumb to any one of many negative social psychological reasons for marrying. They may marry on the rebound, simply transferring emotion from a third party. They may marry as rebellion, in a reactive process of establishing distance and autonomy from significant others, most often parents. They may marry out of pity, obligation, or guilt, each being a form of negative attachment to their partner. They may marry out of romance, blinded by passion and believing that love is all you need, because it will conquer all. Or they may marry to remedy their loneliness, foolishly using another human being to fill the God-shaped void in every human heart, desperately trying to eradicate the core, existential loneliness that is part of the finite human condition. In today's psychologized and pseudo-spiritualized Western culture, many Christians search frenetically for a soulmate or kindred spirit that their ancestors would have assumed could only be created through relationship over time, not discovered among associates at will, if at all.

Having adopted the Western cultural method of mate selection, Christians have nevertheless sought to guide their young people through its many

---

Clark Warren, founder of the internet match-making service eHarmony.com, offers twenty-nine "dimensions of compatibility" to consider before committing to a romantic relationship.

16. Bruce Springsteen, "Brilliant Disguise," *Tunnel of Love* (1987).

perils. Countless aids have been produced to, if not Christianize dating, at least enable young people to negotiate its minefields,[17] offering advice often not much different from secular dating advice. What church youth group has not held earnest sessions on some variation of the standard "What does the Bible say about dating?" The correct answer, of course, can only be "Absolutely nothing." Dating, as we have seen, was a twentieth-century invention of Western society, and its method of marital coupling by supposed personal right. But no one else has heard about it, or practiced it, certainly not the writers of the biblical text.[18] Nevertheless, to the question "What does the Bible say that is applicable to whatever process of marital coupling our culture employs?" the correct answer can only be "Absolutely everything."[19] Perhaps Philippians 4:8 is a useful place to start: "Whatever is true, honorable, just, pure, pleasing, commendable . . ."[20]

Less useful are trendy little tomes like *Marriable: Taking the Desperate Out of Dating*. Though its packaging is clearly designed to capture the current crop of Christian teenagers, its message is, shall we say, dated, and little more than a Christian cover of an equally cynical and stereotyping pop culture bestseller. A decade earlier, Fein and Schneider had attempted to bring clarity to the post-feminist, postmodern confusion in coupling protocols by reasserting the traditional gender roles and tactics of the previous generation in their bestselling *The Rules: Time-Tested Secrets for Capturing the Heart of Mr. Right*.[21] A sampling of the original thirty-five rules for women is as follows:

Rule 2: Don't Talk to a Man First

Rule 4: Don't Meet Him Halfway or Go Dutch on a Date

Rule 5: Don't Call Him and Rarely Return His Calls

---

17. As recent titles suggest, the primary perils continue to be inordinate sexuality and false intimacy. See Eagar, *Dating with Pure Passion*, and Kern, *Seduced by Sex, Saved by Love*.

18. Scott Croft insisted on the concept of "biblical dating," not just Christian dating, in a series of columns by that title in the Focus on the Family webzine *Boundless*. Marshalling an array of Bible verses to back the notion of biblical dating, and contrasting it with modern dating, he nevertheless admitted that "The Scriptural support for the idea of biblical dating is largely by example and implication" (Croft, "Biblical Dating").

19. Phillips and Phillips make this distinction central to their book on Christian dating, *Holding Hands, Holding Hearts*.

20. Burge and Toussaint base each of the chapters in their book on Christian dating, *His Rules*, on a particular verse from the biblical text that contains a general ethical imperative.

21. Fein and Schneider, *Rules*. After the original publication in 1995, several derivations appeared over the next ten years, culminating in *All the Rules* in 2007.

Rule 7: Don't Accept a Saturday Night Date after Wednesday.

Rule 16: Don't Tell Him What to Do

Rule 17: Let Him Take the Lead

Rule 18: Don't Expect a Man to Change or Try to Change Him

Rule 20: Be Honest but Mysterious

Rule 32: Don't Break *The Rules*

Rule 34: Love Only Those Who Love You

The essence of the advice to women was simply to play hard to get. "Men are born to respond to challenge. Take away challenge and their interest wanes . . . this is how it works: if men love a challenge, we become challenging."[22] The gist of the book suggested that "women are abandoning the idea that men will ever choose an open, honest, companionate marriage, and that women think they must use men's emotional limitations to manipulate them into committed romantic relationships."[23]

In writing *Marriable* for Christian young people, the DiMarcos claimed to "set fire to the so-called 'rules for dating success,'" yet they unabashedly echoed them, and failed to take the desperate tone out of dating that they also claimed they would.[24] They begin by introducing dating as playing a game. The object of the game is marriage. The players are simplistic gender stereotypes. The rules are as follows:

1. Men were made to chase.
2. Women were made to be pursued.
3. Men are generally the main providers.
4. Women are the nurturers.
5. Men communicate differently than women.
6. Women want different things out of relationships than men.[25]

The young Christian reader is then told that women should never call men, that women should "shut up and be mysterious," that "men lie to get what they want" (sex and admiration), that men should always pay, that "being just friends is a waste of time," and that it is best to be realistic about your

22. Fein and Schneider, *Rules*, 7.

23. Levant and Brooks, *Men and Sex*, 2.

24. For an actual biblical counterpoint to Fein and Schneider's *The Rules*, see Burge and Toussaint, *His Rules*.

25. DiMarco and DiMarco, *Marriable*, 21.

"marriage market value."[26] A detailed description of how to flirt is even included. Throughout the reactionary, conservative dating advice dressed up in contemporary youth culture chic, nothing distinctly Christian ever appears. And Isaac and Rebekah are undeniably a long way gone.

KISSING DATING GOODBYE

Despite such desperate attempts to take the desperate out of dating and keep the system working, the cultural dis-ease about its devolution has only intensified. Whitehead, for example, offered social critique instead of practical advice in *Why There Are No Good Men Left: The Romantic Plight of the New Single Woman*, lamenting the replacement of the "courtship system" of yesteryear with the "relationship system" of today.[27] From hook-ups to cohabitation, well-educated, career-oriented, later-marrying women are particularly vulnerable to having a series of relationships that fail to generate momentum toward marriage. In such a "system," rules, conventions, and consensus go missing, causing social conditions closer to anarchy, with its characteristic winners and losers. During the sexual revolution a generation ago, Gilder observed that the only undeniable winners in such conditions are powerful men whose sexual and romantic self-interests are thereby best served.[28] As for prospects for successful marriage, "the attributes which mark men as 'good' marriage material—fidelity, commitment, dependability—are precisely those least likely to flourish in an atmosphere of open sexual competition."[29] Whereas the imbalance of power women suffer was once economic and institutional, today it is social and sexual, exacerbated again, but differently, by the ever-evolving rituals of mating.

Some more thoughtful Christian voices resonate with the growing cultural disillusionment with dating, though for rather different reasons. Single youth pastor Joshua Harris's *I Kissed Dating Goodbye: A New Attitude Toward Relationships and Romance* was perhaps the book most widely read

---

26. Greenwald takes the market metaphor quite literally in *Find a Husband After 35: Using What I Learned at Harvard Business School*. She offers a "proven 15-step action program" on how women can package their assets, develop a personal brand, leverage niche marketing, use direct mail and telemarketing to get the word out, establish a husband-hunting budget, and hold quarterly performance reviews to assess the results. Not surprisingly, she prioritizes investment in packaging, going so far as to assert that packaging is more important than the product itself.

27. Whitehead, *Why There Are No Good Men Left*.

28. Gilder, *Sexual Suicide*.

29. Grossman, "Anarchy in Eros," 57.

by churched adolescents at the turn of the millennium.[30] In the chapter on "The Seven Habits of Highly Defective Dating," he gives a Christian critique of dating as follows:

1. Dating leads to intimacy, but not necessarily to commitment.

2. Dating tends to skip the friendship stage of a relationship.

3. Dating often mistakes a physical relationship for love.

4. Dating often isolates a couple from other vital relationships.

5. Dating, in many cases, distracts young adults from their primary responsibility of preparing for the future.

6. Dating can cause discontentment with God's gift of singleness.

7. Dating creates an artificial environment for evaluating another person's character.

The solution to the challenge of marital coupling for Harris is to wait for God to deliver a mate in some mystical manner, while actively making the most of singleness. He even cites Rebekah as an extended example of someone who was willing to "watch, wait, and pray" while faithfully watering camels. But these are not the days of Isaac and Rebekah. God does not routinely deliver spouses through the arrangement of third parties the way Rebekah was delivered to Isaac, because our culture has changed. Given our current system of self-selection, it would still seem best for young people to engage the other sex somehow in order to learn about them, to learn about themselves, and to learn the relational skills that are now mandatory for what marriage has become.[31]

Though mate selection in the Judeo-Christian tradition has evolved from arranged marriages based on socioeconomic factors to self-selected marriages based almost exclusively on romantic love, God appears to have no preference, recommending or prohibiting neither. We can only conclude that self-selected marriage based on love is not necessarily wrong or inadvisable, but neither is it necessarily God's intent. It is left to humans to recommend, cultures to mandate, and individuals to cope. Yet we have through the larger trajectories of cultural change undoubtedly forsaken the clearheaded, community-minded, pragmatic assessments of matchmakers in favor of the misty-eyed, self-centered, idealistic passions of lovers themselves.

30. Harris, *I Kissed Dating Goodbye*. The 1997 publication was followed in 2000 by Harris' account of his subsequent courtship and marriage in *Boy Meets Girl*.

31. Without naming Harris directly, Clark argued that dating was still the best method for Christians to find mates in *I Gave Dating a Chance: A Biblical Perspective to Balance the Extremes.*

The fog of romantic love then too often fades into the fog of marital war, and ill-begotten marriages are challenged beyond their ability to survive.

Young Christians today have little choice but to struggle on with mixed results, burdened by reminders that, next to their faith, this will be the second most important decision of their lives. Some naively assume that being "in love" with a Christian of the other sex satisfies the only two biblical criteria of "loving one another" and not being unequally yoked with an unbeliever (2 Cor 6:14). They thereby mistake the starting point of serious deliberation about whether they should marry each other as the end point, and hastily conclude that it is God's will that they do. Others abandon themselves to serendipity. Few bother to consult their faith community about the wisdom of their choice. All usually believe that they have biblical warrant for what they do. None have compelling cases.

Mandate 2

Connectedness

Should marriage be a separate social unit?

ONCE A MARRIAGE IS formed, it must exist in some relationship with its social environment. One of the first tasks of a newly married couple is to negotiate what kinds of relationships they will maintain with their families of origin and their community. Will the couple become more or less engaged with and attached to other people? Does getting married lead to more integration with others or more distancing from others? Will the social worlds of the spouses become larger or smaller? As with every other aspect of marriage, cultural mandates will have a script for marriages to adopt about their relationship to their social context. Every society will have many social-structural inducements for couples to adopt its cultural mandates, and many social deterrents for couples who might be inclined to ignore the cultural script and do otherwise. An arranged marriage will be as problematic in one culture as self-selected marriage will be in another.

The historical trend of Judeo-Christian marriage has been a shift away from premodern marriages, which were more socially integrated with their community, toward modern marriages in which couples are less integrated. This is the centuries-long process of the privatization of marriage.[1] As marriage has come to be more about the couple itself than about the community, the couple has become increasingly separated from the community. We have already observed one aspect of the privatization of marriage in the shift

---

1. The process has been parallel to, and not merely coincidental to, the better known process of the privatization of religion in the modern world.

from arranged marriages to self-selected marriages as methods of couple formation. How a marriage is formed does not determine how much it is socially connected, but neither are formation and connection coincidental. There is a strong, logical, and historical correlation between the social embeddedness of arranged marriages on one hand, and the privatization of self-selected marriages on the other. While both have their own merits and demerits, privatized self-selected marriages are clearly at greater risk of dissolution, if the exponentially higher divorce rates they have wrought are any measure. But again the question confronts the Christian, what does God intend for the social connectedness of marriages?

As we explore what contrasting cultural mandates normalize regarding the social connectedness of marriage, we will be drawn into pondering the family unit as a whole as much as the marriage at its center. The family, not just the marriage, becomes the unit of analysis, and our interest here is in the family's relative connectedness to its social environment. We begin by collecting concepts of kinship, so as to understand the options that are possible. The shift in social ethos from the premodern to the modern world will then serve as the context for understanding the specific historical forces that created the social location that the modern family inhabits. Issues of individualism and community will need to be untangled before finally contemplating how Christians have related family to community, and how they might best do so. We will find that it may not be best for Christians to surrender to the current cultural mandate that families be separate, standalone social units, struggling to be self-sufficient.

WE ARE FAMILY

No one is an island, entire of itself, and neither is a marriage. When a man and a woman choose to form a new social unit in marriage, they both bring with them many already established social ties, both non-familial and familial. As the saying goes, you can choose your friends, but you cannot choose your relatives.[2] Friendships are achieved voluntarily, whereas relatives are ascribed involuntarily. As such, friendships can also be freely discontinued, whereas relatives are presumably forever. Each spouse comes with a network of friends, who are people with whom we choose to interact in multiple contexts because of their personal qualities, instead of their status or role in a particular context. Each spouse also comes with a network of acquaintances (those whom we know and by whom we are known) and

2. A front-door welcome sign suggests a similar preference: "Friends Welcome; Relatives by Appointment."

associates (those with whom we interact regularly based on common social involvement).[3] Acquaintances, associates, and friends represent increasing degrees of intimacy and attachment, all of which contemporary Western culture expects to be surpassed by the status and role of spouse. Marriage thus adds another identity that calls for the utmost interaction, intimacy, and attachment, inclining the couple to loosen ties to others and turn toward each other. Furthermore, each spouse also comes from a family of origin, with a whole kinship network that forms a long genealogy of identity. Family trees grow ever taller, even as they grow thinner with fewer children. The degree to which a marriage is embedded in its friends and relatives, or carves out a social space for itself separate from them, and what percentage of their life is spent in this private world of their own, varies by culture.

A marriage not only confers on a man and woman the status of husband and wife, it also greatly expands their family ties, or kin relations. As counterintuitive as it may seem, which relative is defined as what kind of kin is not determined by nature. It is only the unrecognized power of culture that makes kinship feel natural. In some cultures, breastfeeding is a more important criterion for kinship than birthing; if you breastfeed a child you become its "biological" mother, even if you have not birthed it.[4] Each culture has a particular kinship system that classifies people who are related to one another by ties of descent or marriage. Kinship systems determine who we identify as relatives, with whatever rights and responsibilities are attached thereto. Determination of descent, for example, is the cultural recognition of children as kin of parents. Some cultures, such as Western culture, trace descent through both parents (bilateral descent). Other cultures trace descent through either the father's family or the mother's family (unilineal)—if it is the father's it is patrilineal, if the mother's it is matrilineal. Among the matrilineal Navajo of North America, the most important man in a boy's life is not his father, and his father is not even in the boy's lineage.[5] Still other cultures let each generation of a family decide whether they will trace their descent through the father's family or the mother's family, but not both (ambilineal).

Sometimes societies also create relationships that are thought of as more or less equivalent to kinship relationships between persons who would otherwise not be considered relatives by either descent or marriage. These so-called "fictive kin" include adopted relatives like the next door neighbors who are like grandparents, ceremonial relatives like godparents, fraternities

---

3. Hiebert, "Toward Adult Cross-Sex Friendship."

4. Miller, Esterik, and Esterik, *Anthropology*.

5. Lavenda and Schultz, *Anthropology*.

and sororities who are like "blood brothers and sisters," exchange students, boarders, and so on.[6] Increasingly in Western societies, fictive kin are caregiving functionaries, all those who help with child or elder care regardless of biological or marital relatedness. On native reserves and in city slums, children are often deemed to belong to the community, or to any adult who can contribute. It is in this regard that theorists talk of "phenomenological families," which are based on the perception of the participants. By such definitions, those groups that think and feel about themselves as family, in spite of the absence of blood or marital ties, are a "family." By now the anthem "We are family, I got all my sisters with me" no doubt refers to more than daughters of our parents.

A more traditional definition of families focuses on the minimum components necessary to constitute a family. Structural definitions require at least one parent and one child, in other words, at least one member of two different generations. The nuclear family—a father, mother, and their children—adds to these minimal components the requirement of a marriage. An extended family is simply two or more related nuclear families, which could be extended vertically to include grandparents, or horizontally to include aunts, uncles, and cousins. Anthropologists also speak in terms of the consanguineal family versus the conjugal family. The consanguineal family is based on genetic or "blood" relations between parents, children, and siblings. It is also known as the family of origin or orientation, the family into which we are born, that is extended through multiple generations. The conjugal family is based on the marital bond of a husband and wife. It is also known as the family of procreation, the family we create by marriage, which is therefore limited to the nuclear family.

Two further aspects of marriage complete the package of conceptual tools necessary to examine the social connectedness of marriages and families in any given culture: residence and households. Newly-marrieds must choose where to live, and the contrasting cultural patterns of geographical location include setting up residence with or near the groom's family (patrilocality), with or near the bride's family (matrilocality), or in some separate place apart from either family (neolocality). The latter is obviously the predominant pattern in Western societies that are organized around the nuclear family. The group of people that actually share the residence is known simply as the household, those whom the house actually holds. The predominant Western pattern of households comprised of single nuclear

---

6. There is also a category known as fictive marriages. These marriages exist legally for the sake of some social benefit, though the parties do not establish a common domicile or sexual relationship. A common motive is immigration and the acquisition of citizenship for one of the parties.

families is a relatively recent historical development. The genealogical fact of the extended family has not and cannot change. But the witness of history has seen the modern household shrink to the nuclear family.

TOO SEPARATE AND TOO LITTLE TO DO

The predominant pattern of the social connectedness of families has not changed on its own, or because of dynamics internal to families, but rather in concert with larger shifts in Western culture. No shift has been more radical or comprehensive than the transition from the premodern to the modern world. Beginning in the nineteenth century, social theorists noted some fundamental differences in the character of these two respective eras.[7] Premodern society was largely a rural way of life, lived in close-knit communities with a collective orientation and identity, a strong sense of physical and social place, and a respect for tradition and social obligation. It was a hard-working, slow-moving way of life, with little geographical or social mobility. Everyone knew everyone else personally, and in a variety of contexts, and therefore could both care for each other and monitor each other's behavior. Not that there was much need for formal social control; there was strong moral consensus maintained by equally strong norms and social bonds, and thus strong social pressure toward conformity. Most everyone also developed a complete set of practical skills for everyday living, resulting in a homogeneous society of self-sufficient people.

The many different forces of modernization relentlessly altered this way of life. Modern society is largely a more urban way of life, lived in loose association with autonomous and often anonymous others, with a lesser sense of physical or social place and lesser regard for history or collective sentiment. It is a self-focused, fast-moving way of life, with change of every kind the only constant. Life is now lived among strangers whom we learn to ignore, except for those whom we engage temporarily and usually impersonally within a single context. Trust is much more difficult to come by, and social exchanges proceed on the basis of a rational calculation of personal interest, instead of social obligation or genuine loyalty. Amid a diversity of values and lifestyles, with less social cohesion and little informal control, formal mechanisms of social control such as a judicial system become necessary to maintain social order. Police officers patrol the street, instead of

---

7. The best known analysis of this is Toennies's distinction between *Gemeinschaft* and *Gesellschaft* in *Community and Society*. Almost as well known is Durkheim's distinction between mechanical solidarity and organic solidarity in *The Division of Labor in Society*.

neighbors looking out for each other. As individual self-sufficiency decreases, a highly specialized and complex division of labor emerges, which creates a new kind of cooperation that replaces the old commonality. Society becomes a collection of people who do only one thing well, and therefore desperately need each other. In this heterogeneous society, people are now bound together by practical interdependence rather than by consensus and similarity. Social integration is now based on difference and dependence rather than similarity and self-sufficiency.

These differences between premodern and modern societies go a long way in explaining the shift in Western societies from multiple, stronger, tighter family ties to fewer, weaker, looser family ties. Premodern societies placed priority on the group over the individual, whereas modern societies place priority on the individual over the group. Premodern societies placed little value on the privacy of individuals and couples, whereas modern societies insist on it.[8] People in premodern societies came together on the basis of kinship and tradition, whereas people in modern societies come together on the basis of self-interest. Individual family units in premodernity were identical and self-sufficient, whereas family units in modernity are diverse and dependent. Social bonds in premodernity were based on common sentiments and shared social values, whereas social bonds in modernity are based on specialization and interdependence.

The differentiation and specialization characteristic of modern society extends beyond that of individuals to entire social institutions, and further explains the new social location of the family in modernity. Social institutions are the major spheres of social life that form around the major challenges of collective living. Before individuals could differentiate from their families in the modern world, entire social institutions themselves had to differentiate and specialize. Put differently, premodern societies were institutionally undifferentiated and non-specialized social worlds. There was no sense of society being comprised of separate social institutions such as the economy, education, religion, and so on, much less that they each performed specialized functions for society. Today, we can identify the family as a separate social institution and list its functions, or what it does for society. In short, it provides a social identity, status, and role for its members; it provides economic, emotional, and sexual need fulfillment for its members; and it provides a secure context for the procreation and nurturant care of children.

But historically, families have done much more than this. The social institution of marriage and family has long been responsible for many more

8. This includes literal physical privacy. Houses in the Middle Ages were rarely divided by walls into separate and private bedrooms and bathrooms compared to public "family rooms," and household nakedness was common.

of what we now take as unrelated aspects of life. Three hundred years ago, families served as units of economic production, in contrast to the units of economic consumption they are today.[9] In the absence of formal public schooling, family members taught and learned from each other. Without a church in every village, parents functioned as priests. Before hospitals, families nursed their ill back to health with folk medicine and cures. Instead of plugging in to an entertainment industry, young siblings played with each other more physically and imaginatively. In each of these aspects and more, the functions necessary for society to exist were separated into the distinct and specialized institutions of economy, education, religion, medicine, leisure, and so on. However, modernity would be characterized by institutional differentiation.

Social theory from the 1930s on suggested that, not only had the family been separated from other institutions, its functions had been significantly reduced over the previous few centuries.[10] Those who fretted about the family's well-being in society feared that not only had it become too separate, but it had also been left with too little to do. Once the hub of everything necessary for life, the family had become just another component of life. As institutions separated themselves from the family, the family did less and less of what was needed to survive, and was more and more dependent on the larger society. Of course, it had not been stripped of all its functions, but most of the functions it retained were now modified or shared with other institutions. For example, the socialization of children is now shared with the institutions of public education, mass media, and newly formed youth subcultures, and the family's role is increasingly that of the monitor and coordinator of inputs from these other socializing institutions. The family has also carved out new roles for itself, such as caring for the heightened emotional needs of its members, as we shall see later. As social relations have become more impersonal and anonymous, familial relations have become more intimate and affectional. In short, instead of being all things, the family became a specialist among specialists, focused primarily on nurturing personal relationship.

FROM UNITED TO UNTIED

A few descriptive historical details can sketch how the industrialization and urbanization of the nineteenth century set off the transition from an extended family system to a nuclear family system.[11] Marital and familial structures

9. Berger and Berger, *War Over the Family.*
10. Ogburn, "Family and Its Functions."
11. Goode, *World Revolution.*

changed only slightly in agrarian and feudal societies, but the Industrial Revolution shattered the longstanding family system, where all members were together at home and equally productive, interdependently ensuring their subsistence. Husband, wife, and children were no longer together in the fields or in the shop producing household necessities. Families ceased being units of production and became units of consumption and service. They became spatially separated and fragmented, as fathers left the house to go to work in the factories, children went to school, and mothers stayed home.

No longer farmers or craftsmen, fathers became absentee "good providers" or "breadwinners" doing what was considered the "real" work because they were paid a wage. At the same time, they were losing control over their children, because they had no significant property or craft to offer as inheritance. Children became an economic liability instead of an asset, as they were now another hungry mouth to feed instead of a source of free labor. Not coincidentally, they came instead to carry supreme sentimental worth, to be considered innocent and needy, economically useless but emotionally priceless.[12] The state struck up public education to nurture intellectual skills and moral values instead of practical life skills.

Married women, devalued and unwelcome in the public sphere, were given a new full-time role of "mothering." Because no monetary value was placed on their services, they decreased in status, and became "housewives" entirely dependent on their husbands. At the same time, women became revalued and idealized with a reformulated femininity. Though they had traditionally been considered hardy workers that were nevertheless morally inferior to men, they now were placed on a pedestal as more delicate and virtuous than men. They needed to be protected from the harsh outside world, preserved in the isolation of their homes where they could cultivate their finer emotions. As for marriage itself, it became emotional and companionate, built on self-selection based on a love that was sentimental and affectionate. Now marriage was supposed to bring personal happiness; to be "happily married" was measured by the emotional relationship, not the meeting of material needs.

Of course, all this was only the idealization of the middle-class family, and not the hard realities of working-class families, but it prevailed as the norm nonetheless. Driven to wherever finding work would take it, the family as a whole became geographically uprooted and socially mobile.[13] Kinship networks deteriorated in function, and all but disintegrated. The family shrank to a refuge and retreat. The net effect was to isolate, privatize, and

12. Zelizer, *Pricing the Priceless Child*.
13. Browning, *Marriage and Modernization*.

emotionally load the family. "Of all the social institutions in our culture, it is the family that is the locus of privatization par excellence. Contemporary [Western] society looks to the family as an emotional and spiritual haven, the place where the affective and consumptive goods of life are enjoyed."[14] Thus the impetus for our current autonomous family values and structures was socioeconomic, not theological or hermeneutical, and is only approximately two hundred years old. Despite being a social construction of the nineteenth century, this model is taken by many conservative Christians as not merely the "traditional family" but the "biblical family."

By the middle of the twentieth century, the pre-eminent sociologist Talcott Parsons noted that kinship had become relatively unimportant in Western societies, that the nuclear, conjugal family had become the normal household unit, and that this isolated mobile family was best suited to the workforce and to urban living.[15] Some subsequent empirical research has suggested that the notion of an isolated nuclear family may not be entirely accurate. Though the friends and relatives of couples tend to be geographically dispersed rather than physically proximate, they nevertheless do tend to maintain regular contact, facilitated most recently by communication and social networking technologies.

However, more refined research has found that, while contemporary couples do exchange goods such as financial and emotional support with their social networks, those networks tend to be low in significant ways. First, they are low in connectivity, meaning that the couple's friends tend not to know and interact with each other. Second, they are low in boundedness, meaning their networks are so extensive that few feel the responsibility to lend support. Third, they are low in overlap, meaning that one partner's network tends not to be a member of the other partner's network. Overall, these types of contacts and exchanges "should not be considered as indicators of profound interdependences between couples and their network members. Network support is limited in various ways. It only concerns a small number of persons, mostly drawn from the couple's families of orientation . . . and it becomes more and more voluntary and associated with personal liking, rather than norms of reciprocity."[16]

Though the claim of the isolated nuclear family can be contested on some technicalities, and therefore must not be overstated, the isolation of the Western nuclear family relative to the full sweep of world history and culture cannot be disputed. After surveying Western societies, Adams

14. Lee, *Beyond Family Values*, 176–77.
15. Parsons, "American Family."
16. Widmer, "Couples and Their Networks," 361.

concluded that "Neither institutions nor individuals are as embedded in kin networks as they have been in many other societies."[17]

IT TAKES A VILLAGE

The picture of the modern nuclear family that emerges from the foregoing analysis is one of a fragile social unit at risk both from within and without. Internally, marriages and families are being undermined persistently by individualism. Externally, marriages and families are being eroded relentlessly by not just loss of function, but by loss of community. Writing at the end of the second millennium, Witte observed:

> A century ago, Friedrich Nietzsche made a dire prediction about the fate of the family. Every millennium, he said, has chosen an ever-smaller organizing unit. Two millennia ago, Jews, Greeks and Romans put the people, the polis and the empire first. In the next millennium, the tribe and the clan became the basic units of social life. In the current millennium, the family has emerged as the foundation of society. But this emphasis will not last, Nietzsche predicted. In the course of the 20th century, "the family will be slowly ground into a random collection of individuals," haphazardly bound together "in the common pursuit of selfish ends" and in the common rejection of the structures and strictures of family, church, state and civil society. The "raw individual" will be the norm and the nemesis of the next millennium.[18]

Wendell Berry drew a shorter timeline for the same progression, employing dance as a metaphor.[19] Two hundred years ago, people in Western societies danced in festive groups in which couples merged with a ring of people in choreographed folk dances that all participants had to learn equally. One hundred years ago, couples danced in ballrooms according to basic rules that allowed for improvisation by the male lead, provided the female partner could follow well. Today, individuals dance alone in crowded bars, moving spontaneously and idiosyncratically to the rhythm of the beat, their partner proximate, but independent.

It is important to note that the current ethos of individualism is not merely the Enlightenment individualism of early modernity, but the advanced individualism of late modernity. As noted above, if individuation is the process of coming to place the interests of the individual above the interests of

17. Adams, *Family*, 324.

18. Witte, "Consulting a Living Tradition," 1108.

19. Wirzba, *Art of the Commonplace.*

the community, hyperindividuation is placing the interests of the individual above even marriage and the nuclear family.[20] Furthermore, we now have an institutionalized individualization in which the person is required to "live a life of their own," beyond the link to marriage and family. Individuals are increasingly urged to break free of such ties, and to act without regard for them. Central institutions of the Western world are now addressed to the individual, not to marriage, the family, or other social groupings. As marriage and family comes into the service of the individual, marriages and families become as diverse as the individuals that comprise them.

> What is now asserting itself is, much more than simple diversity, the normalization of diversity in everything from family law to the self-images of family members. Any collectively shared definition of familial relationships and individual positions is gone . . . Is a society without established traditions a theology without God? Can there ever be a relationship between two (selves) without a conscious, deliberate transcendence of the (self)? Is there anything like an inherent limit to individualization?[21]

Every relationship requires the conscious, deliberate transcendence of the self, whether the relationship is that of the husband and wife, the couple to their friends and relatives, or the couple to their community.[22] Several different senses of community complicate a couple's relationship to it. If community is understood simplistically as a "shared place," it is almost synonymous with a neighborhood, and refers to all those who reside proximate to each other. Historically, your neighborhood or village was also your community. It was a physical area with imprecise boundaries that emerged unintentionally over time. Gated communities are recent artificial simulations of neighborhoods, though they tend to be more about the security of the gates than the vibrancy of the community. They are private access, intentional constructions sealed off from surrounding neighborhoods, the "haves" hidden together in their private fortresses, walled off from the "have-nots." But real community is not a commodity available for purchase.

If community is understood as "shared interests," it is defined by interpersonal contact patterns and networks beyond the confines of the physical location of one's residence. Cyberspace communities that today reach around the globe are the ultimate evidence of the non-locality of shared-interest communities. Both vocational and avocational interests bring people together as associates. In late modernity, friends and even spouses are increasingly drawn

20. Berger and Berger, *War Over the Family.*
21. Beck and Beck-Gernsheim, "Families in a Runaway World," 512.
22. Crow and Maclean, "Families and Local Communities."

from a wider assortment of associates than the narrow selection available in premodern neighborhoods and villages. Finally, if community is understood as "shared identity," it could be based on any one of interests, kinship, or subculture. Just as it is nigh impossible for the individual to answer "Who am I?" without first answering "Who are we?," so too for the married couple. This is where the church, which is a community in all three senses of place, interests, and identity, makes its claim on the couple. Spouses who identify as Christian are a part of the church community. Berry draws together all three senses of community as follows:

> [A] marriage involves more than just the bodies and minds of a man and a woman. It involves locality, human circumstance, and duration. There is a strong possibility that the basic human sexual unit is composed of a man and a woman (bodies and minds), plus their history together, plus their kin and descendants, plus their place in the world with its economy and history, plus their natural neighborhood, plus their human community with its memories, satisfactions, expectations, and hopes.[23]

Berry goes on to suggest much more: marriages and families that are not embedded in community are not just fragile, but meaningless, and ultimately homeless.

> [It] may be that our marriages, kinships, friendships, neighborhoods, and all our forms and acts of homemaking are the rites by which we solemnize and enact our union with the universe. . . . For example, a marriage without a place, a household, has nothing to show for itself. Without a history of some length, it does not know what it means. Without a community to exert a shaping pressure around it, it may explode because of the pressure inside it.[24]

Like the concept of neighborhood, the concept of homelessness has at face value a physical meaning—the lack of permanent shelter—but upon any reflection, it quickly deepens to become much more profound. Bouma-Prediger and Walsh tell of the under-housed beggar living on the streets—displaced socially, economically, psychologically, legally, and geographically—but embedded in an intimate network of face-to-face others. They tell also of the over-housed executive splitting time between three different condos in three different cities—secure socially, economically, and legally—but not knowing his neighbors. Which person then is truly homeless? Which one has a primal

23. Wirzba, *Art of the Commonplace*, 139.
24. Ibid., 140.

place, and which one is displaced? And if both are married and raising a child, which is the isolated nuclear family? When displacement and homelessness are applied to the couple instead of the individual, the dynamics remain the same. "We think that 'home alone' is actually an oxymoron. There is no such thing as being home alone. Home is a matter of community. Home is about belonging, connectedness, and shared memory. Home involves relationships of trust. . . . To be at home in the world, indeed to be at home within ourselves, we must be in a home that is shared."[25]

Two decades ago, Jane Cowen-Fletcher wrote and illustrated a children's book that told the simple, charming story of a young girl. Yemi is off with her family to sell a tub of mangos in a village market in the Republic of Benin. When her mother asks Yemi to keep an eye on her younger brother Kokou, the pleased big sister proudly announces to the women of the market that she is quite capable of doing so "all by myself." The other vendors smile and nod knowingly. Inevitably, as soon as Yemi turns her back to buy a bag of peanuts, Kokou wanders off. While Yemi searches anxiously for her little brother, imagining his terrible fate, he is shown being fed by other adults, napping under their watchful eye, and playing with other kids, as Yemi's mother knew he would. Reunited with Kokou at the end of the day, Yemi thanks each vendor in turn, having learned a little more what it means to belong to a community. The title of the award-winning book was *It Takes a Village*,[26] based on the ancient West African proverb, "It takes a village to raise a child."

Two years later, then First Lady Hillary Rodham Clinton published *It Takes a Village and Other Lessons Children Teach Us.*[27] She argued that, though "parents bear the first and primary responsibility for their sons and daughters," many individuals and groups outside the family have an impact on a child's well-being. Unfortunately, it was the election year of 1996, and the seemingly self-evident point was quickly politicized.[28] Reacting to any hint of communalism, presidential nominee Bob Dole, during his acceptance speech at the Republican National Convention, said, "After the virtual devastation of the American family, the rock upon which this country was founded, we are told that it takes a village—that is, the collective, and thus, the state—to raise a child . . . [W]ith all due respect, I am here to tell you: it does not take a village to raise a child. It takes a family." The deep meaning

25. Ibid., xi.

26. Cowen-Fletcher, *It Takes a Village*.

27. Clinton, *It Takes a Village*.

28. Hunter laments "the politicization of nearly everything." Politicization is "the turn toward law and politics . . . to find solutions to public problems. . . . the predisposition to interpret all of public life through the filter of partisan beliefs . . . . the conflation of the public with the political" (Hunter, *To Change the World*, 102–3, 105).

of community was thereby simply conflated with state intervention, and the specter of the state's intrusion into "private affairs" roused ready resistance. Christian spokespersons, such as Gary Bauer of the Family Research Council and Kerby Anderson of Probe Ministries, chimed in, insisting on the self-sufficiency of the family, and the folly of state-assisted child rearing. A decade later, Senator Rick Santorum wrote a full rebuttal to Clinton entitled *It Takes a Family: Conservatism and the Common Good*,[29] which was praised by conservative Christian media leaders James Dobson and Pat Robertson and promoted through their organizations. The private nuclear family was held up as the biblical ideal.

THE HOUSEHOLD OF FAITH

In the beginning, God may have commanded, or merely observed, that men will leave their consanguineal families and cleave to a woman to form a new neo-local conjugal family, but this was not a pattern in Judeo-Christian history in any literal sense until the modern era. In fact, the family patterns of many non-Judeo-Christian cultures "bear a much closer resemblance to the biblical picture than patterns currently operative in Western countries."[30] The children of Israel organized themselves around and lived in patrilocal extended family households, not even having a word in the Hebrew language for what we mean by the nuclear family.[31] Their households were open and fluid communities, consisting of multiple families and multigenerational clans, and more.[32]

As important as bloodlines were to the children of Israel, their households usually included not just extended family, but resident slaves and, more often than not, widows, orphans, or sojourning strangers. There was none of the exclusivity, privacy, and autonomy that now characterize the self-enclosed fortresses that modern nuclear family households tend to be. There was none of the certainty and control in life the modern person has come to expect and demand. Hospitality was a core value and norm, and it was much more than the safe, evening entertainment of invited friends and relatives that it is today. It meant providing a safe place for the weak, vulnerable, and strange who needed to be protected and respected. To the early church, hospitality meant "transcending social and ethnic difference by sharing meals,

29. Santorum, *It Takes a Family*.
30. Block, "Marriage and Family in Ancient Israel," 34.
31. Ibid.
32. Maugans, *Faith Families Then and Now*.

homes, and worship with persons of different backgrounds."[33] The writer of Hebrews puts the mandate sharply: "Do not neglect to show hospitality to strangers, for by doing that some have entertained angels without knowing it" (Heb 13:2). In a world without formal "community agencies," it was clear which groups would be caring for "strangers"—family households.

There certainly is no evidence that God was displeased with the family structures of the Israelites or viewed them as dysfunctional, as God clearly was with their choices of governance and worship. As appalled as we today may be, Joseph and Mary were not charged with parental neglect when it took more than a day for them to realize that their twelve-year-old son Jesus was not in the traveling party of friends and relatives returning from the Passover festival in Jerusalem. Evidently, their parental assumption was that it did in reality take a village to raise a child. As resistant as we today may be to anything that smacks of collectivism, communalism, much less communism, the first believers of the early church met in homes and notably "had all things in common" (Acts 2:44). Evidently, there was little functional difference between house and church, or between everyday life and faith, and they really did believe that in Jesus, Jubilee had actually come. As insistent as we today may be about personal salvation, Paul and Silas instructed the Philippian jailor to "Believe on the Lord Jesus, and you will be saved, you and your household," after which "he and his entire family were baptized without delay" (Acts 16:31–33). Evidently, there was little individual religious differentiation within the household, albeit because of the power of the patriarch to determine his family's religious affiliation. In truth, the biblical record suggests that the embedded, undifferentiated family and household was very functional for building first the chosen people of God, and then the new family of God.

What might the term "family of God" mean, given the array of possibilities?[34] Jesus himself left little doubt about what he meant by it. Within earshot of his mother and brothers he said, "Who are my mother and my brothers?" And looking at those who sat around him, he said, "Here are my mother and my brothers! Whoever does the will of God is my brother and sister and mother" (Mark 3:33–35). At minimum, the family of God is a new basis of belonging that contextualizes all other forms of family, and renders the term "single Christian" an oxymoron. No longer limited to the lineage of Abraham, Christian marrieds and non-marrieds alike belong to each other. The extent to which there are isolated singles and families in

33. Pohl, *Making Room*, 5.

34. This phrase from Galatians 6:10 appears as "household of faith" in many translations, suggesting that the family included all that the house held. The phrase in Ephesians 2:19 is also alternately translated "household of God" and "family of God."

the church is the extent to which the church itself is a "broken home." All Christians have "things in common" at the highest level. The only question is how far down into the practicalities of everyday life that commonality extends. The disciples, who became the fictive kin of Jesus, had virtually "all things in common," as did later monks in monasteries and nuns in convents. Yet modern nuclear families hold virtually nothing in common.

Clapp suggests that none of the social-scientific concepts of family apply adequately to the family of God.[35] The conjugal family is too marriage-centered, and results in the church ostracizing singles and panicking over divorce. The consanguineal family perpetuates the privilege of exclusive inheritance, contrary to New Testament teaching. Even the consensual family, otherwise known as the phenomenological family, is too feebly a voluntary association. He suggests instead that the church is a "collateral family" built on the primary importance of siblings in voluntary social life. Siblings are unilaterally descended from the same ancestor, are the longest lasting of human relationships, and provide a context for friendship without requiring it. We are brothers and sisters in Christ. We are "joint heirs" in Christ. We are family.

In the face of all this, or more likely oblivious to all this, current Christians nevertheless tend to read the leave and cleave passage in Genesis as calling for our present Western societal practice of relatively detached, privatized, neo-local, nuclear families. New marriages, we say, need to cut the apron strings and establish their own identity, develop their own social networks, take ownership of their own assets, and perhaps home school their own children, because God intended the conjugal nuclear family to be the organizing principle and most prominent feature of society.

Romantic nostalgia about the socially embedded family of the past overlooks that it was also authoritarian, coercive, and stifling of the individual. Nonetheless, there are reasons to conclude that our current cultural mandate has more than its share of dysfunctions, and is not God's original intent. Its internal dynamics remain publicly unseen and unaccountable, ensuring that virtually no one really knows who we are, if who we are is what we are when no one is looking. Its ideals of not just extraordinary but self-sufficient sentiment overburden and discourage its members, leaving us relationally suffocated or stunted for want of alternatives. Its unprecedented norms of privacy provide harbor for personal dysfunction and interpersonal abuse,[36] facilitating the addictions and aggressions that break our spirits. Moreover,

35. See Clapp, *Families at the Crossroads*; and "From Family Values to Family Virtues."

36. See chapter 8, "A Concern for the Christian Family: The Dangers of Idolization and Idealization," in Kroeger and Nason-Clark, *No Place for Abuse*.

its basic premises and practices contradict those of both the church and the community, rendering us profoundly homeless in our own houses.

In assessing the disintegration of community in modernity and the resultant isolated nuclear family, Balswick and Balswick are representative when they conclude, "The self-contained family is an unrealistic ideal that is doomed to fail in modern society."[37] Noting that traditional societies are more successful in fostering community, they call for greater inclusivity in the family as one means of reconstructing community. Both the family and the community need the family to have more permeable boundaries, like living cell membranes. "The church therefore must be willing to commit the culturally inappropriate transgression of drawing families out of their privatism."[38] It may well be unavoidable for Christians to surrender to the social disconnectedness of marriage in Western culture, but they ought not justify doing so by glibly reassuring themselves that, after all, God told them to leave and cleave.

37. Balswick and Balswick, *Family*, 350.
38. Lee, *Beyond Family Values*, 230.

Mandate 3

Calling

*Should our marriage
be our primary calling in life?*

CONTEMPORARY WESTERN CULTURE CONTAINS mixed messages that can easily confound us about the value of marriage. On one hand, our civic leaders hold holy matrimony in highest regard, even when they lack any concept of its sanctity. In times of crisis, people put their entire private and public worlds on hold to save a marriage descending into unholy acrimony. On the other hand, our celebrities play out before our voyeuristic eyes a shocking disregard for the solemnity of marriage, even when we do not expect them to comprehend its gravity. A large and growing proportion of the population disregards completely its necessity, cohabiting as happily ever after, or not, as those who commit to marriage. Reading our culture, one could just as readily conclude that marriage is either far more or far less important than its face value.

Of course, who is to say how important marriage really is? Who determines its value, and on what basis? Do individuals freely choose what marriage means and therefore how important it is to them based on whatever criteria they personally select? Do cultures determine the meaning and importance of marriage based on its function for the community and society? The answer, of course, is yes to both. However, we in Western culture tend to overestimate the power of our own choice and underestimate the power of culture to shape our choice. "In the game of life, we may decide how to play our cards, but it is society that deals us the hand."[1] And whatever the importance or priority placed on marriage by humans individually or collectively for whatever reasons, what relative value does God want us to place on it?

Contemplating the value, importance, or priority of marriage also raises perennial questions about the difference between describing what a cultural practice is in reality, compared to prescribing what it ought to be ideally: description versus prescription, "is" versus "ought," real versus ideal, fact versus value. A particular culture may in *descriptive fact* mandate that marriage become a spouse's primary calling in life, with the resulting cultural norm that it really is lived out as such. Alternatively, such a notion of marriage may exist in a particular culture only as a *prescriptive value* of how marriages ideally ought to be valued, while the normal practice of real life is otherwise. With the tools of sociology, we can observe, describe, and explain the value with which marriages are actually lived out within a particular cultural context, compared to how that culture thinks marriages should be lived out. How that cultural mandate is generated and justified within that cultural context is a much more complicated question that requires much more than examining the ethical and religious basis for the imperative. Myriad social forces produce cultural mandates, and some would even argue that those ethical and religious imperatives are themselves a product of social forces.

So it would be oversimplifying to suggest that the value, importance, or priority of marriage is a more theological question than the supposedly more sociological question of the social connectedness of the family, discussed in Mandate 2. True, some Christians have argued that the primary value of marriage is in what it symbolically represents about God's covenantal relationship with humans, rather than in what marriage does for humans. Yet it would also be misleading to suggest that the value of marriage is a more theological question than the question of its social connectedness. After all, mate selection and marital social connectedness are each also symbolic of God's relations with us. Certainly, a marriage's relative social (dis) connectedness and the functions it performs in a given society are instructive in assessing its value in that society, or more precisely the basis for its value. Because of its focus on the individual self, a self-selected, socially isolated, and emotionally loaded marriage is more likely to be viewed as a primary life calling than an arranged, socially embedded, and functionally integrated marriage. So it is that with each successive cultural mandate of marriage we examine, we see more clearly their cumulative effects in shaping what contemporary Christians take as normative. It is precisely this entanglement of the cultural and the Christian that we are seeking to unravel.

---

1. Macionis and Gerber, *Sociology*, 9.

As with the social connectedness of marriage in Mandate 2, contemplating the value of marriage again quickly calls into consideration the family unit as a whole, not just the marriage at its core. Obviously, many marriages do not produce or provide primary care for children, and as much as they may like to think of themselves as "family," they are not family by any rigorous definition. Yet marriage values are rooted in family values, and it is there we must begin. To reveal the development of current Western ways of thinking and feeling about marriage and the family, and their differing implications for men and women, is to recognize them as the product of history and culture that they are. Those values must then be evaluated in light of the uncomfortably unsentimental words of Jesus about marriage and family. Finally, a look at the marriages of some notable Christian missionaries will be similarly unsettling. Yet we will be led to conclude that for marriage to become a Christian's primary value and focus in life is to surrender to culture's mandate rather than submit to God's calling.

FAMILY VALUES

The "culture war" over "family values" that reached a feverous pitch in the 1990s[2] pitted those who believed the family was in decline, breakdown, or outright crisis, against those who believed the family was simply accommodating to society as it always had historically. The focus was on the particular character of the values that families held, as well as the relative value attached by society to the family enterprise as a whole, both having repercussions for society at large. At one pole of the argument were those lamenting the erosion of the traditional family structure and function, and at the other pole were those bemoaning a retrenchment of the traditional family as too moralistic and out of touch with new social realities. Though the majority of Christians were clearly in the alarmist camp, both camps nonetheless shared an underlying, overlapping, and overarching pattern of values with the surrounding culture. The largest similarities they shared were the "habits of the heart"[3] that permeate our cultural way of understanding life in general, and family relationships in particular. These habits of the heart

---

2. Hunter's analysis in *Culture Wars* framed the debate. Hunter later dialogued with Wolfe about the existence and continuance of a culture war in Hunter and Wolfe, *Is There a Culture War?*

3. Bellah and his colleagues popularized this phrase from the nineteenth-century French social philosopher Alexis de Tocqueville in Bellah et al., *Habits of the Heart: Individualism and Commitment in American Life.*

represent the moral horizons of our culture: background assumptions that guide how we perceive and act on our commitments. ... [O]ur contemporary [Western] culture is dominated by three types of moral discourse, each imposing its own inherent logic: the language of individual rights, the language of the consumer market-place, and the language of psychotherapy. Such is the case both inside and outside the church; the three languages become mingled in practice and in some cases replace the biblical narratives as the functional logic of today's Christians.[4]

In addition to these habits of the heart that Christians shared with their surrounding culture, there were also some differences of emphasis, making the Christian community more of a subculture than a counterculture. The most notable differences were that Christians were more reluctant to accept same-sex marriage, and that they placed greater importance on marriage.[5]

If the "family values" debate make anything clear, it is that marriage and family in Western cultures are now valued as much, or more, for what they represent than for what they actually do. People care passionately about family values, even while they disagree about what they should be, and what the family itself should be or do. Through all its permutations of structure and function throughout history, family has always been important for one reason or another. Even when consensus about what makes family valuable is lost, consensus that it is valuable is not. Family has come to stand for all that is good in the world. It has become a symbol, and has thereby acquired a symbolic role. As such, it is in fact doing something; it is fulfilling a function. When modernity diminished the social functions of the family, thrust the individual out into the world alone, and accelerated the pace of social change, the *idea* of the family became the repository of all our hopes for not just relationship and security, but virtue and meaning itself. "Our beliefs about the family are tied to the understandable need to maintain a meaningful sense of cultural stability and continuity in the face of social and technological change."[6]

We have already seen in Mandate 2 the radical transformations of marriage and family fashioned by the Industrial Revolution. In fuller fact, the evolution of cultural values that would give shape to the modern family was already under way before the nineteenth century. For example, the colonial Puritan families of the seventeenth and eighteenth centuries had held a very high regard for the family, "but family affections were not of

4. Lee, *Beyond Family Values*, 91, 12–13.

5. Ibid., 30.

6. Ibid., 12.

ultimate significance. Children were routinely given over to other households, to be suckled by a wet nurse, to learn a trade by being apprenticed to a craftsman for several years, or simply as servants. Children were therefore under the care and tutelage of some household, even if not the one into which they had been born. The household served the public order, not the sentiments of families."[7] But the rise of pietism, especially John Wesley's "Christian perfectionism" in the eighteenth century, taught that individuals could achieve holiness of heart and life in this world. This spiritual individualism paved the way for the Enlightenment of the eighteenth century, a broader intellectual and cultural movement that stressed the rationality of the autonomous individual. Then, in reaction to the Enlightenment, and while the Industrial Revolution was exerting itself, the Romantic Era of the early nineteenth century provided a further impetus to the new family. It validated strong emotion as an authentic source of knowledge, it prized intuition and imagination as authoritative, and it harnessed their power to envision and to escape from increasingly harsh modern realities.

WHERE THE HEART IS

Through this vortex of macro sociocultural change in Western society, it is no surprise or accident that family became a matter of the heart. Marriage became more about passion than practicality, imbued with emotional significance like never before. Centuries earlier in Greek antiquity, Pliny the Elder had said that "Home is where the heart is," but that sentiment had now become institutionalized. Clearly, it is not as if men and women had never felt the pull of passion for each other before, but they had never given themselves over to it so totally or systematically, never let it rule their individual or collective lives, never idealized it as the ultimate mode of being in relationship. They had never before made a moral virtue, or cultural mandate, of "following your heart." Marriage and family had always been valued for various pragmatic reasons, but it is perhaps more than coincidence that only when it became sentimentalized did it also become idealized. Both are effects of cultural romanticism, which emphasizes the individual, the subjective, the irrational, the imaginative, the personal, the spontaneous, and the emotional.

To sentimentalize something like marriage is not just to characterize it and attend to it in terms of the feelings or emotions it elicits. Rather, it is to define it by those very feelings and emotions, to take them as its essence and significance, its reason for being. Those feelings and emotions must therefore be nurtured above all else. Just as the twentieth century

7. Ibid., 59.

intensified nineteenth-century individualism into hyper-individualism, so too it dramatized the sentimentalization of marriage into hyper-sentimentalization.[8] After the interruptive assaults of the two World Wars when women maintained the wartime labor force, and the Great Depression when men deserted their families in despair, the peaceful and prosperous 1950s took up the vision of reconstructing the sentimentalized "traditional family" with renewed gusto. In undoubtedly the most intensely conservative decade of the century, men and women were coaxed by social ideology and coerced by social policy to settle back into their former gender based marital roles. Babies were booming and families rebuilding. Nevertheless, a warning soon appeared that not all was as idyllic as it seemed. As Betty Friedan wrote on behalf of those housewives who felt trapped, "There was a strange discrepancy between the reality of our lives as women and the image to which we were trying to conform, the image that I came to call the feminine mystique."[9]

By the end of the twentieth century, it was not just the social institution of the family that was thoroughly hyper-sentimentalized, but most other institutions were equally awash in the language of individual rights, the consumer marketplace, and psychotherapy. In a volume on the "sentimentalization of modern society", O'Hear wrote of the hysteria surrounding the death of Princess Diana, whose troubled marriage had played out in the public eye. "Diana's personal canonization, for it amounts to no less, was at the same time a canonization of what she stood for. What she stood for was the elevation of feeling, image, and spontaneity over reason, reality, and restraint. . . . Diana's story is the story of many. We have become a society obsessed with selfhood, self-expression, self-actualization."[10] If to sentimentalize something is to one-sidedly accentuate and exaggerate its positive emotions, then to idealize it is to one-sidedly accentuate and exaggerate its positive values. To idealize something is to view it as constituting the standard of perfection or excellence, to glorify and exalt it as of greatest worth. The idealization of marriage and family meant that they took on mythic dimensions as the source and center of the good life, the fulfillment of our deepest desires, the realization of an Edenic utopia. Idealization forgets or ignores that home is a place of both nurture and violence, "a place to escape to and a place to escape from."[11] This utopia is exactly what the consummate "traditional family," as it was termed and promoted in the 1950s, was

---

8. Berger and Berger, *War Over the Family*.

9. Friedan, *Feminine Mystique*.

10. O'Hear, "Diana: Queen of Hearts."

11. George, *Politics of Home*, 9.

designed to deliver. It was not so much distinguished by its structure and function as by its values and norms. Berger and Berger summarized six that come as no surprise.[12] First, romantic love was the motive for self-selected marriage. Second, gender roles are clearly differentiated and hierarchical, with headship and submission the rule. Third, the spouses are intensely affectionate to one another. Fourth, the wife and mother was paramount in the home, with full-time mothering being the highest, most noble role to which a woman could aspire. Fifth, parents were preoccupied with their children, convinced that personal fulfillment was impossible apart from raising children, that parenting was the experience that gave meaning to all other experience. Sixth, family was the major focus of life, more important than any other commitment or group membership.

TRUE WOMANHOOD AND MANHOOD

What is immediately evident from this list of "traditional" marital and familial values is the disparity of its implications for the respective sexes. We have already noted in Mandate 2 the privatization, sentimentalization, and idealization of women in particular during the nineteenth century. While their social role was being privatized into being a "housewife," their femininity was being sentimentalized into emotional fragility, and their moral worth was being idealized into paragons of virtue. The fuller picture is that the same was happening concurrently to all of family life. So it was that the primary responsibility for transforming the home into a haven fell to wives and mothers, in what historians have termed the "cult of true womanhood." True women "were pious, their lives being one long act of devotion to God, husband, children, servants, the poor, humanity. Second, they were passive, without any desire to strive or achieve for themselves. Third, they were 'pure.' Marriage was their career—spinsters were pitied and regarded as failures—and virginity and total sexual ignorance were crucial."[13] Western society waxed lyrical about the power and privilege of the (female) hand that rocked the cradle, though it was strictly a moral power and privilege bereft of direct socioeconomic rewards. "Thus, while men's work was turning into a career or a job, women's work had the old meaning of a calling, an occupation defined essentially in terms of its contribution to the common good."[14] That marriage was one's primary calling in life was true first and

---

12. Berger and Berger, *War Over the Family*.

13. Fowler, *In a Gilded Cage*, xvi.

14. Bellah et al., *Habits of the Heart*, 88.

foremost about women, not men. An unmarried man had many options for living a full and admirable life that an unmarried woman simply did not.

Women in Jesus' times had been comparatively even more privatized than nineteenth-century women. Both married and unmarried women in first-century Judaism were encouraged to remain literally, physically in the home as much as possible, though practical necessities and duties did take them out into public occasionally. Still, women and the home were not sentimentalized. Husbands were discouraged from talking much with their own wives, and strongly deterred from talking with other women at all. Husbands and wives did not look to each other for comfort or companionship. Both women and the home were valued for and served one primary function: the bearing and rearing of children, preferably sons. A woman's first loyalty and duty was to her sons, not her husband, and when a son became a husband his first loyalty remained to his mother, not his wife. The family was about building lineage, not sentimental relationship.

In contrast to preindustrial expectations for women, Western masculinity was more of a "communal manhood," in which a man's identity was based on what he contributed to the community, not necessarily his family or the economy. Viewed as having less passion but more reason and virtue than a woman, his public usefulness was deemed more important than his personal economic success. A "real man" was one of virtue and responsibility, who cared for and protected his neighbors. With industrialization, his newly defined work role that took him away from his family and apart from his community became central to his personal and social identity. He was encouraged to give free reign to ambition and aggression outside the home, and to channel all his energies into his work in order to become the "self-made man" based on his own achievements, whose only familial role was to be a "good provider."[15] Meanwhile, an ideal middle-class woman, deemed by nature to be pure, fragile, delicate, emotional, and needing protection, was called to the dependency of marriage, to surrender her legal status as a person in order to become the "angel of the hearth," whose domesticity was her honor and her glory.[16] By late industrialization, men who had been disempowered by industrial labor sought new ways of validating their masculinity. A more "passionate manhood" emerged, where male traits were divested of any tenderness or self-restraint, becoming ends in themselves, not merely means to economic ends.

15. Rotundo, *American Manhood.*
16. Margolis, *True to Her Nature.*

AMERICAN IDOL

Beyond its privatization, sentimentalization, and idealization, there is an additional spiritual significance that Christians have now given to the family that comes in both positive and negative forms. The first is the notion of family as a Christian calling or vocation (which comes from the Latin for "call"). One's calling is one's God-appointed task in everyday life, and hence a primary calling is a personalized directive to do that which defines one's entire life. Calvinists distinguish at least two separate callings: a *general* calling to the Christian life and the service of God, and a *particular* calling to take up a station or function in life by which one's usefulness to the greater common good is determined. When Paul begs Christians to live a life worthy of the vocation to which they are called (Eph 4:1), is marriage included?

For the female half of married people throughout history, the primacy of marital calling has been a cultural given beyond question. Traditional gender role ideology has consistently directed wives to find their life and meaning in their husbands and children, placing the needs of other family members ahead of their own in the sanctuary of the home. Christian tradition has historically and enthusiastically legitimated this wider cultural imperative. Conversely, Paul's directive to husbands of the early church that they should love their wives was unprecedented and countercultural at the time. Two millennia later, Christian husbands are now also being told that they too should find their life and meaning primarily in their wives. Family values value family above all else; nothing is permitted to take priority over it. Today, anyone, but especially Christians, can withdraw from any social commitment, with honor, simply by citing a desire to "spend more time with my family," confident that their motive will be unchallenged and their character admired.

The second spiritual significance of the modern family, a darker development in both Western culture and the Christian subculture, is suggested by many of the terms already used to describe its current valuation. Words such as *canonization, angel,* and *sanctuary* suggest that something more than idealization is going on. Without discounting the family's historical, sociological, and theological importance, a growing chorus of Christian scholars contend that the supreme worth and ultimate significance given to it in many sectors of the Christian subculture today constitutes nothing less than the idolization of the family. The family, in this view, has been venerated and deified to where it now invokes the reverence and indeed worship befitting an idol. "The home had never before been sanctified in the way it was in the nineteenth century. . . . Home had become a sacramental site, complete with the redemptive qualities previously associated with holy places."[17] Idolatry does not necessarily find security and meaning in graven images of wood or stone, but in something or someone other than God. Idols today are often aspects of social life that are good in themselves, but become evil when they are cast as the highest good, and we sacrifice for, or to, them other things of equal or greater importance. Our idols tend to be legitimate engagements that we make into false gods, in that, instead of pointing us *to* God, they point to themselves *as* God. Some idols of our time at the popular level include money, sex, and power,[18] and at the cultural level include scientism, technicism, consumerism,[19] and yes, familism.

Fishburn describes the idolatry of familism as a domestic folk religion that adapts Christian language and symbols to reinforce commitments to family. Her concern is the negative consequences of "a severely truncated vision of the nature and mission of the church."[20] Insisting that the church, not "the Christian home," is the primary source of blessing, she states flatly that "The family is not essential to the Christian life. . . . Only the church is essential to the Christian life."[21] If marriage and family concerns and commitments do take precedence over all others, then they must by this definition be deemed idolatrous. If they usurp direct allegiance to God and the church, then they cease to be virtuous.

THE CHRISTIAN'S HOME

The biblical text maintains an uneasy ambivalence about marriage that calls into question the transcendent status of marriage in our current Christian subculture. In the biggest picture, marriage held great importance in the Old Testament, where it was essential and good for everyone, but marriage was downgraded in the New Testament, where it was optional and good, but not intended for everyone.[22] No doubt this was due in part to God's chosen people becoming a church instead of a race. The fact that Jesus himself lived unmarried, along with John the Baptist, the Apostle Paul, and all but one of Jesus' disciples (Peter), does not so much undermine marriage as render it unnecessary for a full and God-honoring personal life. In his actions, Jesus is said to have endorsed marriage by performing his first miracle at a wedding (John 2:1–11), and one of his last acts on the cross was to take care of

17. Gillis, *World of Their Own Making*, 126, 116.

18. Keller, *Counterfeit Gods*.

19. Goudzwaard, *Idols of our Time*.

20. Fishburn, *Confronting the Idolatry of Family*, 36.

21. Ibid., 86.

22. Mace and Mace, *Sacred Fire*.

family matters by looking after his mother (John 19:25–27), as every good Jewish son would do. However, in his teachings, Jesus never addressed marriage and family intentionally, but only in response to questions. He taught that marriage was not desirable for all his followers, was limited to life on earth (Matt 22:30; 24:38), and could hinder full discipleship (Luke 14:20, 26; Matt 19:12), but also those who do marry should take it very seriously (Mark 10:2–12; Matt 19:3–9).

What is most striking about Jesus' comments on marriage and family is that he consistently takes the opportunity to teach a radical discipleship that contextualizes and qualifies the importance of marriage and family. We have already noted his redefinition of family in Mark 3:33–35, where he—a Jewish son—ignores the cultural status of his biological mother, insisting that only whoever does the will of God is his family. Contrary to all Jewish custom, he refuses to grant Mary the highest status available to a Jewish woman, that of mother, insisting that her foremost status would be that of follower of God. In a similar vein, when a woman in a crowd calls out "Blessed is the womb that bore you and the breasts that nursed you!" his startling response was "Blessed rather are those who hear the word of God and obey it!" (Luke 11:27). Again he rejects the ideal of the Jewish woman as primarily a child-bearer, in favor of a person whose principal calling is to obey God.

These assertions become clangingly repetitive during the course of Jesus' ministry. Those who, fulfilling their cultural obligations, put priority on saying farewell to family or burying their kin are not "fit for the kingdom of God" (Luke 9:59–61). The consequence of his coming will be to divide the family (Luke 12:52–53; Matt 10:21). If we do not "hate" spouse and family, we cannot be his disciples (Luke 14:25–27). Most forthrightly, "Whoever loves father or mother more than me is not worthy of me; and whoever loves son or daughter more than me is not worthy of me" (Matt 10:37). While disciples may lose their biological families, they will receive new ones a hundredfold (Mark 10:29–30). Though he remained respectful of marriage and responsible to his own family, Jesus nonetheless repeatedly and forcefully placed marriage in the service of the kingdom, denying that investing in marriage and family was the central task of his followers. The demands of the kingdom were ultimately to pre-empt the demands of marriage, though not necessarily in every daily situation.

For his part, Paul had some very positive things to say about marriage, likening it to the relationship of Christ and the church (Eph 5:21–33) and identifying false teachers by those who tried to forbid it (1 Tim 4:3). But overall, the New Testament pays surprisingly little attention, for us, to marriage. When it does, many passages downplay its importance, relative to the emphasis on building the church under the conviction of the world's imminent end. A certain Christian asceticism had tempered the high view of marriage and family in Old Testament Jewish culture. Though any absolute priority of the family was soundly denied, its natural order was not dissolved. It remained good, and good for something, especially when brought into the service of the new order. So we return to the functions of marriage and the family to look for what may be distinctly or uniquely Christian.

One approach would be a simple overview of Bible passages that address marriage. For example, the purposes of marriage listed in the Biblical Cyclopedic Index of *The Open Bible* (NASB) are as follows: continuance of the race (Gen 1:28); Godly offspring (Mal 2:14–15); prevention of immoral behavior (1 Cor 7:2, 9); complete satisfaction (Prov 5:19); and man's (*sic*) happiness (Gen 2:18). One problem with this approach is that it is a product of the interpretive lens through which the Bible is read, reflecting assumptions about marriage brought to the text. A second, related problem is that it simply reproduces standard sociological functions of the family: procreation, socialization, social control, need fulfillment, and sentiment. Another approach would be to argue that marriage holds spiritual or theological significance because it is symbolic of Christ the bridegroom and the church his bride. This of course is a metaphor, a simile, or an analogy, meaning that the relationship is *like* a marriage in some significant ways, but not an actual marriage. Analogies are illustrative teaching tools that, by the laws of logic, prove nothing in argument, though they provide enough similarity to make a comparison useful, and enough dissimilarity to eventually break down.

Rodney Clapp has perhaps articulated best both the Christian function and the Christian importance of marriage and family.[23] In his view, the primary Christian function of the family is to serve as a mission base, in much the same way as some social theorists have viewed it as an agent for the common good. Marriage is not an end unto itself, but a means to a greater end, just as a mission base is not a mission base if it does not continually send its members out into the world to do things of greater importance than enjoying the security and comfort of the base. There are times when the mission is carried out right at the base, such as in the institutionally undifferentiated society of the Bible discussed in Mandate 2. For example, their hospitality ethic was one way in which family as mission base was lived out in ancient Hebrew culture. Households served not just as havens for the family, but as hostels, homeless shelters, halfway houses, and hospices. In the new covenant, kingdom building remains more important than marriage building, and it will not do to claim that we build God's kingdom by always giving first priority to marriage and family. God's call on our lives

---

23. Clapp, *Families at the Crossroads*.

is bigger and broader than our marital status and role. As Levinas puts it, "The privileged role of the home does not consist in being the end of human activity, but in being its condition, and in this sense, its commencement."[24]

As for the family's relative importance, Clapp distinguishes between the first family and the second family. Centered on the unequivocal words of Jesus, the sum total teaching of the biblical text is that the church is the Christian's first family, and the domestic family is the Christian's second family.

> Recovering the purpose of Christian family, on the distinctive terms of the Christian story, requires two declarations—one negative and one positive. The negative declaration: The family is not God's most important institution on earth. The family is not the social agent that most significantly shapes and forms the character of Christians. The family is not the primary vehicle of God's grace and salvation for a waiting, desperate world. And the positive declaration: The church is God's most important institution on earth. The church is the social agent that most significantly shapes and forms the character of Christians. And the church is the primary vehicle of God's grace and salvation for a waiting, desperate world.[25]

As such, a Christian man and woman are brother and sister to each other in Christ, long before and long after they are husband and wife in marriage to each other. While the kingdom of God does not deny or abandon the family, the demands of the kingdom ultimately pre-empt the demands of family. We must not "put the family on a spiritual pedestal to be worshipped, or reduce the church to the role of service provider. The Lord is quite clear that the advent of the reign of God relativizes all human institutions, including the family."[26] What Christians must recover from their cultural idealization and idolization of the family is that it is not their calling to put family first in everything. They are instead called to more readily sacrifice family for kingdom building than sacrifice kingdom building for family, while recognizing that complete either/or one-sidedness is simplistic and misguided. That said, it must be added quickly and clearly that such a God-ordered priority is no license to be irresponsible toward the family, as some driven ministers and missionaries are wont to do.

---

24. Levinas, *Totality and Infinity*, 152.
25. Clapp, *Families at the Crossroads*, 67–68.
26. Lee, *Beyond Family Values*, 178.

BREAK THE HEART OF GOD

Bob Pierce (1914–1978) founded World Vision in 1950, which has become one of the largest Christian relief and development agencies in the world. After clashing with his board over his near maniacal style that was leaving him increasingly unstable, he left World Vision and later founded the similar Samaritan's Purse in 1970. His passion for Christian humanitarian ministry was unequalled and knew no bounds, rebounding on his marriage and family.

> He traveled as much as 10 months of the year, and his family suffered. "I've made an agreement with God," he said, "that I'll take care of his helpless little lambs overseas if he'll take care of mine at home." In 1963 he had a nervous breakdown. For nine months he almost disappeared, preferring to travel the world rather than return home. . . . On a 1968 good-bye tour of Asia, his daughter Sharon reached him by phone. She asked if he could come home, but he refused, saying that he wanted to extend his trip to Vietnam. His wife, Lorraine, started home immediately, but by the time she arrived, Sharon had tried to commit suicide. Later that year, she tried again and succeeded. . . . In 1970 he legally separated from his wife. . . . Just once, in September 1978, the family was able to gather for an evening of reconciliation. Four days later, Pierce died.[27]

Lorraine Pierce, the temperamental opposite of Bob, was a rather insecure woman determined not to do what her own mother had done, which was to separate from her overly zealous evangelistic father. Lorraine believed in Bob and his work to the end, always hoping for meaningful partnership and stability, refusing to give in to his attempts at divorce. The tone of another daughter's raw account of their family life, *Days of Glory, Seasons of Night*,[28] reveals her own anguished but unwavering attachment and hope, and insistence that the suffering was justified by the cause; in the end, she maintained, it was worth the price.

So what can be drawn from the Pierce marriage and family in the context of their cultural mandates and Christian calling? Other than their pronounced gender role distinction,[29] it would appear at first light to be outrightly countercultural in its opposition to sentimentalization, idealization, and idolization. And it would appear to be outrightly unchristian in Bob's abandonment of his family. This was neither the model cultural family nor

---

27. Stafford, "Imperfect Instrument."
28. Dunker, *Days of Glory*.
29. The original title of their daughter's book was *Man of Vision, Woman of Prayer*.

the model Christian family. For all the kingdom-serving humanitarian good that Bob did, he clearly failed at home. On the back cover of their daughter's book, *Moody Monthly* rendered a judgment about "the misconception that man [*sic*] can best serve God by putting ministry before family." But what about the words of Jesus? And what about the call of women? And if there is a culturally captivated Christianity to be found operative here, could it be in the assumptions and expectations of Bob's wife and daughters, as well as in the values of the "traditional family" by which the Christian subculture judged him? Would the story have played out the same 150 years previously, before the rise of the "traditional family"? It so happens that there is a case with some useful parallels. If Bob Pierce could be cast as the father of modern evangelical humanitarian missions, William Carey (1761–1834) had long since been labeled the father of modern Protestant evangelistic missions.[30] Like Pierce, he seemed to be mismatched in his first marriage to Dorothy, and was an appallingly neglectful father. When he left for India, she at first refused to go along, but acquiesced at the last moment. One year after arriving, their first child died, and Dorothy, unable to adapt culturally or cope mentally, suffered a complete breakdown from which she never recovered. Quite literally raving with madness, she was kept by William in virtual house arrest for thirteen years before she died. Yet Carey was judged less harshly by his Christian contemporaries than Pierce was, partly because it was his wife who broke down, not he himself. But neither was he living with the same cultural mandates of marriage and family that haunted the Pierce family.

The past two centuries have seen a succession of notable missionaries who did not use their family as a mission base. David Livingstone (1813–1873) was well matched in marriage, wedding the oldest daughter of English missionaries in Africa who was "sturdy and matter-of-fact," as was their marriage. Yet Mary gave up trying to follow David on his cross-continental treks, returned to England, and became an alcoholic. Their children grew up effectively fatherless. C. T. Studd (1860–1931), the founder of Worldwide Evangelisation Crusade, wrote the same kind of romantic letters from Africa to his wife Priscilla as Bob Pierce would later write to Lorraine, yet never saw Priscilla from 1916 until her death in 1929. The history of modern Protestant missions is full of similar stories of men who chose their mission over their marriage, of women who chose mission instead of marriage, of mission compounds communally caring for young children, and of those children then sent off to boarding school at an early age. As often as not, Protestant missionaries have not exemplified marriage and family as

---

30. The following accounts are drawn from Tucker, *From Jerusalem to Irian Jaya* and *Guardians of the Great Commission*.

their primary calling in life. Our discomfort with their stories exposes our surrender to our culture. ——⟶ Disagree

Bob Pierce's famous epithet was written on the flyleaf of his Bible: "Let my heart be broken with the things that break the heart of God." At least by his language, evidently he too was thoroughly embedded in a culturally romanticized Christianity. Even so, there is no doubt that human suffering and social injustice do break the heart of God, and Pierce was exemplary in responding to that call. But did not Pierce's own marriage and family also break God's heart? If so, did Jesus' similar words to his mother break not only his mother's heart, but God's heart too? How can Christians give primary allegiance to their first family and calling, the church, and still be fully responsible to their second family and calling, the home? These are not easy questions, or negotiations. But Christians must begin by resisting the cultural mandate to privatize, sentimentalize, idealize, and idolize their marriages and families.

> Gillis makes a helpful distinction between the families that we "live by" and the families that we "live with." The former refers to our cultural family ideals, the family as it should be, the bearer of our hopes and dreams. The latter refers to the people with whom we must actually live. Compared to the families we live by, the families we live with often disappoint us with their fallibility, fragility, and selfishness. The question for society and the church is whether we have become so captivated by the families we live by that we soon cease to deal compassionately and realistically with the families we must live with.[31]

---

31. Lee, *Beyond Family Values*, 62.

Mandate 4

Need Fulfillment

Should our spouse be our primary source of personal need fulfillment?

MARRIAGE, WE HAVE SEEN, is valued for what it does. The various functions it performs for society as a whole go a long way in determining how much it is valued. But modern Western individuals contemplating marriage are unlikely to be altruistic in their assessment of its merits. They are unlikely to be thinking about what their marriage might do for their family or community, and more likely to be focused entirely on what marriage could do for themselves. In the euphoric romantic fog of being "in love," their thoughts will focus on "you" and "us," not "others." There will be lots of talk about wanting to grow as individuals, to nurture each other, and to celebrate togetherness. But behind such talk will lurk myriad, perhaps unacknowledged, and probably uncomfortable thoughts about "me." "What will marriage do for *me*?" Even the noblest focus on giving to one's spouse implies that marital partners receive something from the other by the very process of being in intimate relationship with them, and that giving makes getting possible. Therefore, at some point the question "What do *I* get out of it?" becomes unavoidable.

Our Western cultural pattern of forming couples by self-selection based on love, described in Mandate 1, increases the probability that choice will be driven by self-interest. Our isolation and privatization of the family, described in Mandate 2, increases the dependence of the spouse on the marriage. And our moral horizon of modern individual rights and psychotherapy, described in Mandate 3, legitimates that "what is good for me is right for me." If a marriage matures well, it will likely be described as "fulfilling," without specifying what exactly is fulfilled, though the connotation will be that marriage meets the personal needs of each spouse. If the marriage falters, each spouse will likely question it by again asking, if only silently, "What's in it for me?" The moral or pragmatic question about "What should I do" will likely arise next, but the social question of "What is good for my kin and community" is unlikely to be asked at all. As such, personal needs tend to take precedence, perhaps subconsciously, over theological meanings, with little or no regard given to the well-being of the community.

Our propensity to think of marriage first in terms of love and personal "need fulfillment" is a further manifestation of the individualism, explicated in Mandates 2 and 3, that has come to characterize, distinguish, and virtually define contemporary Western culture. It contrasts sharply with the collectivistic cultures of the ancient world of the Bible, and the contemporary world of non-Western societies. To formulate an analysis of human relationships in terms of the presumed needs of individuals is to analyze from the inside out, which is an already enculturated enterprise, representative of our particular time and place, or what has been termed our "standpoint."[1] Christians have likewise only begun to do so in relatively recent history, in concert with Enlightenment values and their dispensations.

Current Western Christian reflection on marriage tends to focus on the personal thoughts, feelings, and behavior of each individual spouse regarding the other spouse. Popular Christian marriage talk is largely preoccupied with the interpersonal relational dynamics of marriage. It tends to think of the relational nature of humans in psychological, interpersonal terms at the expense of equally important sociological, collective terms. This fixation on the internalities of marriage at the expense of the externalities of marriage is both a cause and effect of the reality that most recent leading Christian experts on marriage and family have been psychologists. Yet as the science of the individual, psychology is not necessarily best equipped to unpack the social or relational phenomena of marriage and family.[2] Nevertheless, most Christian marriage and family analyses and admonitions are spiritualized self-help pop psychology, products of "the psychological captivity of evangelicalism."[3]

This is not to suggest that the interpersonal, relational dynamics of marriage are merely fictions of culture, and not real. It is only to suggest that

---

1. Standpoint theory, which posits that knowledge is specific to social structure and position, is most associated with Dorothy Smith.

2. Anderson and Guernsey, *On Being Family*.

3. Balswick, "Psychological Captivity of Evangelicalism."

the rise and embrace of psychologized individualism has placed a historically and culturally unprecedented emphasis on them. That Christians now pursue marriage with equal and sometimes seemingly greater emphasis on interpersonal dynamics is further evidence of their surrender to culture. As we continue tracking the conflation of cultural and Christian concepts of marriage, we must turn from the historical and sociological questions we have put to marriage toward more psychological questions in this and the next few Mandates. What are the basic human needs as perceived by psychology? Which of them are best met by marriage? How effective is marriage in meeting them? What are some other sources of need fulfillment? How realistic and yes, psychologically healthy, is it to expect spouses to be the primary source of need fulfillment? We will find the psychological way of thinking beguiling, and ultimately diversionary and discrepant from what the biblical text models.

FROM SURVIVAL TO TRANSCENDENCE

Understanding human needs frequently begins with distinguishing them from human wants. Not surprisingly, what gets classified as a need or a want varies markedly from person to person and culture to culture, but what constitutes a need or a want does not vary. A need is simply something necessary for a human to live a healthy life, something whose absence would cause dysfunction or death. Needs stem from the condition of being human. They are few, finite, and classifiable,[4] and they remain constant throughout all human cultures and across historical time periods. What changes over time and between cultures is the strategies by which needs are satisfied. For our interests here, some personal needs met by Western marriage today, such as companionship, were met otherwise in other times and places. A want, in contrast, is simply something desired to enrich life, but is unnecessary to sustain healthy life. Wants go beyond health to pursue happiness, and as such are infinite and insatiable. As the billionaire replied when asked how much was enough, "Just a little more." Both needs and wants drive human behavior, arousing a person to action toward a goal, giving purpose and direction to behavior.

Unfortunately, as soon as psychological substance is inserted into the tidy and mutually exclusive definitions of needs and wants, clarity dissipates. The different types of human "needs" range from objective and physical needs, such as food, to subjective and psychological needs, such as self-esteem. More specifically, needs are typically categorized as physical,

4. Max-Neef, *Human Scale Development*.

emotional, social, sexual, psychic, spiritual, intellectual, vocational, and so on, each with endless details to be understood, academic disciplines to understand, and professions to provide care. By far the best-known academic classification of human needs, familiar to anyone who has taken an introductory psychology course, is Maslow's hierarchy of human needs.[5] Usually portrayed in the shape of a pyramid, the most basic levels of needs at the bottom must be met before the individual will focus motivation upon the secondary or higher-level needs.

The largest and most fundamental level of need is physiological, the need for sheer bodily survival. Air, water, food, and sleep are metabolic requirements, clothing and shelter provide necessary protection from the elements of nature. At the second level are safety needs, including the security of body, resources, and human rights that are threatened by violence, poverty, and power. The third level of human needs are social, comprising the need for love and belonging, affection and affiliation. Families, friends, or other groups and engagements are required to provide the intimate and emotionally significant relationships that foster a sense of value and acceptance. Fourth, humans need to be seen as significant and respected for their contributions, what Maslow termed the need for esteem. He deemed attention, recognition, and prestige in the eyes of others as less important than the conceptually separate competence, independence, and confidence of self-esteem. Finally, at the top of the pyramid is the need for self-actualization, the realization of one's full potential. "What a [person] can be, [they] must be."[6] Maslow explicitly defines self-actualization to be the desire for self-fulfillment, to become more and more what one is, to become everything that one is capable of becoming. What distinguishes this highest human need from the previous four in the pyramid is that self-actualization is growth motivated rather than deficiency motivated, a "being need" rather than a "deficiency need."

Maslow's theory was generated within his devotion to humanistic[7] and developmental psychology, and has been criticized in those terms. One criticism is that, despite its widespread acceptance, there is little empirical support for the ranking of human needs.[8] Chilean economist and philosopher Manfred Max-Neef developed a well-regarded taxonomy of interrelated and interactive needs that draws a rather different picture of humans. According

5. The hierarchy was first expressed in Maslow, "Theory of Human Motivation," and fully developed in his *Motivation and Personality*.

6. Maslow, *Motivation and Personality*, 91.

7. In contrast to other branches of psychology such as psychoanalytic, behavioral, experimental, and so on.

8. Wahba, "Maslow Reconsidered."

to Max-Neef, the fundamental human needs are subsistence, protection, affection, understanding, participation, leisure, creation, identity, and freedom.[9] Another criticism is that casting self-actualization as the apex of human being is clearly the predictable conclusion of a selfist, individualist, American culture. As an ethnocentric theory not applicable to collectivist cultures that place the community above the individual, self-actualization as the ultimate state is more a product of culture than an accurate insight into universal human being.[10] Perhaps the most damning criticism of Maslow's theory, from both a cultural and Christian perspective, comes from another, this time European, humanistic psychologist writing at the same time as Maslow. Viktor Fankl, a survivor of the Holocaust, maintained that self-transcendence, not self-actualization, is the pinnacle of human development. The highest state of being is to rise above narrow absorption with self and give one's self to someone other and something bigger than one's self.

In the latter part of his life, Maslow took these criticisms as correctives, and though he never altered his basic hierarchy of needs, he did elaborate what self-actualization entailed.[11] First, it requires a cognitive need to know, understand, and explore the depths of life that made it meaningful, thereby echoing Frankl's *Man's Search for Meaning*. Second, it requires an aesthetic need for symmetry, order, and beauty that gives life form and balance. Only when cognitive and aesthetic needs have been met can the individual self-actualize and, having done so, finally self-transcend to the point of helping others find self-fulfillment and realize their own potential. Indeed, Maslow went on to establish the transpersonal school of psychology, which held full spiritual awakening and liberation from egocentricity as ideals.

RELATEDNESS

These are the range of questions and considerations involved in exploring whether, how, and to what degree marriage fulfills personal needs. From basic breathing to self-transcendence, marriage is not necessary for meeting any one particular need, but it can be an effectual means of meeting some personal needs, however they are defined. Conceptually, there is at least a clear difference between personal need fulfillment and self-fulfillment, the latter being a small and culturally driven subset of the former. To examine need fulfillment carefully requires not only distinguishing between needs and wants, but distinguishing further between drives, obsessions,

9. Max-Neef, *Human Scale Development*.

10. Cianci, "Maslow's Hierarchy of Needs."

11. Huitt, "Maslow's Hierarchy of Needs."

compulsions, addictions, longings, interests, preferences and so on. Some are healthy, some unhealthy; some are innate, some acquired. Objective, physical needs are products of universal human nature, and thus innate. Subjective, psychological needs are as much products of particular human cultures as human nature, and thus can be acquired.[12]

Sex is a pertinent example, and a significant part of marriage. As customarily as sex is granted the status of a need, it certainly is not necessary for individual survival, or living a healthy life, or even living a fulfilling life. Millions of celibates including Jesus and Paul have done so their entire lives, and all persons have done so for parts of their lives. That sex is deemed a need is more likely a manifestation of androcentrism and male bias in psychological theory. Males may have a stronger sex drive than females,[13] and have self-servingly used their social power to define sex as a need and obligate women to provide it. Hull's drive theory is a case in point.[14] According to this perspective, people have a set of innate physiological needs that reflect bodily tissue deficits, result in "drive states," and must be met for the organism to remain physically healthy. As examples, Hull included sex along with the metabolic requirements of food and water. Maslow can also be criticized for placing sex on the foundational level of physiological needs, thereby reducing it to an individualistic physical need and ignoring its emotional, relational, and in fact communal implications and consequences.[15] Sex is best understood as a drive or a longing that varies not only from person to person and culture to culture, but within the individual. Sexual expression can be encouraged and nurtured, or discouraged and repressed, but no one has died or become dysfunctional for lack of it. When the sex drive becomes pathologically excessive, it becomes obsessive/compulsive, or addictive, and only thereby dysfunctional and destructive. But to conceive of sex as a need is only justifiable in a more delimited relational context, such as the health of a marriage, where lack of it may produce anxiety in some cultures. And even there, questions remain about innate needs versus acquired wants.

Two other psychological theories facilitate narrowing discussion of needs to those met by or in marriage. The first is Alderfer's ERG theory, which streamlines Maslow's hierarchy into three collapsed categories. The lower order needs of physiology and safety are combined into Existence needs; interpersonal love, belonging, and esteem are combined into

12. Murray, *Explorations in Personality*.

13. Though women have never had the power and privilege to explore, develop, and enjoy their sexuality on their own terms in the way men have. Effective contraception has only recently liberated women somewhat.

14. Hull, *Principles of Behavior*.

15. Kenrick et al., "Renovating the Pyramid of Needs."

Relatedness needs; self-esteem and self-actualization are combined into Growth needs. Of these three, marriage would seem to be most associated with Relatedness needs, but that is true only of the current Western historical moment. Premodern marriage was more preoccupied with Existence needs than Relatedness needs, and only with modernity did marriage undergo the "great transformation from survival to sentiment."[16] In plainer terms, the focus of marriage shifted in step with culture from securing human needs to pursing human wants, including happiness, fulfillment, and eventually self-actualization. Though for some today marriage may be their principal means of growth, and indeed the most immediate test of self-transcendence, marriage today serves and satisfies Relatedness needs more than Existence or Growth needs.

A second theory also draws attention to relatedness needs. Self-determination theory identifies competence, relatedness, and autonomy as essential needs for optimal psychological growth and well-being. "A need for competence reflects the need to feel effective in one's efforts and capable of achieving desired outcomes. The need for relatedness involves a need to feel connected to and understood by others. Finally, autonomy reflects the need to feel volitional in one's actions, to fully and authentically endorse one's behaviors, and to act as the originator of one's own behavior."[17] Of these three, competence needs are least associated with marriage, relatedness needs are again most associated with marriage, and autonomy needs may actually be jeopardized by marriage. Research has consistently shown that relatedness need fulfillment is the strongest and often the only unique predictor of relationship functioning and well-being.[18]

The point here is not so much that marriage meets certain needs, but that marriage meets certain needs much more than other needs. No one form of relationship or engagement meets all human needs. While marriage is a positive and powerful though limited means to an end, it is no guarantor of full human need fulfillment. Marriage is one way of meeting some human needs. Those needs seem to be clustered in the middle range of Relatedness needs, more so than the earlier, primary Existence needs or the later, secondary Growth needs. The question remains whether, once entered, marriage ought to become the primary or even exclusive means of meeting the most important human needs, if we can speak with any confidence of such.

16. Mace and Mace, *Sacred Fire*.

17. Note that autonomy should not be confused with independence or detachment from others. Rather, it involves a sense of volition, agency, and initiative. See Patrick et al., "Role of Need Fulfillment," 434.

18. Ibid.

ONE OR TWO?

Christian discourse on the need fulfillment of marriage today seems more grounded in and informed by the modern cultural phenomenon of psychology than in the ancient practice of biblical hermeneutics. Christian psychology, or more precisely Christian counseling, has addressed it directly and extensively. One of the most influential Christian counseling theories applied to marriage in the last generation has been supplied by Larry Crabb in his book *The Marriage Builder: A Blueprint for Couples and Counselors.*[19] Writing from a fully developed counseling theory grounded in psychology and Scripture,[20] he asserts that people have two deep needs that cannot be met outside of relationship. Psychologically, they need the security of being loved freely and unconditionally, and the significance of having a meaningful impact on another person. Yet theologically, ultimately only Christ can meet these needs. When spouses try to derive their personal security and significance from each other, the relationship becomes manipulative and exploitative as they use the other for the satisfaction of their own needs.

The goal of marriage, according to Crabb, is not the meeting of personal needs, but the relationship of Oneness. Spirit Oneness entails a simultaneous, complete dependence on God for the satisfaction of primal personal needs.[21] Soul Oneness entails "the mutual, intelligent, and unreserved commitment to be an instrument of God to deeply touch a spouse's personal needs in a unique, powerful, and meaningful way."[22] This is interpersonal ministry instead of manipulation, helping the other to become more aware of, and subjectively experience, their sufficiency in Christ, adding to the feelings of their already given security and significance, not adding to the fact. Along the way, it is important to differentiate between goals and desires. A goal is an objective that is under personal control, whereas a desire is an objective that may be a legitimate want, but cannot be reached through our efforts alone. Hence legitimate desires can become illegitimate goals when we confuse or conflate them. For example, we may desire that a spouse change what disappoints us in them, but to voice our disappointments in such a way as to make it our goal to change them is to be coercive. Even making the other carry our disappointment in some essentially unchangeable aspect of their person is to subtly make a desire into a goal, foregoing the silent strength, grace, and peace of accepting what

19. Crabb, *Marriage Builder.*

20. Crabb, *Basic Principles of Biblical Counseling, Effective Biblical Counseling.*

21. There is a certain problematic mysticism in this notion that God meets personal needs directly, instead of through other people.

22. Crabb, *Marriage Builder,* 47.

disappoints us. The danger of such silence, of course, is that it becomes a form of disengagement, or false martyrdom.

Like Maslow, Crabb later modified his language, and thus his concepts, if not his analytic schemes. "[M]y preference now is to speak of *deep longings in the human heart for relationship and impact* rather than *personal needs for security and significance.*"[23] This seemingly subtle shift reduces essential requirements to drive states, suggesting they are not in fact necessary, but still highly motivating. What Crabb did not modify was his gendering of the two primal needs or longings. He consistently described men as more intent on significance, and women as more intent on security. In effect, his definition of masculinity is a virtual portrait of significance: "The satisfying awareness of the substance God has placed within a man's being that can make an enduring contribution to God's purposes in this world, and will be deeply valued by others, especially his wife, as a reliable source of wise, sensitive, compassionate, and decisive involvement."[24] Likewise, his definition of femininity is the picture of security: "The secure awareness of the substance God has placed within a woman's being that enables her to confidently and warmly invite others into relationship with God and with herself, knowing that there is something in each relationship to be wonderfully enjoyed."[25] This bifurcation of humans is problematic. If the needs, longings, or essences of men and women are that different, how can we know if each carries them differently as well, and how can we even talk about both simultaneously?

Crabb's gendering of human needs, tempered somewhat by academic responsibility, pales in comparison to a more popularized Christian portrayal of marital needs that has likely enjoyed even broader influence in the last generation. Willard Harley's analysis is not grounded in any full psychological theory of being human, and is less theological or exegetical than Crabb's. Consistent with his Marriage Builders website,[26] the title of his bestselling book, *His Needs, Her Needs: Building an Affair-Proof Marriage*, not only genders human needs, but conceptualizes marriage simply as mutual need fulfillment, and threatens marital breakdown if needs are not met. He delineates the respective "most important emotional needs" of husbands and wives as follows:

> Her Needs:
> *Affection*—the first thing she can't do without

23. Crabb, *Understanding People*, 15.
24. Crabb, *Men and Women*, 160.
25. Ibid 163.
26. http://www.marriagebuilders.com/.

Conversation—she needs him to talk to her
Honesty and Openness—she needs to trust him totally
Financial Support—she needs enough money to live comfortably
Family Commitment—she needs him to be a good father

His Needs:
Sexual Fulfillment—the first thing he can't do without
Recreational Companionship—he needs her to be his playmate
An Attractive Spouse—he needs a good looking wife
Domestic Support—he needs peace and quiet
Admiration—he needs her to be proud of him[27]

Such a portrayal of respective spousal needs is little more than traditional gender roles and stereotypes redefined as male and female needs, culture cast as nature. She is sexually ambivalent, expressive, relational, emotional, dependent, and nurturing. He is sexually driven, non-relational, agentic, demanding, and self-focused. There is also a conspicuous difference in power and privilege, in that he can seemingly demand compliance in sex and anything else he wants to do, oblige her to be obsessed with her appearance so as to be sufficient eye candy on his arm, expect to receive as much space as he wants at home, and be the apple of her eye in the process. One wonders what her and his needs would be if they were not married. Do these supposed needs arise only in marriage, and if so, are marital needs separate from human needs? Then does marriage fulfill needs or create needs? And do she and he have anything in common? From Harley, men and women come off sounding as if they are two entirely different species that are alien to each other. Instead of being far more alike than different in their humanity—perhaps 98 percent the same—it sounds as if men are from Mars and women are from Venus,[28] not from the same rib.

FRIENDS AND LOVERS

The most contentious point about need fulfillment and marriage is not that marriage should meet personal needs, or even what those needs might be, but to what degree spouses should be responsible for mutual need fulfillment. The full range of potential involvement can be conceptualized as a five-point continuum: 1) spouse as a non-source, 2) a secondary source,

27. From the table of contents in Harley, *His Needs, Her Needs.*

28. The Christian version of John Gray's wildly popular *Men are from Mars, Women are from Venus* is Bill and Pam Farrel's *Men are Like Waffles, Women are Like Spaghetti.* Men are like waffles because they think in small separate boxes. Women are like spaghetti because their thoughts are all interwoven.

3) an equal source, 4) a primary source, or 5) an exclusive source. Crabb's assertion that spouses are not called to be, or even capable of being, the ultimate sources of each other's need for security and significance, and that they become dysfunctionally manipulative when they try, suggests that more reliance is not always better. The best they can do is to be mutual ministers who help the other get in touch with and feel the already established fact of their security and significance in God. In Crabb's view, spouses should contribute to need fulfillment, but not be responsible for or demanding of it. In the language of social-scientific methodology, they are contributing factors, but not necessary or sufficient factors.

It is not difficult to envision spouses being healthy and happy 1) non-sources or 2) secondary sources of need fulfillment in certain aspects of life. Vocational and avocational interests are two examples, despite Harley's insistence on a male need for a female playmate in recreational pursuits. Many marriage counselors actually recommend at least some separate interests as healthy. At the other extreme, sexuality is clearly an area of 5) sole or exclusive need fulfillment in marriage, by both cultural and Christian standards. The most contentious areas lie in between, at points three and four of the continuum. Which needs are best 3) shared equally with non-spousal others and which are best met 4) primarily by spouses is much less clear. What culture mandates in this regard is more discernible than what God mandates, as the biblical text does not address this level of specificity. Any attempt to articulate a Christian position will unavoidably be an enculturated interpretation, if not extrapolation.

At least three variables seem to be operative in assessing the propriety of need fulfillment being either shared equally with others or reserved primarily for spouses: which need, which gender, and which other. Of the range of needs identified by Maslow, Max-Neef, and others, the vast majority are met most appropriately and effectively by multiple others. The need for esteem, for example, is hardly met by the admiration of a spouse alone. By cultural standards, a sense of being loved and belonging should come primarily from a spouse, but that is not borne out in the biblical text. True, Paul exhorts husbands to love their wives "as Christ loved the church and gave himself up for her" (Eph 5:25), but that admonition is a special point of emphasis for a culture in which it was not normative for husbands to love their wives. A few verses earlier, Paul had established the overarching imperative by instructing all the men and women of the church to "live in love, as Christ loved us and gave himself up for us" (Eph 5:2). Furthermore, that ultimate expression of love is matched by Jesus' assertion that "no one has greater love than this, to lay down one's life for one's friends" (John 15:13). The ultimate act of love is not reserved for marriage.

Regarding growth needs, we have already noted how autonomy needs, in the sense of volition, agency, and initiative, may have been jeopardized by marriage historically, especially for wives. For them, self-fulfillment has traditionally had to come in the form of role fulfillment, not in the form of truly unfettered self-actualization. If truth be told, theirs has also been a tragic kind of self-transcendence, because it has been enforced by patriarchy, not achieved after authentic self-actualization. Yet it is also true that for any genuinely caring husband as well, marriage is a boot camp for self-transcendence. Men and women have also differed in their relatedness needs. Historically, women, including Christian women, have experienced far more intimacy with their own mothers, children, and friends than they have with their husbands. For many women from Ruth and Naomi on, family and friends continue to meet more of their emotional needs than their husbands do. The current ideal of spouses as best friends is a historical and cultural anomaly, and a dubious reality. The current norm is for wives to name another woman as their best friend, and for husbands to name their wife—an intriguing double standard.

Of the five subtypes of relatedness needs found to be fulfilled by romantic relationships—intimacy, companionship, sexuality, security, and emotional involvement[29]—four are equally fulfilled by non-romantic relationships. Parent and sibling relationships obviously continue to provide relatedness need fulfillment, but because of the fragmentation and isolation of the modern family, friendship appears to have supplanted family as the still secondary alternative to spouses. There was a time in Western history when friendship in fact was pre-eminent. To the ancients, friendship was "the happiest and most fully human of all loves; the crown of life and the school of virtue."[30] It was regarded a greater love than marriage, and the consummate source of need fulfillment.[31] Aristotle devoted two of the ten books of his *Nicomachean Ethics* to friendship, picturing it as "a single soul dwelling in two bodies," a portrayal we today would want to reserve for marriage. As the biblical paragon of the ancient veneration of friendship, it is written that "the soul of Jonathan was bound to the soul of David, and Jonathan loved him as his own soul" (1 Sam 18:1). In response, David lamented Jonathan's death by saying "your love to me was wonderful, passing the love of women" (2 Sam 1:26). Later, we see Jesus expressing his deepest

29. Drigotas and Rusbult, "Should I Stay or Should I Go?"

30. Lewis, *Four Loves*, 55

31. This is argued most convincingly in Lewis, *Four Loves*; and Olthuis, *I Pledge You My Troth*.

emotional attachment to his disciples in the upper room by calling them his friends, as he lay down his life for them.

Friendships existed across sex, age, and class distinctions in early Christian communities,[32] medieval Europe, and early colonial life much more so than in modern industrial society.[33] It is no coincidence that mass, modern, technological society has become increasingly friendless in direct proportion to the idealization and emotional loading of modern marriage. In the storied loss of community that is modern history, it is no surprise that visions of best-friends marriage should arise to fill the vacuum. This is due in large part to the transformation of the notion of friendship itself. Predictably, ancient notions were highly gendered, reflecting the traditional male myth of friendship in bravery, loyalty, duty, and heroism.[34] This male bias was still evident in C. S. Lewis' modern picture of friends standing side by side, while lovers stand face to face.[35] In fact it is only male friendship that is founded on the companionship of shared "side-by-side" activity.[36] Female friendship, like lovers, is founded on the intimacy of shared "face-to-face" talk, and has led to a greater value, need fulfillment, and participation in friendship by women than by men. Thus, the perception and practice of friendship itself has reversed completely from a male civic virtue in antiquity to a female private indulgence in modernity. As with other dimensions of social life, when friendship was considered a male preserve, it had high social status and value, but when it came to be considered a female preserve, it lost its prestige, though not its ability to meet relatedness needs.[37]

Because men and women practice friendship differently, they derive different need fulfillment from it. When they engage each other as friends, they gain a clear window into the neighboring sex, and an opportunity for greater personal well-being. "[F]riendship between the sexes may take us not out of ourselves but beyond ourselves—may make us more whole, more balanced and sane, than we could otherwise be."[38] However, cross-sex friendships face at least four further negotiation challenges: "1) determining the type of emotional bond represented by the relationship, 2) contending with the issue of sexuality, 3) dealing with the barrier of inequality, and 4) the challenge of public relationships—presenting the relationship as au-

32. Rader, *Breaking Boundaries.*
33. Lopata, "Friendship."
34. Sapadin, "Friendship and Gender."
35. Lewis, *Four Loves.*
36. Wright, "Men's Friendships, Women's Friendships."
37. Ibid.
38. Meilaender, "Men and Women," 13.

thentic to relevant audiences."[39] Even if a married person is not suspected of adultery, they are likely to be accused of emotional adultery if the intimacy of the cross-sex friendship matches or surpasses that with their spouse. Yet the charge of emotional infidelity is unlikely to be leveled if the other is a parent, sibling, or same-sex friend. The charge of emotional incest is unlikely to be leveled if the other is one's child. And the charge of emotional fornication is unlikely to be leveled if the cross-sex friends are unmarried. Moreover, emotional primacy in marriage is a current Western cultural mandate nowhere to be found in the biblical text.

In his book *Sacred Unions, Sacred Passions*, Dan Brennan writes that "Friendships between the sexes are increasing in contemporary culture and, even more significantly, trans-marital friendship love is emerging as a sacred option for husbands and wives in Christ-honoring marriages. More than ever, friendship love between a man and a woman is poised to become a receptive love coexisting *with* marriage, not a rival love *to* it."[40] With deep understanding of the profundity of sexuality and the sacredness of marriage, Brennan tells of the other sacred unions and passions of friendship in the Bible and throughout Christian history. His exposition of the passionate and pure cross-sex friendship between Jesus and Mary Magdalene is particularly poignant. Yet he too holds up the ideal of best-friends marriage, without biblical warrant, and without noting the difference between marriage and friendship. Friendship by definition remains voluntary or formally unconstrained by roles,[41] thus rendering marriage as friendship problematic. Perhaps only when men and women get to know and love each other deeply in the freedom and equality of friendship will they be able to move beyond the alienation and antagonism of gender socialization toward true gender reconciliation. Marriage partners "may need help in recognizing that some needs will never be met anywhere, that lots of needs can be and should be met by people other than one's spouse, and that such relationships need not be sexualized."[42]

39. Hiebert, "Toward Adult Cross-Sex Friendship," 275.

40. Brennan, *Sacred Unions, Sacred Passions*, 17.

41. Wright defines friendship as "voluntary or unconstrained interaction in which the participants respond to one another personally, that is, as unique individuals rather than as packages of discrete attributes or mere role occupants" (Wright, "Self-Referent Motivation," 116).

42. Fay, "Turning Down the Temperature," 89.

FRAMES OF DEPENDENCE

In light of the many questions and complexities of personal need fulfillment, it is startling that contemporary Western culture should require that
spouses be the primary resource for meeting as many of them as possible,
that we should look first to and gain most from our spouse in every aspect
of human being. Even a cursory appraisal of such a norm suggests that it
severely reduces personal resources for living, applies enormous pressure to
marriages, and demands superhuman spouses for us all. A case can readily
be made that such a norm also makes spouses inordinately dependent on
each other. Types of marital dependence can be represented visually by four
capital letters depicting frames of relationship. K-frame dependence is an
asymmetrical relationship in which one weak spouse leans and relies on
a strong spouse in the strongest sense of "need." If the strong one lets go
for any reason, the weak one falls, but if the weak one lets go, the strong
one feels relief. A-frame codependence is an involuntary and uncontrolled,
though symmetrical and mutual reliance on each other, in which spouses
commend themselves as a couple, a single unit, not as partners or attached
units. If either lets go, they both collapse. H-frame independence is self-
reliance and self-sufficiency, with little attachment, mutuality, or sense of
oneness. If one lets go, they are simply detached and disconnected, not even
destabilized. Finally, M-frame interdependence is the chosen, controlled
mutual reliance of mutual influence and support. If one lets go, the other is
destabilized and feels the loss, but recovers balance. Of these four frames,
current Western culture holds A-frame marriage as an ideal, despite the
acknowledged psychopathology of symbiotic codependency.

Christians fed and formed by pop psychology tend to agree, despite insufficient biblical warrant for marital codependency. Instead, God calls Christian spouses to interdependency, to love and loyalty, mutual submission and
satisfaction, not to idolatry of self or other, just as not to idolatry of institution
discussed previously. Crabb is sternly critical of the ascendency of psychological need fulfillment that fosters virtual codependency in marriage.

> "Fulfillment" has taken on a greater urgency and value than
> "obedience." Psychologists do great damage by encouraging this
> reversal of priorities. . . . Scriptures about dying to self, finding
> one's life by losing it, being crucified with Christ, and living only
> for Christ make it clear that realizing true fulfillment depends,
> not on preoccupation with fulfillment, but preoccupation with
> knowing God. . . . To validate a plan of action by appealing to its

potential for meeting needs is to replace the authority of [the] Bible with a humanistic value system.[43]

Though not all Christians are as confident as Crabb about what obedience to the authority of the Bible looks like in marriage, preoccupation with fulfillment is by any measure a product of individualistic culture and humanistic psychology. Individuals so encultured are likely, perhaps subconsciously, to place psychological needs ahead of theological meanings, with little or no regard for community well-being. This rank ordering of the implicit importance of psychology, theology, and community is actually completely reversed in causal effect. Though Christians claim that their theology takes precedence over everything, including marriage, their practice is usually to let their culture shape their theology and psychology equally. The consequential results are in. In his now classic Christian critique of humanistic psychology, *Psychology as Religion: The Cult of Self-Worship*, Paul Vitz concluded that "There is every reason to believe that the spread of the selfist philosophy in society has contributed greatly to the destruction of families."[44]

Whether it be friendship, vocation, avocation, ministry, or something else, nothing, Western culture insists, is supposed to "take us away" from our spouses. Christians have surrendered equally to this cultural mandate of spousal all-sufficiency. We have been led to believe and fear that any personal need met outside a marriage destabilizes and threatens that marriage. We are now culturally obligated to gamble almost all our personal and interpersonal chips on a single wager—the stakes, and the vulnerability, are at an all-time high. How we got here, the Scriptures know not.

---

43. Crabb, *Marriage Builder*, 10–11.

44. Vitz, *Psychology as Religion*, 57.

Mandate 5

Love

Should marital love be romantic?

WE COME NOW TO the heart of marriage: love. More than anything else, marriage is characterized by love, both by the current Western cultural mandate and by Christian mandate. Yet here again, what characterizes a relationship does not necessarily distinguish it from other relationships. Yes, of course Christian wives and husbands should love each other, but according to Jesus' two great commandments they should also love God and neighbor (Matt 22:37–39). Husbands and wives may be each other's closest neighbors, but spouses are not singled out for a special, greater love. Love is not just the heart of marriage, it is the heart of life, the "greatest of these" (1 Cor 13:13). From pondering specifics about marriage, we are now confronted with the most profound question of human life, and make no pretense of doing it justice. The more manageable question here is whether marital love ought to be a certain, perhaps unique kind of love. To address that question—answering it would be pretentious—many aspects of love must at least be explored. What is love? What are the dimensions, components, and kinds of love? What is mistaken for love? How is love portrayed in current popular culture? Where does romantic love come from? What kind of love do Christians advocate for marriage? And what more could possibly be said about love that has not already been said better by sages, poets, and songwriters throughout history?

Much has already been said about love in the preceding mandates. In Mandate 1, we noted that perhaps the easiest distinction between biblical and cultural mandates regarding marriage is that, though the Scriptures insist that spouses love each other, nowhere do they stipulate that potential partners should select each other for marriage because they already love each other. In Mandate 2, we traced the historical development of how marital love became sentimental and emotional, companionate and affectionate. In Mandate 3, we understood that to sentimentalize marriage is to one-sidedly accentuate and exaggerate its positive emotions, and define marriage by the feelings it elicits. In Mandate 4, we observed that, though love is perceived as a "mid-level" human need for relatedness, it became the focus of marriage in the "great transformation" of marriage "from survival to sentiment."

This collection of disparate insights into marital love already suggests much about its current cultural status and character, but does not adequately portray the pure emotional grip romantic love has on Western individualists. An old folk rhyme does a little better in exposing how easily taken in we are by romantic love.

> They strolled the lane together
> The sky was studded with stars
> They reached the gate in silence
> He lifted down the bars.
> She neither smiled nor thanked him
> Indeed, she knew not how
> For he was just a farmer's boy
> And she, a Jersey cow.

To be enamored—the word itself means to be inflamed with love—with romance and sentiment is pleasurably innocent enough, unless one is addicted to trashy romance novels that serve as surrogate pornography for women. We are culturally, and often personally, in love with love, as Augustine confessed. The word is so overused that it easily loses meaning. After all, we say we love fun, food, and football, and thereby understate its often life-and-death power in human relationships. We are even capable of drawing life from death and calling it love, or putting to death what is alive and calling it love. As the novelist Margaret Atwood put it, "On the streets, love these days is a matter for either scavengers, who turn death to life, or for predators, who turn life to death."[1] Of all that can be taken and mistaken for love, Christian spouses who want to know what "true (marital) love" is best not simply surrender to romance.

---

1. Atwood, "On the Streets, Love," 24.

HOW DO I LOVE THEE?

To define love is as daunting as to define life, and requires an equally interdisciplinary approach. Oord's recent effort to synthesize philosophical, scientific, and theological perspectives of love defines it as follows: "To love is to act intentionally, in sympathetic response to others (including God), to promote overall well-being."[2] Fortunately, such a distant and generalized abstraction can be brought into closer view by describing more concrete dimensions, components, and kinds of love. There certainly can be an emotional dimension to love, a strong feeling that seemingly arises without effort, and at its height, overwhelms the lover. Strong emotion even creates a physiological effect, a literal physical feeling, such as the "flutter of the heart" or the "churn of the stomach." Yet as Arlie Hochschild detailed in *The Managed Heart*,[3] every social situation has "emotion rules" that often require "emotion work," sibling relations being one example of where love may not arise naturally. There is also a cognitive dimension to love, a persistent, thoughtful reflection about the beloved, a desire to know and be known, that functions as the information processing that guides emotion. However, just as emotion does not necessarily lead to irrationality, so too cognition does not necessarily lead to rationality, as all kinds of fantasy and idealization can occur.

There is a behavioral dimension to love, an acting out or demonstration of thoughts and feelings. What is motivated by altruistic care becomes, happily in marriage, an exchange of material and non-material "goods and services." Mutual love eagerly shares all of life, beyond the simple social norm of reciprocity. Finally, love produces an interpersonal attachment that is the basis of its persistence, a grown-up version of the separation anxiety experienced by infants. One Christian antidote to the extreme emotional bias of romantic love has been to accentuate its behavioral dimension, to emphasize that *Love Is Something You Do*.[4] Even so, though it may be true that "love is a verb," love cannot be reduced to behavior alone. Many otherwise loving acts can be purchased from unfeeling, unthinking, and unattached prostitutes, housekeepers, counselors, teachers, nurses, and so on.

Turning from the dimensions of love to the components of love yields several concepts useful for further understanding. In Sternberg's triangular theory of love, the three primary components of love are depicted as the points of a triangle.

2. Oord, *Defining Love*, 15.

3. Hochschild, *Managed Heart*.

4. Bisagno, *Love Is Something You Do*.

1. Intimacy is the friendship aspect, and involves sharing confidences and various details of personal life.

2. Passion is the emotional and motivational aspect, and is driven by arousing attraction.

3. Commitment is the cognitive and volitional aspect, and leads to both short-term and long-term decisions.[5]

These three primary components produce seven types of relationship. When all three components are equal, there is consummate love, which is the goal of marriage. If only intimacy is present, it is liking; if only passion is present, it is infatuation; if only commitment is present, it is self-giving love. The midpoints along each side of the triangle comprise the other three types of relationship. Romantic love is a mix of intimacy and passion; companionate love is a mix of intimacy and commitment; fatuous love[6] is a mix of passion and commitment.

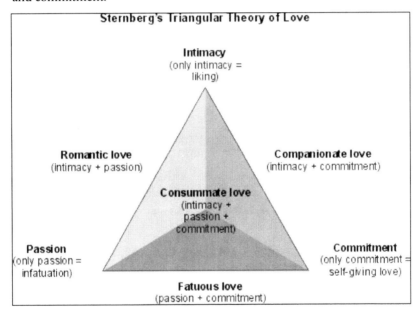

Sternberg's Triangular Theory of Love

Intimacy
(only intimacy = liking)

Romantic love
(intimacy + passion)

Companionate love
(intimacy + commitment)

Consummate love
(intimacy + passion + commitment)

Passion
(only passion = infatuation)

Commitment
(only commitment = self-giving love)

Fatuous love
(passion + commitment)

Sternberg's theorizing about the effects of time on the respective primary components is particularly salient to our concerns here. He noted that whereas both intimacy and commitment grow slowly and steadily, passion grows rapidly at first and then declines with habituation and routinization.

5. Sternberg, "Triangular Theory of Love."

6. This is the product of dizzy, whirlwind courtship, where a quick decision is made on the basis of passion without really getting to know each other.

This waning of arousal is experienced and resisted as a crisis by couples adhering to the mandate that love ought to be romantic and sentimental. Other couples are content to live in companionate love after the passion wanes, and still others live out a self-giving love in a stable but emotionally empty marriage.

Some of these types of relationship produced by various combinations of the components of love—intimacy, passion, commitment—are actually understood elsewhere as completely different kinds of love. One such psychological taxonomy employs various Greek words for love to delineate what it terms "styles of love." The theorist, John Lee, characterized the following styles as the "colors of love," the first three being the primary colors and the second three being compound mixtures.

1. *Eros* is passionate love, intensely sentimental with powerful physical attraction. Plato refined *eros* as a longing for beauty and sensuality that led to spiritual truth, but moderns have reduced it to sexuality. It can come and go rather quickly, because it is not possessive of relationship.

2. *Ludus* is game love, dodging deep emotional engagement while playing the field in the fun sport of challenge and conquest. It is permissive and pluralistic, not jealous or possessive, and ultimately self-centered and exploitative.

3. *Storge* is friendship love, affectionate and companionate, secure and trusting, built up over time. Respect and shared interests deepen mutual commitment without generating or depending on excitement.

4. *Mania* [*eros* + *ludus*] is obsessive love, the moodiness and possessiveness of being "madly in love." Low self-esteem leads to jealous insecurity and insatiability, and a virtual bipolar rollercoaster of euphoria and depression.

5. *Pragma* [*ludus* + *storge*] is logical love, the undemonstrative practicality of getting along, meeting basic needs, and finding contentment. Its rational and realistic assessment of assets and liabilities seeks a fair exchange while avoiding emotional extremes.

6. *Agape* [*eros* + *storge*] is altruistic love, an unconditional concern for the beloved, a generous gift without ulterior motives, compassionate and self-sacrificing. Because it does not demand love in return, it requires high self-esteem of the lover.[7]

---

7. Lee, "Typology of Styles of Loving."

Conceptually, the overlap between Sternberg's components of love and Lee's styles of love is readily apparent. Intimacy is much like *storge*, passion like *eros*, and commitment like *agape*. In Sternberg's terms, romantic love is a mix of intimacy and passion, while in Lee's terms it is primarily *eros*, with a dash of the drama of *mania*. Culturally, collectivist cultures that practice arranged marriages begin with *pragma*, Latin cultures are stereotypically *manic*, and Western cultures mandate romance. Biblically, *agape* is the word used most often in the Greek New Testament to signify love. John, the "apostle of love," declares that God is *agape*,[8] Paul instructs husbands to *agape* their wives, and 1 Corinthians 13 famously explicates *agape* in definitive detail. None of *eros*, *ludus*, *storge*, *mania*, and *pragma* even appear in word, though some are certainly illustrated in deed. When the word *epithumia*, meaning a strong desire of any kind, appears it is usually translated as "lust" when in a negative context and "desire" when in a positive context. *Philia*, or the virtuous "brotherly love" of equals, is a kindred of *storge*, and is the most common alternative to *agape* in the canon, exemplifying the ancient veneration of friendship. The first two times Jesus asks whether Peter loves him, he uses *agapao*, but switches to *phileo* the third time. Peter consistently replies with *phileo* (John 21:15–17).

One of the most influential books on love written from a Christian perspective is C. S. Lewis's classic *The Four Loves*. He too builds on Greek words for love: *storge*—affection; *philia*—friendship; *eros*—romance; *agape*—unconditional love. Love is indeed a many-splendored thing, romance just one part.

LOVES ME NOT

An alternate approach to describing the indescribable is to describe what it is not, to set it apart from its closest correlates, and at times imposters, in a sort of description in reverse. There are certain things that love is not, though they may be a part of love, or even look like love at first glance.

For one, love is not mere attraction. The first glance of love takes in little more than physical appearance, and physical attractiveness often serves as a trigger mechanism for couple formation. Of course, physical beauty is almost entirely culturally defined and variant, and thus is not only in the eye of the beholder. It creates a problematic halo effect, which infers additional positive qualities to a person based on their attractive appearance, because it assumes that the beautiful is also good. It also mistakes the non-moral value

---

8. In *Defining Love*, Oord makes a compelling case that God's love is not just *agape*, but *philia* and *eros* as well.

of aesthetics for the moral value of virtue, though both derive from God. G. K. Chesterton observed that "Love means to love that which is unlovable; or it is no virtue at all."[9] Otherwise it is just attraction, which, like attractiveness itself, is a non-moral value, not a virtue. Truly loving someone to whom one is physically attracted is no easy or simple achievement.

Nor is attraction only to physical appearance. One can be attracted to all kinds of qualities and attributes of someone—personality, intelligence, status, power—without necessarily loving their person. The philosopher Jacques Derrida distinguished between loving someone and loving something, the "who" and the "what."[10] We can love someone for the absolute singularity of who they are, or we can love their qualities and attributes. There is a difference between loving someone and loving something about that someone, the former being closer to authentic love, and the latter being mere attraction. Much the same point is made in a very different forum. *The Big Kahuna* is a 1999 movie about three marketing representatives at a trade show. Larry (Kevin Spacey) is a relentless, world-wise old cynic who is again hounding Bob (Peter Facinelli), a soft-spoken, devout young Baptist. It is one of the more respectful Hollywood portrayals of an evangelical.

> Larry: How long have you been married, Bob?
>
> Bob: Six months.
>
> Larry: Do you love your wife?
>
> Bob: Do I love my wife? Why wouldn't I?
>
> Larry: Well, people get married for a lot of different reasons, Bob. You seem like a real principled guy to me.
>
> Bob: So?
>
> Larry: I've known people—I'm not saying you're one of them— it's just that I've known some who were real principled, and then they met somebody else who was real principled, and then the two of them got married, only to find out one day that it was their principles that got married. The two of them just kind of came along for the ride.
>
> Bob: Oh.
>
> Larry: Love has a lot of counterfeits, Bob, not to get too deep.

Liking is another correlate of loving that in itself is not equivalent. It is ordinary to like someone without loving them, such as casual acquaintances or workplace associates. More profoundly, it is also possible to love

---

9. It must be noted that this has the problematic implications that a loveable person can never be loved authentically, and that to love a loveable person is not a virtue.

10. Kirby Dick and Amy Ziering Kofman, *Derrida*, 2002.

someone without liking them, siblings again being a helpful example. They may annoy us endlessly, but they are us, and blood runs deep. In social psychologist Rubin's seminal distinction,[11] consistent with what has already been said here, loving is associated with attachment, caring, and intimacy. Attachment is a strong desire to be in the presence of the other, and to be approved by the other because of the value placed on the other. Caring is the opposite of attachment in its focus on contributing to the welfare of the beloved, going beyond cherishing to nourishing the beloved. Intimacy is sharing private thoughts, feelings, and desires with each other.

Liking, on the other hand, is associated with affection, enjoyment, and respect. Affection is a moderate feeling of fondness that is comparatively inert and free of anxiety, sensuality, and passion. Enjoyment finds pleasure in the other's personality, temperament, or demeanor. Respect is the result of favorable evaluations of the other's competence and character. Together, these aspects of liking give it a subdued emotional volume, the way one would like an associate without necessarily loving them. To love someone is not only quantitatively more than liking, it is qualitatively different.[12] Much to Christian confusion and consternation, though the biblical text calls spouses to love each other, nowhere does it mandate that they like each other.

Infatuation differs from love in the opposite direction of liking, because it turns up the volume of emotion to where it becomes deafening, drowning out reason and reality. Recall that Sternberg equated passion alone with infatuation, and its similarity to romance is substantial. Occurring most frequently among younger people, but clearly not limited to them, infatuation begins "as prolifically inventive, producing enthralling illusions about each other . . . only to be disappointed into truth."[13] Infatuation appears quickly and remains unstable and erratic, whereas love grows slowly and gains stability and consistency. Infatuation is to be the passive victim of a spell cast by the other, whereas love is an active appreciation of the intrinsic worth of the other. Infatuation is personally disorganizing and destructive, whereas love is personally organizing and constructive. Infatuation is self-centered taking from selected features of the other, whereas love is other-centered giving to the whole person. Finally, infatuation withers when challenged, whereas love grows.

---

11. Rubin, *Liking and Loving*.

12. By now it will be evident that different theorists have slightly different conceptions of the components and correlates of love, which makes for some confusion and understandable frustration. For example, recall that Sternberg equated intimacy alone with liking, yet Rubin linked intimacy with love, not liking.

13. Phillips, *On Flirtation*, 40.

The recent concept of limerence[14] demonstrates the potential of attraction to become personally disorganizing and pathological. It is substantially similar to what Lee termed *mania*, or obsession, in its acute longing for reciprocation, its fear of rejection, and its intensification through adversity. Thoughts about the person who is the object of limerence are persistent, involuntary, and intrusive, and persons experiencing limerence "are notoriously frantic epistemologists, second only to paranoiacs as readers of signs and wonders."[15] The actual physical presence of the object of limerence may lead the person experiencing limerence to personal incapacitation expressed through awkwardness, stuttering, or unsettling shyness. Physically, there may even be dizziness and loss of appetite. Overall, the person experiencing limerence is more to be pitied than envied.

Human capacity to distort the good and beautiful, or provide counterfeits for it, seems infinite. Any good thing, including "love," taken to the extreme becomes grotesque. Love is not blind idealization of the other, "falling in love" with a fabricated image instead of a real person, overlooking faults and magnifying virtues. There is no single God-appointed mate for everyone, we cannot mystically know our ideal mate at first sight, love is not all we need, and love does not conquer all. Love is not possessing or controlling another person, or manipulating them in order to meet our own needs. We cannot close our hands around the life we treasure without suffocating and ultimately destroying it. We must live with open hands, constantly be setting it free to see if it returns to us. Even *agape* is subject to human distortion, in this case the distortion of self, when it becomes a virtual self-martyrdom. As self-sacrificial love, *agape* says "I am something, and I choose to forego my own interests in this situation for you." But when it says "I am nothing—go ahead and walk all over me," it is self-abdication. Masquerading as virtue, it becomes complicit self-victimization for the purpose of securing attachment, sometimes growing silently angry, sometimes becoming terminal. True martyrdom for principle may be noble, but martyrdom to maintain relationship is pathological.

"Love has a lot of counterfeits, Bob, not to get too deep."

THE HALLELUJAH CHORUS

Popular love songs make for a readily accessible reading of the one-dimensional emphasis on romantic love in Western culture, likely matched only by romantic movies in both reflecting and shaping how love is currently

14. Tennov, *Love and Limerence*.
15. Phillips, *On Flirtation*, 41.

experienced. A sampling of some of the most popular love song lyrics from the last generation conveys in most passionate tones that love is primarily a feeling. The suggestively named band Foreigner's best known hit, "I Want to Know What Love Is,"[16] pleaded to both know and feel love, and implied that knowing love is impossible without feeling it. The presumption in the plea is that love is not a cerebral abstraction to be explained conceptually, but an affective behavior to be demonstrated relationally in such a way that deeply moves the one loved. Only the emotional experience of love will satisfy.

In "The Rose,"[17] Bette Midler answered the question of what love is by offering several metaphors, most of which portray it as overwhelming and painful. Love is likened to a river that drowns reeds, a razor that cuts souls, and a hunger that aches endlessly. Conversely, Joe Cocker and Jennifer Warnes characterized love as euphoric, lifting lovers up to where they belong, soaring with eagles in clear mountain air, far from the mundane life of mere mortals.[18] Celine Dion also depicted love as personal transport and occasionally apprehensive adventure driven by the unfathomable "Power of Love."[19] Bryan Adams sang of love as supremely desirous and motivating. Love is worth trying for, fighting for, lying for, and ultimately dying for, such that everything the lover does is ultimately for the beloved.[20]

In calmer tones, the Eagles found love to be comforting and sustaining, not so much to die for as to live for. Love provides both a reason to live and the will to live, and is not so much a hunger in itself as the satiation of a primal hunger.[21] Finally, and ironically in light of practical empirical reality, Celine Dion rhapsodized about romantic love as enduring, even eternal: "Love can touch us one time / And last for a lifetime / And never let go till we're gone . . . / You're here, there's nothing I fear / And I know that my heart will go on / We'll stay forever this way / You are safe in my heart / And my heart will go on and on."[22] This was the Academy Award–winning theme song for the equally

16. Mick Jones, "I Want to Know What Love Is," on Foreigner's *Agent Provocateur* (1984).

17. Amanda McBroom, "The Rose," on Bette Midler's *The Rose* (1979).

18. Will Jennings, "Up Where We Belong," performed by Joe Cocker and Jennifer Warnes, on the soundtrack to *An Officer and a Gentleman* (1982).

19. Jennifer Rush, "The Power of Love," on Celine Dion's *The Colour of My Love* (1993).

20. Michael Kaman and Robert John "Mutt" Lange, "(Everything I Do) I Do It for You," performed by Bryan Adams, on the soundtrack to *Robin Hood: Prince of Thieves* (1991).

21. Jim Capaldi, Paul Carrack, and Peter Vale, "Love Will Keep Us Alive," on The Eagles' *Hell Freezes Over* (1994).

22. James Horner and Will Jennings, "My Heart Will Go On," performed by Celine Dion, on the soundtrack to *Titanic* (1997).

melodramatic and romantic movie blockbuster, *Titanic*, which was rated by Beliefnet as one of the top ten movies to put your faith in love.[23]

Some popular music does probe love for deeper meaning, not just deeper feeling. Leonard Cohen can be as romantic as any singer-songwriter—"there ain't no cure for love"[24]—and as erotic—"O baby, we'll be making love again / We'll be going down so deep / the river's going to weep / and the mountain's going to shout, Amen!"[25] But Cohen can also perceive that "Love is not a victory march / It's a cold and it's a broken Hallelujah."[26] In his own most haunting and provocative simile, "every heart to love will come, but like a refugee."[27] If that sounds more like a reluctant human beloved wooed by God the Great Lover in the cosmic sacred romance,[28] Cohen is not alone in suggesting the romantic similarities of human and divine love. The referent in many love songs is ambiguous, applying as readily to God as to a human lover. It is unclear to whom Paul Janz sings "And when I close my eyes / I feel you are near / Near me again and when I close my eyes / I feel the air you breathe / and hear you say my name / When we're alone."[29] As further indication of the pervasiveness of romantic love, contemporary Christian worship choruses are equally rife with romantic imagery—"Lord you are more beautiful than diamonds / And nothing I desire compares with you."[30] In the feminization of Christianity, love songs to Jesus are often not unlike those to an adolescent boyfriend. Occasionally, they are even as erotic—"Your love is surprising, I can feel it rising / All the joy that's growing deep inside of me."[31]

23. http://www.ranker.com/list/beliefnet_s-top-10-movies-to-put-your-faith-in-love/movie-info.

24. Leonard Cohen, "Ain't No Cure for Love," *I'm Your Man* (1988).

25. Leonard Cohen, "Democracy," *The Future* (1992).

26. Leonard Cohen, "Hallelujah," *Various Positions* (1984).

27. Leonard Cohen, "Anthem," *The Future* (1992).

28. Curtis and Eldredge, *Sacred Romance*.

29. Paul Janz, "Close My Eyes," *Presence* (1992).

30. Lyn Deshazo, "More Precious than Silver" (Integrity's Hosanna! Music, 1982).

31. Brian Doerkson and Brenton Brown, "Hallelujah (Your Love is Amazing)" (Vineyard Songs, 2000).
    Composition/Song Title: HALLELUJAH (YOUR LOVE IS AMAZING)
    Writer Credits: BRENTON BROWN & BRIAN DOERKSEN
    Copyright: © 2000 VINEYARD SONGS (UK/EIRE) (PRS)
    ADMIN. IN NORTH AMERICA BY MUSIC SERVICES
    Song Time:
    License % Controlled by Licensor: 100.00%
    Per Unit Rate (Based on 100% Control): 0.0200
    Dollar Rate (Based on Licensor's Share): 40.0000
    All Rights Reserved. Used By Permission.

What most popular romantic love songs have in common is that they address love at its formative beginning, at its outset or onset, not so much in its mid- or later-life maturity. Neither is such love associated with the commitments of marriage. Romance is seen as the cauldron of fire in which love is born, and, in Western culture, marriage is begun, but rarely is on-going marital love celebrated as romantic. So what becomes of love after twenty years of marriage? Can the structures and strictures of marriage sustain romantic love, or does it evolve into something else? What happens when spouses, driven by their "natural desires," cultural scripts, and con-stant Christian admonitions, earnestly attempt to keep that flame alive, and evaluate their marital love according to their ability to do so?

KNIGHTS IN WHITE SATIN

The location of romantic love in the earliest stage of couple formation and outside of marriage is itself a product of two identifiable eras of Western so-cial history, the first medieval and the second modern.[32] Such love made its first appearance as a social fact beginning in the twelfth century as "courtly" or "chivalrous" love. "Romance" originally signified an extravagant me-dieval tale of imaginary characters involved in events remote in time and place, and usually heroic, adventurous, or mysterious. Courtly love was so called because it was literally played out in aristocratic courts according to "sophisticated and highly refined courtliness that emulated religious love in its ability to create a holy union between the participants."[33] Stereotypi-cally, the smitten knight would engage in jousting tournaments or other acts of heroism in order to win the heart of "his lady," who was pure, helpless, and swooning on the balcony. He would race through corn fields on holy crusades in his desire to be worthy of her, to honor her and please her by acts of devotion and sacrifice. If they met face to face at all, it would be in secret, where the tryst would escalate mentally and emotionally, but never physically. All this had nothing to do with sexual consummation, as she was likely already married to another, given to a vow of chastity, or wearing a chastity belt, and therefore sexually unavailable. It was thought to be a splendid platonic ideal that ennobled both the lover and the beloved. Ah,

---

32. Irving Singer has written an outstanding three-volume work on the philo-sophical history of love: *The Nature of Love*—vol. 1, *Plato to Luther*; vol. 2, *Courtly and Romantic*; vol. 3, *The Modern World*.

33. Singer, *Nature of Love*, back cover. The rules of engagement were codified in *The Art of Courtly Love*, written in the twelfth century, which included rules such as "Marriage is no real excuse for not loving."

that was true romance! Notably, all this also had nothing to do with marriage, which remained a political, economic, or kinship arrangement of convenience among both the nobility and the commoners.

The second era of Western history to provide an impetus to romantic love was the Romantic period of the nineteenth century. Romanticism was a cultural reaction to the industrialization and rationalization of modern life, and was a key component of the Counter-Enlightenment movement. As noted in Mandate 3, the idealization and sentimentalization of marriage are both effects of cultural romanticism, which emphasizes the subjective, the irrational, the imaginative, the spontaneous, and the emotional. For example, theology at the time, as led by Schleiermacher, was affected by rooting faith in the inner world, as spirituality, like love, became feeling based. Romanticism indulged the agony and ecstasy of unrequited human love, whether in a tragic or comic sense, or in the sublimation of desire as a form of romance itself. It affirmed the capacity of love to effect a merging between two people who thus became one. The giant of German literature, von Goethe, is representative of the rapturous hyperbole of romanticism when he wrote that: "This is the true measure of love: When we believe that we alone can love, that no one could ever have loved so before us, and that no one will ever love in the same way after us."[34]

Not that the viability of romantic love in marriage was without its skeptics in modern Western culture. Sages like Shakespeare and Kierkegaard shared the view that marriage and romance were not harmoniously in tune with each other. Oscar Wilde opined that "One should always be in love. That is the reason one should never marry."[35] We have already heard in Mandate 1 George Bernard Shaw's take on the prospects of romantic love in marriage: "When two people are under the influence of the most violent, most insane, most delusive, and most transient of passions, they are required to swear that they will remain in that excited, abnormal, and exhausting condition continuously until death do them part."[36] Contemporary marriage therapist Frank Pittman compares romantic love to a dangerous drug that creates "a state of temporary insanity, akin to a manic episode. It is a narcissistic intoxication that has no relationship to loving but is rather a response to crisis that triggers a bigger crisis."[37] According to leading psychoanalyst Karen Horney, that greater crisis is not just the disappointment and even disillusionment to which euphoric romance must inevitably come.

34. Quoted from http://www.great-quotes.com/quote/475016.
35. Quoted from http://www.great-quotes.com/quote/140949.
36. Quoted in Jacobs, *All You Need Is Love*, 9.
37. Pittman, "Just in Love," 309.

More gravely, the possessiveness of romantic love eventually creates a desire to escape from the other, and when escape is prevented by the strictures of marriage, leads inexorably to the dishonesty of secret alienation and even secret hostility. Romantic lovers thereby come to secretly resent each other, and look elsewhere.[38] More positively, in a recent academic journal article entitled "Does a Long-Term Relationship Kill Romantic Love?," the researchers gather evidence to show that romantic love—including intensity, engagement, and sexuality—can endure, but only when passion and obsession are left behind, and a rather tepid notion of romantic love remains.[39]

MIXED MESSAGES

So how then shall we love? The Christian scriptures are not shy or short on instructions; no general theme is more fully modeled or developed. For better or for worse, examples of marital love in the Old Testament include Adam and Eve, Isaac and Rebekah, Jacob and Rachel, Boaz and Ruth, Samson and Delilah, Elqanah and Hannah, David and Michal, among many others. Most of the dimensions, components, styles, and counterfeits of love can be found in multiple marriages on the list of characters. Codes for marital love are developed in the New Testament primarily in Ephesians 5, Colossians 3, and 1 Peter 3 as part of the unified household codes. Because contemporary Western culture has abhorred the slavery that was assumed for proper household functioning in these codes, the codes have clearly been understood as cultural, not transcultural. Therefore the other components of the household codes—marriage and parenting—must be evaluated in the same light, and also not applied literally or universally.

Yet when the sundry descriptions and exhortations of love in the biblical text are applied to contemporary marriage, they repeatedly suffer a giddy distortion that would have been preposterous to the writers and original audience. For example, it is inconceivable to align the serious suggestions of some contemporary advisors—recall the example of Doyle's *Surrendered Wife* from the second chapter—with the explication of what love is in 1 Corinthians 13. Too often in so-called marriage ministries, it is romantic love that is prescribed for couples, as if the ability to sustain it is the measure and lifeline of a marriage. That this can apparently be achieved through some combination of flowers, chocolates, candles, dinners, and gazes does nothing but trivialize further the sense of adventure or mystery that romance

---

38. Horney, "Problem of the Monogamous Ideal."
39. Acevedo and Aron, "Does a Long-Term Relationship Kill Romantic Love?"

once conveyed. But such are the distortions of self and other integral to and necessitated by the lingering cultural infatuation with romantic love.

Some Christian marriage literature and ministries appear to be working to temper if not counter our cultural yearning for romantic love. Titles such as *Love Is Something You Do*[40] and *Love Is a Decision*[41] emphasize the behavioral and cognitive dimensions of love over the emotional. One of the most popular approaches has been Gary Chapman's *Five Love Languages*,[42] which posits that each person has a primary way of expressing and interpreting love. For reasons he cannot identify, people are usually drawn to those who speak a different love language than their own. "No matter how hard you try to express love in English, if your spouse understands only Chinese, you will never understand how to love each other."[43] The five "universal and comprehensive" love languages are each in their own right good and loving acts: words of affirmation, quality time, receiving gifts, acts of service, and physical touch. Love in any language means discovering your spouse's love language and behaving accordingly; love is a choice to do something, not a feeling.

The film *Fireproof*, referenced in the second chapter, is another extremely popular and powerful depiction of what it takes to gain and sustain a Christian marriage. The plot follows the struggles of a frustrated husband to win the heart of his despairing wife by following a forty-day Love Dare. Each day Caleb will choose to do something to show Catherine that he loves her, beginning day one with saying nothing negative to her at all, day two with doing an unexpected act of kindness, day three with buying something to show her is thinking of her, and so on. When Caleb gets discouraged by Catherine's cold response, his father exhorts him that "this is a decision, not based on feelings." Caleb is admonished to "Don't just follow your heart; you gotta lead your heart." Many lines in the script seek to deemphasize the emotional self-focused dimension of love and emphasize the sacrificial other-oriented nature of love.

But stepping back from the many admirable practices taught by these well-intentioned Christian marriage ministries yields a fuller view of their deeper character. Regarding the "languages of love," it is important to bear in mind that language is a form of expression, a method of communicating something, not the thing itself. In the language of semiotics, which is the study of representation, language is the signifier, not the signified. These

---

40. Bisagno, *Love is Something You Do*.

41. Smalley and Trent, *Love Is a Decision*.

42. Chapman, *Five Love Languages*. The website is at http://www.5lovelanguages.com/

43. Chapman, *Five Love Languages*, 15.

so-called love languages turn out to be particular ways of showing love, not love itself. By talking about what love does, we are left still one step short of what love is. To communicate, in this case through actions, is a behavior motivated by some other impulse, whether it be duty, desire, principle, reward, manipulation, and so on, and that impulse is not necessarily love. Furthermore, Chapman is actually as fixated on emotion as any romantic: "The purpose of this book is . . . to focus on that kind of love that is essential to our emotional health."[44] He repeatedly characterizes the love languages as "emotional love languages," designed to "keep the emotional love tank full," by enabling spouses to "say or do just the right thing guaranteed to make that special someone feel loved."

As for *Fireproof*, one could hardly name or imagine a more melodramatically romantic movie. The message may be that spouses should grow beyond romantic love, but if it is true that the medium is the message, the underlying message of this medium, or film genre, overpowers the viewer, no doubt leaving many in tears. Right up to when they kiss for the first time amidst the promise of "happily ever after" in the climactic scene, Catherine wearing a pretty dress for the first time and Caleb in his firefighter's garb, the filmmakers use romance to supposedly criticize romance. Summoning every traditional gender stereotype—she cries with friends, he gets angry alone—it is said that "a man's got to be a hero to his own wife before anybody else, or he ain't a real man." And a hero Caleb becomes. In the classic mytho-poetic sense of masculinity described in Eldredge's *Wild at Heart*,[45] Caleb has a battle to fight, an adventure to live, and a beauty to save. As he threatens his new rival for Catherine's affections, he leads his heart back to falling in love with her again. In the end, his love is little different than the courtly love of the twelfth-century knight engaged in acts of devotion, sacrifice, and heroism in order to honor and please his lady, and thereby win her heart. Ah, now that's Christian romance! Is there a sweeter surrender than to romantic love?

THE GREATEST OF THESE

When the biblical canon was being written, marital love was largely behavioral, and a good marriage was one in which the husband was well served and the wife was well cared for. Romantic love first grew in Western culture as chivalry in medieval courts, long after the biblical canon was sealed. By the nineteenth century, with its Romantic reaction to the Enlightenment,

44. Ibid., 20.
45. Eldredge, *Wild at Heart*.

its novel notions of the emotional delicacy of femininity, and its bourgeois insistence that marriage produce melodramatic happiness, love became feeling-based, and sentimental. By the end of the millennium, awash in a therapeutic culture, love had been hyper-sentimentalized to the point that emotional considerations were the measure of a marriage. Being happily married was more important than being holy, helpful, or healthy in marriage.[46] Today, "our culture generally elevates the romantic experience of falling in love above religious commitment, teaching us that this emotional experience is both beyond our control and beyond all reproach."[47]

Paul Stookey, of the 1960s folk group Peter, Paul, and Mary, wrote "The Wedding Song,"[48] which became a staple at Christian weddings for the next generation. "Well then what's to be the reason for becoming man and wife? / Is it love that brings you here or love that brings you life? / For if loving is the answer, then who's the giving for? / Do you believe in something that you've never seen before? / Oh there is Love, there is Love." Perhaps love is the belief that takes individuals beyond themselves, to something they've never before seen in a romantic movie, read in a romance novel, or heard in a love song. The colors and contours of covenantal love between a particular man and a particular woman are unknowable in advance, undefinable in the moment, and unreplicable by others. Perhaps that is the true romance. If so, the search for a special formula for marital love is futile, and Christians should stop looking beyond 1 Corinthians 13, where love is again characterized by what it does, not by what it is. "Love is patient; love is kind; love is not envious or boastful or arrogant or rude. It does not insist on its own way; it is not irritable or resentful; it does not rejoice in wrongdoing, but rejoices in the truth. It bears all things, believes all things, hopes all things, endures all things. Love never ends" (vv. 4–8a). As for love's effects on the lover, "All love endures the fortunes of another; all love makes the lover vulnerable; all love suffers the weak-kneed hope of love returned."[49]

Romantic love is but one immature kind of marital love, culturally compulsory, but functionally problematic and biblically unnecessary. No doubt husbands and wives are called by God to love each other, nothing more and nothing less, and we refrain at our own peril. C. S. Lewis wrote of love as a passion of the heart, but warned of the alternative.

> Love anything, and your heart will certainly be wrung and possibly be broken. If you want to make sure of keeping it intact,

46. Thomas, *Sacred Marriage*.

47. Smit, *Loves Me, Loves Me Not*, 33.

48. Noel Paul Stookey, "The Wedding Song (There Is Love)," *Paul And* (1971).

49. Dean, *Practicing Passion*, 137.

you must give your heart to no one, not even to an animal. Wrap it carefully round with hobbies and little luxuries; avoid all entanglements; lock it up safe in the casket or coffin of your selfishness. But in that casket—safe, dark, motionless, airless—it will change. It will not be broken; it will become unbreakable, impenetrable, irredeemable. The alternative to tragedy, or at least to the risk of tragedy, is damnation. The only place outside of Heaven where you can be perfectly safe from all the dangers and perturbations of love is Hell.[50]

50. Lewis, *Four Loves*, 111–12.

Mandate 6

Intimacy

Should the goal of marriage be intimacy?

We have now considered half of the ten conceptions of marriage that Christians commonly mistake as God's intent, concerning how marriage is formed, connected, valued, pursued, and characterized. In current Western culture, Christian marriage is formed by self-selection, disconnected from its community, valued above all else, pursued as the primary means of need fulfillment, and characterized by romantic love. Upon closer examination, we have seen that these imperatives are cultural, not biblical. They are social norms that, like all cultural norms, feel right and natural, and enable Christians to fit comfortably into their society, but are not distinctly Christian, or even necessarily Christian at all. Some, we have argued, are less than Christian. What then of the way marriage is focused, energized, troubled, ended, and perceived?

More than being feeling based and sentimental, contemporary marital love has come to be equated with intimacy. Whether intimacy is mixed with passion to form romantic love, or mixed with commitment to form companionate love,[1] it is seen as the essential ingredient of marriage, and thus the primary focus of marriage. In the broadest strokes of Western culture, marriage has evolved from a task and role orientation to a companionate and intimate relationship. Where once marriage meant forging a new socioeconomic unit, entering into a sexual bond, and caring for consequent children, now marriage means all that plus knowing one's spouse deeply,

1. From Sternberg's triangular theory of love discussed in Mandate 5.

and being known deeply in return. The spousal role today adds to historical expectations that each spouse should also be devoted to delving into the furthest recesses of the other's personhood. The purpose and goal of Western marriage today is for spouses to share their most private thoughts, feelings, and desires with each other as completely as possible. The cultural demands of marriage are greater than ever before.

Of course, this development is not an isolated, independent social phenomenon—none are. As we have seen repeatedly, and by now assume, the rise of the intimacy ethic in marriage has come about in concert with broader historical and cultural shifts already explicated in the preceding Mandates. Those same shifts have equally influenced Christian life more broadly. In the Balswicks' theological model of marriage, the marriage relationship begins with covenant (to love and be loved) and is completed with intimacy (to know and be known), even as covenant, grace, empowerment, and intimacy spiral ever deeper.[2] Love alone does not ensure intimacy. So too, God is *agape* love, but God is also in intimate relationship within the Trinity and, we now emphasize, in intimate relationship with us.[3] Instead of the transcendence of God, Christians now tend to emphasize the immanence of God. God knows us in detail—the number of hairs on our head (Matt 10:30)—and intimately—understanding our groanings that cannot be uttered (Rom 8:26–27). What is relatively new, historically, is that we now seek to know God equally in return, with all sorts of appropriate qualifications and admissions about the ultimate impossibility of doing so. We now seek intimacy with God, desiring and expecting to be able to know God, unwilling to be content to know about God.[4] Like marriage, we are no longer satisfied to love and serve God. Like marriage, the demands of the Christian life are greater than ever before.

Whether or not intimacy with God is a spiritual imperative, or whether the character of that intimacy in any way resembles what occurs between humans, we nonetheless now extrapolate from a biblical metaphor a culturally induced biblical mandate to be intimate with our spouses. The bridegroom Christ may have loved his bride the church by laying down his life for her, but the modern bridegroom must love his bride first by sharing his private thoughts, feelings, and desires with her, and second by exploring, mapping, and inhabiting the vast and fascinating territory of her mysterious

2. Balswick and Balswick, *Model for Marriage* and *Family*.

3. William Paul Young's *The Shack*, an imaginative and popularized depiction of the intimacy within the Trinity, and between the Trinity and a human interloper, was a runaway bestseller. Tim Keller emphasizes intimacy and the Trinity in *The Meaning of Marriage*.

4. Packer, *Knowing God*.

self. She must do the same with him in return. But is that intimacy? How does intimacy compare to love? What notions of self and identity undergird intimacy? How does intimacy vary in marriages? What is the role of communication, and what are its challenges? To what extent have Christians pursued marital intimacy? What biblical basis do they have for doing so?

Anderson and Guernsey tell of missionaries who invited a famous Christian author from the West to their country of ministry to address communication in marriage.[5] As part of his presentation, the expert asked the couples in the audience to draw their chairs together and face one another knee to knee and eye to eye. The nationals became terribly uncomfortable and were unable even to look their spouses in the eye. In their culture, public communication between a husband and wife was grossly inappropriate. When the missionaries suggested to the expert that intimacy and communication could take alternate forms depending on culture, he insisted that this was the biblical way. Yet Christian husbands and wives in the early church culture of first-century Judaism, where husbands were discouraged from talking much even with their own wives, would have been no more comfortable, and the self-assured seminar leader would be no more correct in insisting to them that his marriage prescription was the Christian expectation. To the question "How can I develop intimacy with my spouse?" the baffled Christian couple in the early church would first reply, "What is that?" and when informed, "Why would anyone want to?"

It is painful to imagine the much greater disorientation and distress of either those national couples or the early church couples should they appear on the *The Dr. Phil Show* today. Even so, many contemporary Christian couples take the frequently useful and principled relationship advice of Phil McGraw as gospel truth. Indeed, his highly commodified television spectacle employs the religious narrative of conversion to frame the personal experiences and problems of the participants.[6] As they proceed through confessionals and testimonials, a transformation of self is depicted, producing a sense of moral authority, self-empowerment, and an imagined community. Yet for these earnest and often troubled souls, no substantial transformation of the self actually occurs in some moment of conversion or surrender. Their very presence at the feet of a popular guru like Dr. Phil indicates an already completed formation of the self by the culture into which they have been socialized. They already belong and believe; they just seek help in how to behave. They already value intimacy and are motivated to pursue it; they just need the right techniques to enact. When guidance

5. Anderson and Guernsey, *On Being Family.*

6. Egan and Papson, "You Either Get It or You Don't."

comes to seekers of intimacy in the most effective blurring of secularization and sacralization, as it does from both our television studios and church pulpits, its force is compelling, its grip is tight.

THE SELF LAID BARE

A common misperception of intimacy can be corrected quickly. For the unduly discrete or bashful, intimacy is often used as code for sex, though they remain two very distinct relational dynamics. Intimacy is knowing and being known cognitively and emotionally, not just touching and being touched physically or sexually. While intimacy can certainly include sexual relations, sexual engagement is no guarantee of intimacy, *eros* no promise of communion, as any prostitute can attest. As such, when the Authorized Version (King James) of the Bible rendered sexual intercourse as "knowing" (e.g., "Adam knew Eve is wife, and she conceived," Gen 4:1), it was not just prudish by modern standards, it was also misleading. Moreover, sexual intercourse between a husband and wife in certain circumstances may produce the most profound sense of intimacy for him, and simultaneously the most profound sense of alienation for her. Even the phrase "physical intimacy," though it is more suggestive of sex, is an inadequate euphemism for sex, in light of the heightened non-sexual bodily contact between a parent and child, or between Olympic wrestlers.

As a verb, "intimate" suggests knowledge, as in "to intimate that things are going well." As an adjective, "intimate" means thorough and detailed, as in "an intimate knowledge of things." As a noun, "intimate" means a person in whom one confides, or with whom one has a close relationship, as in "I rely on my intimate." Taken together, intimacy is detailed knowledge of a close relation. The most common aspect of intimacy in academic literature on close relationships is a feeling of closeness and connectedness that develops through communication between partners.[7] But intimacy is also more than complete familiarity with the mundane details that are exposed naturally from the simple process of sharing domestic life with another person. Intimacy is not merely private though superficial knowledge of another, but rather a knowledge of the depth of their being, of what makes them tick. That is why pop psychologist Matthew Kelly is overreaching for a perfect number when he describes seven levels of intimacy as the exchange of 1) clichés, 2) facts, 3) opinions, 4) hopes and dreams, 5) feelings, 6) faults, fears, and failures, and 7) legitimate needs.[8] The first half do not yet tap

7. Perlman and Fehr, "Development of Intimate Relationships."
8. Kelly, *Seven Levels of Intimacy.*

the personal depth of intimacy. That is also why Elaine Storkey's definition of intimacy as "knowing that I am not alone in the universe"[9] unhelpfully stretches the concept beyond meaning. In her Christian ode to intimacy, *The Search for Intimacy*, she also lists lack of self-disclosure as only one of five different problems related to intimacy in marriage.

The leading psychological theory of intimacy, known as the interpersonal process model,[10] suggests that intimacy is not something we possess, but something we do. One half of the process is for a speaker to disclose personally relevant and revealing information. The other half is for the listener to respond by conveying understanding, validation, and caring for the speaker. Such responsiveness by the listener assures the speaker that she or he is valued, and encourages further self-disclosure. As soon as appropriate, the listener self-discloses in return and in equal kind, and the roles are reversed. Intimacy is the transactional process of self-revealing disclosure met by partner responsiveness, in short, voluntary reciprocal self-disclosure. Self-disclosure that is not voluntary, as in interrogation, or not reciprocated, as in therapy, is not intimacy. Voluntary self-disclosure that is not welcome and not reciprocated is often experienced as manipulative, or just socially awkward—"too much information."

A primary pattern found by research is that self-disclosure by itself is a necessary but not sufficient predictor of intimacy in marriage.[11] In fact, partner responsiveness to disclosure has been found to be of greater general importance than the initial self-disclosure of the speaker. Some other patterns include the greater importance placed on self-disclosure by husbands compared to the greater importance placed on partner responsiveness by wives, the greater effect of emotional self-disclosure compared to factual self-disclosure, and the critical importance of speaker perceptions and interpretations of partner responsiveness. One specific maladaptive communication pattern linked to marital intimacy dysfunction is the demand-withdraw pattern.[12] The more one partner pushes an issue, the more the other pulls away, and the less each feels acceptable response from the other. Such a failure of the disclosure-responsiveness exchange erodes intimacy, as each perceives a lack of valuing, understanding, and care from the other. Disappointments with intimacy frequently drive couples to marital counseling, and enhanced intimacy is just as frequently the goal of marital

9. Storkey, *Search for Intimacy*, 4.

10. Laurenceau, Barrett, and Rovine, "Interpersonal Process Model of Intimacy in Marriage."

11. Ibid.

12. Gottman, *What Predicts Divorce*.

therapy. Dissatisfied spouses often invalidate the feelings about relationship problems disclosed by their spouses, and perceiving their spouses as unresponsive is more significant than outright conflict in leading to divorce. When intimacy fails, it does not just stagnate, but reverses into its opposite: distance, and ultimately disconnection.[13]

Just as love is not merely attraction, infatuation, or liking, so too intimacy is not merely sex, or even love. Just as it is possible to love someone without liking them, it is likewise possible to love someone without being intimate with them. Loving a sister or brother without being intimate with her or him again serves as the best, most understandable example. While both love and intimacy are voluntary, intimacy requires reciprocity in a way that love does not. Intimacy requires self-disclosure in a way that love does not. Intimacy requires time, effort, and interaction in a way that love does not. In some ways it could be argued that, though love remains the greater moral achievement, intimacy is a greater relational achievement. George MacDonald said that "To be trusted is a greater compliment than to be loved,"[14] as can be seen by our love for persons to whom we would not entrust the details of our most private thoughts, feelings, and desires. Nevertheless, intimacy is unlikely to occur where love is not also present, and so intimacy requires more than love in a way that love does not require intimacy. And while love always makes the lover vulnerable, intimacy does so in a unique and heightened manner, as the self is laid bare before the other.

FROM YOKEMATES TO SOULMATES

If intimacy is the process of voluntary, reciprocal self-disclosure, the self must be understood as the agent or practitioner of intimacy. And as strange as it may sound, humans have not always lived with the same sense of self as we in contemporary Western culture do. "The (modern) Western conception of the person as a bounded, unique, more or less integrated motivational and cognitive universe . . . is, however incorrigible it may seem to us, a rather peculiar idea within the context of the world's cultures."[15] It was the emergence of the modern notion of self in society that gave rise to the intimacy ethic of modern marriage. For much of premodernity, the self and soul were synonymous. Human consciousness of a separate, identifiable, individual self only arose around the time of Christ. For example, the self as found in the Hebrew scriptures was only identifiable as it responded to

13. Balswick and Balswick, *Model for Marriage* and *Family.*

14. Quoted from http://www.great-quotes.com/quote/46895.

15. Geertz, *Local Knowledge,* 59.

God.[16] God searches us and knows us (Ps 139:23), but without God, there is little sense of a separate self in the text. The premodern self was not so much located *in* its context as it was part *of* its context, identifiable only as it responded *to* its context.[17] There was in fact little emphasis on individual existence at all, because life was communal[18] and people saw themselves only in terms of the group.

Though early Christianity helped "discover" the self, it was the Protestant Reformation in particular that provided the doctrinal basis for accepting the self. The Calvinist doctrine of election or predestination, for example, was a radically individualistic understanding of salvation compared to the "blanket coverage" of Catholicism. With the advent of modernity, the self became autonomous, and now synonymous with the mind, and Christianity embraced and celebrated the self in the cultural context of the new individualism. Instead of being predetermined by the group, the self became what Giddens termed a "reflexive project," something to be reflected upon by self-exploration and molded in intimate social relationships.[19] Awareness of self heightened as it came into tension with society, and the central problem of selfhood became authenticity—being true to one's self.[20] Then, by the beginning of the current millenium, the fixed inner core of the objective modern self had been disolved into the contingent, indeterminate image of the constructed postmodern self.[21] Perhaps the most salient feature of the current postmodern self is its relationality; the self is no longer a defined object, but rather is defined in relationship.[22]

The intersection of the evolution of the self with the intimacy ethic of marriage is obvious. In *Modern Love: Romance, Intimacy, and the Marriage*

16. Muck, "After Selfhood."

17. Ibid.

18. Some have argued that the socially embedded premodern self has more in common with the socially constructed postmodern self than with the modern self. See for example McCarthy, *Whole and Divided Self.*

19. Giddens, *Modernity and Self-Identity.* The transformation of intimacy led to what Giddens also termed the "pure relationship," in which "a social relation is entered into for its own sake, for what can be derived by each person from a sustained association with another" (Giddens, *Transformation of Intimacy*, 58).

20. Gecas and Burke, "Self and Identity."

21. Hiebert, "Toward a Post-Postmodern Concept of Self." I argue here that the most culturally and existentially viable concept of self is located on the middle ground between modernism, which sees the self as centered, bounded, and singular, and postmodernism, which sees the self as decentered, unbounded, and multiple. Such a post-postmodern view is also the most congruent with a Christian understanding of self.

22. Balswick, King, and Reimer, *Reciprocating Self.*

Crisis,[23] Shumway in fact locates the emergence of the discourse of intimacy as recently as the last third of the twentieth century. Emotional closeness is as definitive of intimacy as passion is definitive of romance, and the two discourses of intimacy and passion now coexist in Western culture. Marriage became the primary means of self-realization, for the modern spouse through self-discovery of what was already there, for the postmodern spouse through self-construction of what was not yet there. To the prototypical modern question "Who am I?" the good postmodern spouse would answer "I am my marriage." As both culture and Christians now, in what some have termed post-postmodernity, struggle to reconstruct the self that postmodernism so radically deconstructed, marital intimacy will be likewise affected.

The self and intimacy are also related to identity.[24] Self is that subset of personality that is aware of itself, whereas identity is comprised of the categories individuals use to specify who they are relative to other people. In Stone's pithy definition, identity is "the coincidence of placements [by others] and announcements [by self]."[25] Identity is the most public aspect of the self, the self we know and enact.[26] Just as self and identity emerged in culture over centuries, so too they must emerge within the individual; we are not born with a fully formed self and identity. In Erikson's well-known stages of psychosocial development,[27] adolescence is a period of tension between either forging an identity or suffering from confusion. If the "identity crisis" is resolved positively, it produces the "ego virtue" of fidelity, or the ability to be faithful to a known self, a self-certainness that integrates the past and future of the self and takes responsibility for it. Notably, the tension of the young adult stage that follows is between intimacy and isolation, precipitated by the desire to fuse the just established identity with another. Intimacy for Erikson is the willingness to risk deep friendship or marriage, the capacity to commit and share deeply without losing one's own identity. To do so well is to acquire the ego virtue of love; to fail to do so is to wallow in isolation or promiscuity. Identity is thus the developmental prerequisite for intimacy.

Olthuis's less-known stages of marriage is another developmental model that turns on identity and intimacy.[28] Intimacy between a husband and wife is complicated by their respective stages of personal develop-

23. Shumway, *Modern Love.*
24. Ibid.
25. Stone, "Appearance and the Self," 188.
26. Michener, Delamater, and Meyers, *Social Psychology.*
27. Erikson, *Childhood and Society.*
28. Olthuis, *Keeping Our Troth.*

ment, specifically how well formed the identity of each partner is prior to marriage. Olthuis agrees with Erikson that identity is necessary for authentic intimacy to develop, that "genuine intimacy requires self-identity, which is intimacy with the self."[29] If husband and wife do not bring sufficient individual identity with them into marriage, several problems can arise as they strive to find their identity in the context of intimacy. A husband may isolate himself in false autonomy, resisting his wife to the extent that it feeds his anger and desire to have someone to blame. A wife may debase herself in false submission, controlling her husband by pleasing him to the extent that she can blame him for any marital discontent. They may limit their identity formation to one of "I am my body, my mind, my principles, my cause, or my marriage." Or they may simply collude to prolong their adolescence by postponing personal identity formation.

What we have here are two twentieth-century theories from developmental psychology that highlight identity and intimacy, and are themselves manifestations of the increasingly problematic nature of the self in the macro shifts from premodernity to modernity to postmodernity. Social-scientific theories of the self, like philosophy, theology, and literature before them, are themselves historical and cultural manifestations of the rise of the self in modernity and the fall of the self in postmodernity, and the turn toward intimacy to seek solutions and solace for the increasingly elusive and troubled self.

From his survey data, Regnerus concluded that "Most young Americans no longer think of marriage as a formative institution, but rather as the institution they enter once they think they are fully formed."[30] As such, they more often than not badly underestimate marriage and overestimate themselves. Where premodern marriage may have cast spouses as yokemates,[31] today, as the cynical saying goes, you go to bed soulmates and wake up cellmates.

ALONE TOGETHER

The amount of intimacy varies from one marriage to another, though the current preoccupation with intimacy seldom wavers or wanes, even when it is not the intended focal point. One social-scientific typology of contemporary marriage[32] is built on four factors—power, conflict, intimacy, and rewards—but the six types betray a bias toward the definitive centrality of intimacy.

29. Ibid.
30. Regnerus, "Case for Early Marriage."
31. Coontz, *Marriage, a History.*
32. Kersten and Kersten, *Marriage and the Family.*

1. Traditional marriage typecasts the husband as the head that decides and provides, and the wife as the heart that submits and nurtures. The power is unequal, overt conflict is minimal, and the rewards are differentiated. Intimacy is determined by traditional gender roles, and thus one-sided, with the stereotypically expressive female offering self-disclosure and emotional support, while getting little in return from the stereotypically inexpressive male.

2. Extrinsic marriage is focused on engagements with the world outside the marriage, not on the marital relationship itself. The power is equal, the conflict is limited, and the shared reward is companionship. Intimacy is also minimal, because the partners are too preoccupied with their separate or shared activities to have much time, energy, or interest to devote to each other's inner selves.

3. Empty-shell marriage is a pragmatic arrangement of convenience, or a dogged commitment to the institution of marriage, that shares few common interests. Power and conflict are seldom issues, and the reward is relational stability. Intimacy is absent, as interaction is superficial, life is devitalized, and emotions are disconnected, though the emotional isolation is still deemed preferable to the alternative of living alone.

4. Pseudo-intimate marriage is two weak, insecure, and always-together partners in an A-frame codependent commitment to a merged identity discussed in Mandate 4. Power is avoided, conflict is denied, and the reward is affirmation. Intimacy is illusionary and self-deceiving, as physical togetherness is a cover for lack of cognitive and emotional closeness, while lack of differentiation from each other produces enmeshment.

5. Negative-exchange marriage is a series of hostility rituals between two conflict-habituated individuals who find fault-finding and fighting rewarding, even when it is unproductive. Power is contested, conflict is constant, and the reward is scapegoating. Intimacy is fearfully avoided as it leads only to vulnerability, being used to attack and hurt the other, with the end result often being intimate partner violence.

6. Intimate marriage is the idyllic ideal of this supposedly value-free descriptive typology. Each partner in this M-frame interdependence has a secure sense of self, and seeks relationship out of strength, not personal weakness, inadequacy, desperation, or fear. Both husband and wife put effort into maintaining a balance of power, managing conflicts, offering sensitive self-disclosure, and realizing companionship.

Instead of being "objective" social science, this typology is obviously part of the contemporary "cult of intimacy," even when the aspect of intimacy is not accentuated, as we have here. The alternatives to intimate marriage are labeled with decidedly negative, emotionally loaded terms such as empty-shell and pseudo-intimate. Extrinsic implies unfaithful. Yet a case could be made that all but the negative-exchange model has approximated the cultural and even Christian ideal at some time and place in history. The traditional marriage certainly has. The extrinsic marriage is the model of most companionate, mission-minded Christian couples throughout history, and comes close to Clapp's notion of marriage as mission base discussed in Mandate 3. Even empty-shell marriage, if relabeled more neutrally as pragmatic marriage, has been championed in eras such as that of the Puritans. Many Christian couples today do whatever works for them, and thereby live out marriages that are more pragmatic than principled or passionate. While this may appear to be a non-cultural concession to personal practicalities, it too is a cultural script—good old American pragmatism having finally triumphed over one of the last bastions of the private realm.

The pseudo-intimate marriage is the strongest testament to the power of the cultural mandate that marriages be intimate. Even those couples that are not intimate know they should be, and want to be, or at least want to appear to be. Pseudo-intimacy took on near comical overtones in the 1970s with Marabel Morgan's "Total Woman" script for Christian wives. In another case of gender surrender, Morgan instructed Christian wives to adapt themselves totally to their husbands and draw their identity from them. They were to phone him at work to whisper huskily that "I crave your body," and then when he came home, meet him at the door dressed only in plastic wrap. The pseudo-intimacy was unmistakable in the exhortation to shower him with compliments and admiration, even if dishonest, and avoid all complaints and disagreements by withholding all negative feelings. "Never let him see you without your makeup" was undoubtedly meant both literally and figuratively. Both her body and soul were masked, and hence her true self hidden. Her husband would therefore be left aching, as Leonard Cohen confessed, to see her naked in her body and her thought.[33]

More recently, pseudo-intimacy was implicit in the wistful title of a comprehensive, scholarly update on the state of marriage at the turn of the millennium, *Alone Together: How Marriage in America Is Changing.*[34] The same phrase was used soon after in another book title, *Alone Together: Why*

33. Leonard Cohen, "Ain't No Cure for Love," *I'm Your Man* (1988).
34. Amato et al., *Alone Together.*

We Expect More from Technology and Less from Each Other.[35] The latter is the description of another case of material culture (technology) shaping non-material culture (values and norms). Sherry Turkle gathered empirical evidence to show how digital technology has become the "architect of our intimacies," offering the illusion of companionship without the demands of intimacy. The constant connectedness of social networking technology leads to a new solitude, while manageable sociable robots replace unmanageable people. Beyond the confines of marriage, our innate capacity for intimacy is being eroded by social network technology, and even marital intimacy will not likely remain unaffected. Some more positive version of pseudo-intimate marriage may be the norm for marriage in the future.

WORDS

If intimacy is the process of voluntary, reciprocal self-disclosure, and the self is the primary agent of intimacy, then communication is the primary vehicle of intimacy. By transmitting information about thoughts and feelings, communication discloses the self, and in the context of the intimacy ethic, is often viewed as the primary prerequisite, strength, and measure of a good marriage. Verbal communication is the most effective means of communicating thoughts, whereas non-verbal communication excels most in communicating feelings, though the two are intricately connected. The non-verbal is also usually considered more trustworthy, as it is more difficult to deceive another with our body than with our words. Words can bring either life or death, can heal or hurt, and it is often hurt people who hurt people.[36] Sticks and stones can break our bones, but words can break our spirit. Yet the absence of words altogether, the classic silent treatment, can be the most painful. There may be no loneliness more acute than sharing sexual and domestic life with someone, knowing every curve and crevice of their body, manner, and daily routine, without being intimate with them because they cannot or will not self-disclose.

Greater self-disclosure may lead to greater conflict, but it will at least shatter illusionary intimacy. Like the proverbial onion, continuous self-disclosure will lead to successively deeper levels of knowing as the layers are peeled away. How much self-disclosure can be gained or tolerated depends on the self-esteem of each partner and the strength of the bond between them. When both have low self-esteem, each believes the other is deceived, which sustains an illusion neither can afford to acknowledge. The result is a

35. Turkle, *Alone Together*.
36. Wilson, *Hurt People Hurt People*.

pseudo-intimate marriage that is preoccupied with togetherness, bound by fear. For even the most secure partners, marital intimacy results in the most acute personal vulnerability. The people who are closest to us, our intimates, affect our self-concept most powerfully, making it more consequential to self-disclose to a spouse than to a stranger.

One hundred years ago, before the rise of the intimacy ethic, the theorist Georg Simmel[37] developed the concept of the "stranger" as someone who, among many other attributes, serves as an ideal confidant because of being both distant and near at the same time. Self-disclosure to a stranger is facilitated because it is isolated and detached from everyday life, and therefore freer of daily consequences than disclosure to an intimate. Simmel also advanced an elaborated theory of secrecy, observing in passing that to reveal all in marriage would be a mistake. All social relationships require "a certain proportion of truth and error," making it impossible to remove all error. Complete self-revelation would make marriage matter-of-fact and remove all possibility of the unexpected. Only those with a great storehouse of the self can afford numerous self-revelations without being left denuded and uninteresting.

Though both the stranger and secrecy are suspect in contemporary Western marriage, constituting grounds for discontent or potentially divorce, Simmel's observations raise questions about whether there are limits to healthy self-disclosure in marriage. Are some well-intentioned truths better left unsaid? Can too much openness and honesty be injurious to the relationship? Honesty is saying what you mean and meaning what you say, not necessarily revealing every detail. It is, in truth, impossible to tell the "whole truth," to relay every thought and feeling. Part of the self always remains private and unknown, even to the self. Moreover, complete honesty is not always constructive. Just because something is true is not reason enough to say it, as it may reveal destructive anger, or be destructive only in effect. Criticism without correction or the suggestion of ways to change is not constructive, just as criticism of what someone cannot change is ineffectual and hurtful. Furthermore, demanding complete disclosure may be a form of controlling the other person. Finally, complete disclosure may make future relationship difficult or awkward, as the disclosure of sexual fantasies is wont to do.

Regardless of the degree of openness and honesty desired, couples seeking intimacy must overcome multiple barriers to communication. Traditional gender norms are again a major impediment. Men are socialized to be verbally inexpressive, especially of feelings, like strong, silent, solitary

---

37. Ritzer, *Sociological Theory*.

cowboys. When they do talk, it tends to be about objects, like cars, about activities, like sports, or about ideas, like politics. They seek their sense of intimacy through sexual engagement, whereas women seek their sense of intimacy through emotional engagement. Women are socialized to be verbally expressive, to want and offer more talk. There is also a difference in the quality of talk, not just the quantity. Men engage in what Tannen termed "report talk," whereas women engage in "rapport talk."[38] For a husband, debriefing at the end of the day is information transference, for a wife, emotional connection. A wife thinks her marriage is working as long as they keep talking about it; a husband thinks his marriage is not working because they have to keep talking about it.

Traditional gender norms also create an imbalance of power, and the less the equality between intimates, the less the intimacy. It is difficult to "experience intimacy with someone who is in a position to make decisions about your life. . . . When the structures allow the other person to control your life, then you normally protect your innermost self from being known by that person."[39] Unequal power makes reciprocal self-disclosure less likely, and therefore traditional marriage less intimate. "He fears engulfment; she fears invasion."[40] Perhaps it is power that explains the paradox of the stereotypically expressive yet inaccessible and unfathomable female on one hand, and the inexpressive male on the other. She tries to get him to talk so as to monitor and moderate his power, while never revealing more than she can afford. So even when a traditional husband might seek deep self-disclosure from his wife, he is sabotaged by his own power. This may be the self-defeating scenario Bruce Springsteen laments: "She'll let you in her heart / If you got a hammer and a vice / But into her secret garden, don't think twice . . . / She'll look at you and smile / And her eyes will say / She's got a secret garden / Where everything you want / Where everything you need / Will always stay / a million miles away."[41]

Other reasons why spouses do not communicate include feelings of inadequacy as a communicator—"I'm not good with words; I don't know how to say it"—or inadequacy as a person—"If you really knew what I was like, you would not like me." Sometimes the reason is suppression of what the person considers to be unacceptable feelings, which causes them to pretend to others, and even themselves, that "I am not angry, or hurt, or jealous." Sometimes the reason is guilt or shame about the substance of their

---

38. Tannen, "You Just Don't Understand."

39. Lester and Lester, *It Takes Two*, 120.

40. Rubin, *Intimate Strangers*, 110.

41. Bruce Springsteen, "Secret Garden," *Greatest Hits* (1995).

feelings—"I should not be attracted to someone other than my spouse." And sometimes the reason is fear of conflict—"If I told you how I really felt, you would get angry"—fear of vulnerability—"If I told you my real feelings, you might hurt me"—and even fear of the harmful potential of their own feelings—"If I expressed all my anger, I might destroy you." All of these barriers to communication are forms and degrees of risk deemed too great to contemplate, culminating in "How can I let you see what I dare not even face myself? How can I expect you to know me and still love me?"[42] What ensues is "a living out of two different lives; the joint life which is cautious, full of avoidance, and empty, and the private emotional life which is resentful, defeated, or escapist."[43]

Though some narratives of marriage in the biblical text demonstrate great love and sensitive communication, none display what we today pursue as intimacy. One story perhaps comes close to displaying its absence, or its opposite. Rabbi Joseph Telushkin[44] retells the story of how King David and Michal's intense love turned tragic because of their sharp-tongued manner of communicating. In the early days of their love, each had performed heroic deeds to literally save the life of the other. But later in their marriage, when David danced naked and wild in front of the ark of the Lord and his people, he was confronted with Michal's cold sarcasm: "How the king of Israel honored himself today, uncovering himself before the eyes of his servants' maids, as any vulgar fellow might shamelessly uncover himself!" Instead of absorbing her withering scorn, David shot back by ignoring the substance of her rebuke and attacking the most vulnerable part of her personal identity, God's rejection of her father, King Saul. "It was before the Lord [that I danced], who chose me in place of your father and all his household, to appoint me as prince over Israel." The very next verse suddenly records the seemingly unrelated fact that "Michal the daughter of Saul had no child to the day of her death," and the story ends abruptly. But the implication is that they never had sexual intercourse again, their growing estrangement now final and complete. (2 Sam 6)

THE CULTURE INDUSTRY

The intimacy ethic had its historical roots in the ancient notion of a soulmate, as the ancient equation of the self and the soul suggests. In *The Symposium*, Plato told of how humans originally had four arms and four legs

42. Storkey, *Search for Intimacy*, 3.

43. Ibid., 185.

44. Telushkin, *Words that Hurt, Words that Heal*.

with a single head made of two faces. Zeus feared their power and split them all in half, condemning them to spend their lives searching for the other half to complete them. *Bashert* is an ancient Yiddish word meaning "destiny," used to denote the divinely foreordained spouse or soulmate that completes an individual. This ancient notion was resurrected in the modern Romantic Era, as articulated by Victor Hugo in *Les Miserables*: "When love has melted and merged two persons in a sublime and sacred unity, the secret of life has been revealed to them: they are no longer anything but the two aspects of a single destiny, the wings of a single spirit."[45] As Storkey put it more succinctly, "The boundaries of the self shift; I become inclusive of the one I love."[46] A historical survey of paradigm shifts in notions of marriage over the last several centuries shows that the discourse of romantic love embedded in the individualistic assumptions of capitalism has given way to the more recent discourse of intimacy embedded in the communal assumptions of environmentalism.[47]

Though it was Western culture that raised intimacy to the purpose and goal of marriage, it is remarkable how zealously Christians have responded to the higher call. In current biblical interpretation, what began in the beginning as becoming "one flesh" is now also expected to become one heart and mind and soul. Larry Crabb, whose influential Christian counseling theory we encountered in Mandate 4, is a pertinent example. Crabb states unequivocally that the goal of marriage is oneness, which he defines as "a deep experience of personal intimacy through relationship with a person of the opposite sex."[48] He identifies and examines the different kinds of oneness as spirit oneness, soul oneness, and body oneness. The goal of marriage is to return as much as possible to the pre-fall garden where Adam and Eve were naked "in their body and their thought," and not ashamed. It is as if the goal of marriage is to somehow negate the consequences of human disobedience, the pretense, covering up, games of deception, and fear of unworthiness and rejection. It is also as if God intended marriage to be a joined circle of two facing inward, not outward, to exist for its own sake, not for others, to be an end in itself, not a means to an end.

As we have seen in Mandate 3, Christian critics of this perspective such as Rodney Clapp hold it to be "childishly egocentric,"[49] marriage "fixated on itself and its emotional coddling,"[50] and insist that God intended

45. Hugo, *Les Misérables*, 805.

46. Storkey, *Search for Intimacy*, 166.

47. Leslie and Morgan, "Soulmates, Compatibility, and Intimacy."

48. Crabb, *Marriage Builder*, 19.

49. Clapp, *Families at the Crossroads*, 135.

50. Ibid., 164.

marriage to be more of a mission base than a self-serving "haven in a heartless world."[51] They argue that the scriptural context of it not being "good for man to be alone" and the need for a "helper" suggests that the task being given to the human was too big for one person, and that the partnership of two was designed from the outset to be extrinsic in focus, to work side by side in the world. The primary problem being addressed was human capacity, not loneliness; the issue was the external need, not the internal gendered intimacy of the workers. In an attempt to find the middle ground between Crabb's intimacy and Clapp's mission-base visions of marriage, Allender and Longman offer a vision of marriage partners as *Intimate Allies* that brings theological, psychological, and sociological interests together. "The goal of marriage is twofold: to reveal the glory of God and to enhance the glory of one's spouse. . . . Life is war, and marriage provides us with a close and intimate ally with whom we may wage this war."[52] Oliver writes of marriage as a "community of being," which focuses on relationship, and a "community of purpose," which focuses on accomplishing particular tasks in the world and advancing a particular vision for the world.[53] Gushee insists that marriage ought to be a balance of both.[54]

Some critics and reservations notwithstanding, the Christian embrace of marital intimacy has been so ardent that a further caution of a different kind must be voiced. Critical theory is a school of social thought that arose in the first half of the twentieth century, aligned with what was known as the Frankfurt School of social research. Critical theorists coined the term "culture industry" to designate the processes and products of commercialized mass culture. The process involved turning the values, expressions, and communications of culture into commodities to be produced and sold for profit, literally capitalizing on culture, the entertainment industry being a prime example. The products of mass culture exhibited the same features as other products of mass industrial production: commodification, standardization, homogeneity, and predictability. Together with the "knowledge industry," the culture industry was said to be the primary means of maintaining prevailing ideology and mass conformity to it by pacifying, repressing, and stupefying the masses.[55]

Christians must constantly be concerned about the degree to which they may be complicit with the culture industry, and further, may potentially be

---

51. Lasch, *Haven in a Heartless World*.

52. Allender and Longman, *Intimate Allies*, 22 and 113.

53. Oliver, *Conjugal Spirituality*.

54. Gushee, *Getting Marriage Right*.

55. See Storey, *Cultural Theory and Popular Culture*; and Ritzer, *Sociological Theory*.

adding to its commodification of culture the equally disturbing process of the sacralization of culture. There is a real danger in all the aspects of marriage being examined in this book that Christians are not just blindly following cultural mandates, or mistaking them for biblical imperatives, or even turning the secular into the sacred, but that they are doing so subconsciously at least as much for profit as for principle. Christian ministries of every stripe will insist that they are only obeying God, serving a cause, meeting a need, building the kingdom, and so on, but what looks like ministry to the practitioner from the inside often looks like commodification to the observer from the outside. If identity is the coincidence of announcement by self and placement by others, but the claims of the actors do not coincide with the assessments of the observers, which is more true? If the claimed intention or conscious motive of the actor is ministry, but the operative dynamic is opportunistic marketing of a hot commodity, which is more definitive? The motive of an actor alone certainly does not determine the essence or moral status of an action; there would be little sin in the world if it were so. Motive for ministry is always at least somewhat mixed, because there is no such thing as pure altruism. The only question is what percent of the motive is serving the cause, and what percent is serving the self. Or is it, as T. S. Eliot observed, that we start out serving the cause, and end up making the cause serve us?[56]

For example, conservative Christians embraced personal counseling toward the end of the twentieth century. It was clearly a derivative of the psychotherapy, or "talking cure," at the beginning of the century that itself was a product of the growing modern fascination with nurturing the self, relationships, and intimacy. It was also attuned to their individualistic, psychologized reading of the biblical text that emphasizes personal righteousness and relationships.[57] That alone does not make all Christian marriage counselors opportunistic entrepreneurs of the culture industry, but it does give pause.[58] A Christian talking cure for couples who do not talk with each other well enough is a thoroughly modern enterprise not far removed from the commodification and sacralization of *The Dr. Phil Show.*

By now there are grounds to talk in terms of a veritable Christian intimacy industry. Christians may have produced more books, magazines, articles, DVDs, seminars, retreats, premarital programs, websites, organizations,

---

56. Eliot, *Murder in the Cathedral.*

57. In contrast, conservative Christians did not embrace social activism as readily because they have been culturally deafened to the emphasis on collective social justice in the biblical text.

58. In *More Perfect Unions: The American Search for Marital Bliss*, Rebecca Davis traces the rise of the marriage counseling industry in the twentieth century, and how it was both shaped by and shaped prevailing cultural norms.

task forces, etc. on marriage, family, and intimate relationships than on any other topic.[59] The market seems insatiable.[60] It is often the largest section in a Christian bookstore. Searching the Christian Periodical Index for intimacy and marriage delivers unending analysis and advice, proportionally far more than equivalent secular online databases. Googling the same terms delivers that much more. The *Couples' Devotional Bible*,[61] one of Zondervan's many specialty Bibles published in cooperation with *Marriage Partnership* magazine, is one sample product. Designed to improve marital communication, it offers devotionals on myriad marriage issues sprinkled throughout the biblical text. Notably, none of the devotionals on intimacy are able to extract an imperative from the text for voluntary, reciprocal self-disclosure. One entitled "Genuine Intimacy"[62] separates it from sex, but conflates it with love. Each individual ministry and product in the Christian intimacy industry is no doubt well intentioned, but probably less than fully aware of how it fits into and functions within the big cultural picture, where some misgivings remain.[63]

WHOLE AGAINST THE SKY

As we shall see more fully in Mandate 10, there is a profound difference regarding intimacy between viewing marriage as a covenant and viewing marriage as a contract. Covenant marriage seeks intimacy with the other through the self. Put differently, the self is the medium through which intimacy with the other is achieved, or as we have said here, the self is the agent or practitioner of voluntary self-disclosure. In contrast, contract marriage only seeks intimacy with the self through the other; the other is the medium through which intimacy with the self is achieved. Note the radically different objectives and effects. The intimacy of covenant marriage creates an interpersonal bond, whereas the intimacy of contract marriage leads only to the self-fulfillment discussed in Mandate 4. Note also the need for and the role of the other.

The other is someone distinct from, different from, or opposite to oneself. The concepts of "the other" or "othering" go back to Hegel, who introduced the idea that the other was an essential part of self-consciousness. How a person defines the other is part of what defines or even constitutes him or herself. It has since been applied more pejoratively to groups who are

---

59. This may have been the best reason for not writing this book!

60. This was not the reason for writing this book!

61. *NIV Couples' Devotional Bible.*

62. Ibid., 1373.

63. For example, many Christians have expressed misgivings about Zondervan, the world's largest publisher of Bibles, being owned by Rupert Murdoch's financially aggressive and ethically suspect News Corp. media empire.

marginalized and stigmatized, and to women from a male perspective, but more positively to God as the Infinite Other.[64] For example, Old Testament scholar Walter Brueggemann writes of God as "The Other" in *The Covenanted Self*, stating that the other "is not simply a counter-object, but it is the risky, demanding, dynamic process of relating to one who is not us, one to whom we are accountable."[65] He goes on to suggest that spirituality is "the enterprise of coming to terms with this other in a way that is neither excessively submissive nor excessively resistant . . . [C]ovenanting (and spirituality) consists in learning the skills and sensitivities that include both the courage to assert self and the grace to abandon self to another."[66] Brueggemann makes it clear that this applies both to the ultimate Other and to the marital other. Surely this is a richer, thicker conception of intimacy with God and spouse than popular notions that cast God as a human equal, and spouses as clones or soulmates.

Christians must come to grips with the fact that neither the word nor the concept of intimacy is anywhere to be found in the biblical text with reference to marriage. In its pages, as in analytic academic precision, marital love is not synonymous with intimacy, and God requires only love, nothing more and nothing less. As disconcerting to the contemporary Western spouse as it may be, biblical, God-honoring marital love does not require intimacy any more than it requires liking. Loving a spouse without necessarily being intimate with him or her has in fact been the norm throughout most of Western history, and is still the norm in most non-Western cultures. To insist on or work toward an intimate soulmate in marriage is a sweet surrender to current culture, however desirable and rewarding it may be if realized. The German poet Rainer Rilke offers an "othering" counterpoint to the soulmate, an antidote to the intimacy ethic, that is in many respects closer to the biblical model of marriage: "Once the realization is accepted that even between the closest human beings infinite distances continue to exist, a wonderful living side by side can grow up, if they succeed in loving the distance between them which makes it possible for each to see the other whole against the sky."[67]

---

64. Levinas, *Totality and Infinity*.

65. Brueggemann, *Covenanted Self*, 1.

66. Ibid., 2 and 8.

67. Rilke, *Rilke on Love and Other Difficulties*, 28. Kahlil Gibran expresses a similar perspective on marriage in *The Prophet* (16):

"But let there be spaces in your togetherness.
and let the winds of the heavens dance between you.
Love one another, but make not a bond of love:
Let it rather be a moving sea between the shores of your souls."

Mandate 7

Sex

Should sex be primarily the pursuit of physical pleasure?

LOVE, INTIMACY, SEX—MANY CONTEMPORARY Western Christians hold these to be the holy trinity of marriage. Other conjugal benefits such as companionship and domestic efficiency may be mentioned in characterizing marriage, but usually not in the same breath as the big three. Love, intimacy, and sex are often and easily conflated with one another, as in describing sexual intercourse as "making love" or "being intimate." One is also often said to lead inevitably to the other, as in the rhyme of the old schoolyard serenade: "Max and Mia sitting in a tree, K-I-S-S-I-N-G. First comes love, then comes marriage, then comes baby in a baby carriage." The implied theory in this sometime taunt is that sexual attraction generates love, which leads to marriage, which in turn produces family, with intimacy inevitably developing along the way. At the same time, love, intimacy, and sex remain conventionally associated with different aspects of the person and parts of the body. As reciprocal self-disclosure, intimacy is a cognitive dynamic most associated with the mind, and now deemed the primary focus of marriage. As sentimental affection, romantic love is an emotional dynamic most associated with the heart, and now deemed the "heart" of marriage. As erotic passion, sex is a sensual dynamic most associated with the genitals, and now deemed the energizing force of marriage.

Significantly, the mind, the heart, and the genitals have also taken their turn in history and culture being viewed as the center of personhood.

The ancient Hebrew considered the core of their being to be located in the procreative powers of their loins and wombs. For example, when calling for the death of adversaries, Deuteronomy 33:11 speaks of crushing their loins, not piercing their hearts or cutting off their heads. To "gird up your loins" was not merely to tuck your tunic up between your legs to free yourself for greater movement, but to prepare the essence of your being for resolute action. The modern rationalist, in contrast, considered the core of their being to be located in the reasoning powers of the mind. Descartes' famous conclusion to doubting everything including himself, *cogito ergo sum*, "I think, therefore I am," is representative of Enlightenment thought.[1] The essence of the self came to be seen as minded behavior, that self-consciousness which distinguished humans from non-humans, and made meaningful personal action beyond mere animal reaction possible. As already seen in Mandates 3 and 5, the post-Enlightenment romantic now considers the core of his or her being to be located in the passionate powers of the heart. As postmodernism has cast aspersions on rationality, we now follow our hearts, not our heads.

Just as the mind is more than the brain, so too the "heart" is more than the physical organ that pumps blood from the chest to the rest of the body. Both mind and heart are disembodied cognitive constructs that in their own way have shaped Western culture. In sharp contrast, the genitals and the sexuality that flows through them are as embodied and sensate as possible. Unlike the ideas of mind and heart, sex is a thoroughly physical reality also practiced by animals that have no notion of mind and heart. At the same time, the creational, creaturely reality of sex is also more than a merely bodily function, just as the biblical construct of "flesh" is more than merely physical tissue. "Our ideas about sexuality filter up to us through our embodied biology and down to us from our embedded social environment."[2] Due to our distinctive, God-given, human capacities, sexuality is also emotional, psychological, sociocultural, and spiritual. "To think of the body as separate from the soul or as soulless, either to subvert its appetites or to 'free' them, is to make an object of it."[3] More grievously, to divide up the person endlessly is ultimately to destroy personhood.[4]

1. One of the many derivatives is intended to expose the contemporary self as primarily a consumer instead of a citizen: "I shop, therefore I am." My personal favorite is the inscription on a colleague's coffee mug: "I think, therefore I am . . . overqualified to work here."

2. McMinn, *Sexuality and Holy Longing*, 5.

3. Wirzba, *Art of the Commonplace*, 108.

4. The counter to such reductionism of person is the emergence of personhood, which "refers to the process of constituting a new entity with its own particular

For example, the Freudian psychoanalytic revolution at the beginning of the twentieth century not only brought human unconsciousness to the fore, but thoroughly sexualized it as well. Our sex drive, according to Freud, is the principal motivating force of "the pleasure principle." The *libido* of our life instinct (*eros*) is channeled through socially approved outlets, and all culture is a product of displaced sexual energy. One of Freud's famous students, Wilhelm Reich, broke with his mentor in part because Reich believed that in order for humans to flourish, the *libido* must be freed, not channeled.[5] Concurrent with Freud, the social theorist Pitrim Sorokin observed that throughout history societies had swung between the opposite extremes of sensate periods that emphasize materialist values at one pole, and ideational periods that emphasize ideals and spiritual concerns at the other pole. Early twentieth-century society, according to Sorokin, was the most sensate in Western history. By the end of the century, another social theorist, Daniel Bell, concurred, observing that the self-discipline, restraint, and delayed gratification of modern industrial society had given way to the hedonistic liberation, pleasure, and eroticism of postmodern, post-industrial society. This would have come as no surprise to the premodern Paul, who centuries earlier had warned that in the "last days" people will be "lovers of pleasure rather than lovers of God" (2 Tim 3:4).

These are some of the broadest contours of the comparative cultural milieu in which Christian couples today understand sex in marriage. More manifest expressions of current Western culture's regard of sex are evident at almost every turn. These include the no longer shocking sexual saturation of the mass media that now present as commonplace what just a few decades ago would have been reckoned pornographic. There is now a full-blown multifaceted sex industry of products and services, including a pornography industry that grosses more (in the sense of generating revenue) than all professional sports combined. As defined by the Urban Dictionary, "junk" in popular culture parlance denotes male genitalia. With its slogan "Life is short. Have an affair," Ashley Madison is an online social networking site with over ten million married members looking for extramarital sexual relationships.

Few would dispute that contemporary Western popular culture has reduced sex primarily to physical pleasure, the tie to procreation having been severed by modern contraceptive technologies. The primary relational

---

characteristics through the interactive combination of other, different entities that are necessary to create the new entity but that do not contain the characteristics present in the new entity" (Smith, *What Is a Person?*, 25–26).

5. Reich's belief that neurosis was due to lack of orgasm led Anna Freud, a lifelong virgin who had been analyzed by her father because she was masturbating, to force Reich out of the psychoanalytic movement in 1934.

meaning left in sex is the surprising and curious resilience of the cultural norm—not practice—of marital sexual fidelity. Of more serious dispute is that the Christian subculture has adopted this reduction, though evidence abounds for the myriad ways in which Christians are undistinguished in contemporary sexual practices. Cast by our capitalist culture as consumers rather than citizens, and taught by our therapeutic culture to practice self-actualization rather than self-discipline, Christians have likewise surrendered to the seductions of sex. Most recent surveys indicate there is no longer much difference between Christian and non-Christian sexual practices, even where it is most admonished and likely. Despite a strong majority of evangelicals believing that sex outside of marriage is morally wrong, the many Christian premarital sexual abstinence programs of the last few decades have come to nearly nothing.[6] Their promise of greater sexual pleasure in marriage was hollow all along. "The abstinence industry perpetuates a blissful myth; too much is made of the explosively rewarding marital sex life awaiting abstainers. The fact is that God makes no promises of great sex to those who wait."[7]

What have Christians thought about sex historically? How is an individual's sexuality formed? What evidence is there of the rise of the pleasure principle regarding sex? Is it true that "one of the tasks of the church should be to help make marital sex more pleasurable," as Gudorf asserts?[8] What meanings can sex communicate? How is sex best understood biblically?

FORMS OF OBSESSION

Most Christians are well aware that Christian attitudes toward sex have been rather less than positive throughout history, or even consistent. Indeed, most individuals would confess changes in their own attitudes within their own lifetime. Sex has a checkered past, with some of the most suspicious shifts occurring in the recent past. With their focus on building the chosen people of God, the Old Testament Hebrews had a very positive view of sex. It was celebrated as a good and sacred gift from God, and the presence of concubines, especially among the wealthy, suggests that sex was more than

6. Data and commentary on current Christian premarital sexual practices are offered in Regnerus, *Forbidden Fruit*; Regnerus and Uecker, *Premarital Sex in America*; and Winner, *Real Sex*. One more recent survey found that 88 percent of unmarried 18–29-year-olds are having sex, and of those surveyed who self-identified as "evangelical," 80 percent have had sex, 64 percent within the last year, and 42 percent are in an ongoing sexual relationship. Reported in Charles, "(Almost) Everyone's Doing It."

7. Regnerus, "Case for Early Marriage."

8. Gudorf, "Graceful Pleasures," 125.

merely procreative. Whereas today we swear an oath by placing our hand on the sacred Bible, Abraham made his servant swear an oath by placing his hand on Abraham's penis, the most sacred object available to them then and there (Gen 24:2–3). In their context, the Song of Solomon and passages from Proverbs are as erotic as any in ancient Near Eastern literature. However, by New Testament times, Jesus taught that sexual desire must be firmly controlled (Matt 15:18–20), and Paul, who was outraged by the low standards of sexual behavior of the Greco-Roman world,[9] taught that sexuality could get in the way of spirituality (1 Cor 7:3, 5).

By the time of the early church, the attitudes toward sex of the church fathers had swung infamously to a negative extreme, in stark contrast with other ancient religions. Sexuality was equated with the fall, and some even interpreted the original sin to have actually been sexual intercourse, because of the symbolism of the story. The serpent by its shape was actually Adam's penis sliding toward Eve, the tree was carnal "knowledge" that bore the "fruitfulness" of sex, the covering of their genitals after the event implied sexual guilt, the capacity for reproduction implied vulnerability to death, and so on.[10] Even marital sex came to be disparaged due to a theological dualism that separated the spirit from the body, a practical asceticism that denied the latter, and the flood of feeling that overwhelmed rational controls during sexual encounters. Saint Jerome, best known for translating the Bible into Latin (the Vulgate), maintained that "Anyone who is too passionate a lover with his own wife is himself an adulterer."[11] Church edicts that forbade sex on certain days multiplied to the point where, by one calculation, only forty-four days a year remained available for marital sex.[12] The Greek church father Origen of Alexandria castrated himself in order to be completely free of sexual desire, as celibacy was held to be the highest spiritual state. Pope Gregory the Great explained early in the sixth century that although marriage was not sinful, "conjugal union cannot take place without carnal pleasure, and such pleasure cannot under any circumstances be without blame."[13] The net effect, not surprisingly, was not just the degradation of sex, but the degradation of marriage and women more generally.

---

9. Among the Greeks, prostitutes where a regular part of temple worship, and men practised pederasty, the purchase of young boys for sexual services and mentoring. Among the Roman rulers, Julius Caesar was bisexually "a man to every woman, and a woman to every man," while Caligula sponsored orgies of bestiality and sadism.

10. Mace and Mace, *Sacred Fire*.

11. Quoted in Yancey, "Holy Sex."

12. Quoted in ibid.

13. Quoted in Coontz, *Marriage, a History*, 86.

Attitudes toward sex in Christendom gradually grew more appreciative thereafter. The Protestant reformers abandoned celibacy for the enjoyment of marital sex, and even the Puritans maintained a positive regard for sex that was counter to their subsequent reputation. One Puritan preacher, William Gouge, even recommended that sex should be entered into "with good will and delight, willingly, readily, and cheerfully."[14] When one Puritan husband announced that he would abstain from sex for a year as personal penance for disobeying God, the church leaders pronounced that he had no right to deny his wife her rights to sexual fulfillment.[15] That was certainly more liberal than the Victorian descendants of Puritans would be. In a surprising reversion to the sexual aversion of the early church, the nineteenth-century Victorian era was perhaps the most sexually repressed in Christian history. Indeed, it has become virtually synonymous with sexual repression, and some of it now seems humorous. Even piano legs were covered with skirts to maintain proper modesty. It may be debatable whether Victorian sexual scruples constituted repression (unconscious control of self), suppression (conscious control of self), or oppression (control of self by others), but there is no debate that sex was sternly controlled, and explicitly condemned again. Foucault has argued that Victorians were actually obsessed with sex, and that their repression was just the first form that obsession with sex took. That same obsession would simply morph into sexual expression in the twentieth century.[16]

It was not just sexual expression that was anathema to nineteenth-century Victorians, but sexual desire itself, which was kept as separate from marital love as possible. Desire was considered animal in nature, and men were encouraged to wed a woman for whom they had only pure thoughts, not sexual desire. Once married, men were to show their love for their wives by refraining from sex as much as possible; husbands felt guilty if they wanted intercourse too much, wives if they wanted it at all. Decent wives submitted only for altruistic reasons, lying stoically motionless throughout the ordeal. Because husbands thought they were doing their wives a favor by looking elsewhere for sex, prostitution flourished like never before. Women were again forced into one extreme role or the other—the temptress Eve or the virtuous Mary. "Although the stereotypes changed from women as 'base, carnal, and licentious' (medieval period) to women as 'the fount of all purity' (Victorian period), they were nevertheless still identified with

14. Quoted in Mace and Mace, *Sacred Fire*, 175.

15. Doriani, "Puritans, Sex, and Pleasure." In 2011, a woman in France demanded and was granted court-ordered financial compensation from her ex-husband for lack of sufficient sexual relations over their twenty-year marriage.

16. Foucault, *History of Sexuality*.

the 'problem' of sex. Either they were sexually dangerous and needed to be ruled by men so that chaos would not break out, or they were morally superior and needed to be protected."[17]

Stories from the era surprise, amuse, and sadden us today. In the 1830s, Rev. Sylvester Graham preached that ejaculation drained men of "vital fluids" and endangered their health. Convinced that sexual appetite could be controlled by a diet of whole-grain flours, he developed a cracker called the Graham Wafer. Seventh-Day Adventist John Harvey Kellogg invented corn flakes as a food designed to reduce sexual desire and curb masturbation.

> The art critic John Ruskin, despite having seen the classical statuary of Paris and Venice, was allegedly so shocked when he saw his young wife Effie's pubic hair for the first time that he went into apoplectic spasms and later confided in the Queen herself that there was something wrong with his wife. It is hard to imagine Effie Ruskin's self-esteem, as we would term it now, let alone sexual desire, surviving her husband's horrified reaction to her body; he never consummated the marriage. (The poets) Robert and Elizabeth Barrett-Browning short-circuited any such marital awkwardness by never seeing one another naked—a very common occurrence in nineteenth century marriages.[18]

Lady Hillingdon, wife of the Second Baron Hillingdon, wrote that "I am happy now that Charles calls on my bed chamber less frequently than of old. As it is, I now endure but two calls a week, and when I hear his steps outside my door, I lie down on my bed, close my eyes, open my legs, and think of England."[19]

The twentieth century brought a sudden sexual reawakening, especially among women, and its unmistakable focus was the sheer pleasure of sex. With little to explain their unexpected and abrupt change of mind, experts began arguing that good sex was the glue needed to hold marriages together, now that patriarchy had supposedly lost its force. The 1920s foreshadowed the sexual revolution of the 1960s, as sex appeal replaced submission as a wife's first responsibility to her husband. This upped the ante for successful marriage to the point where, "in 1928, in a book titled *The Marriage Crisis*, sociologist Ernest Groves worried that pursuit of 'the pleasure principle' was creating unrealistic expectation that marriage could 'furnish individual satisfaction' that outweighed all its traditional burdens."[20]

17. Storkey, *In Search of Intimacy*, 191.

18. Margolis, *O: The Intimate History of the Orgasm*, 277.

19. The Oxford English Dictionary cites Hillingdon's use of the phrase from Jonathan Gathorne-Hardy's *Rise and Fall of the British Nanny* (1972).

20. Coontz, *Marriage, a History*, 202.

By the mid-twentieth century, despite the conservative character of the 1950s, the Kinsey reports on sexual behavior and the founding of *Playboy* magazine kept pushing sexual obsession further. In 1960, C. S. Lewis provided his well-known critical comparison of our society's obsession with sex to a hypothetical society's perverse obsession with food, in which the dramatic unveiling of a pork chop has the same effect as a striptease. That was even before the "swinging sixties" brought free love to all, emboldened by the broader social revolution, the birth control pill, and the human potential movement. There was a brief, slight reaction to sexual liberality in the 1980s, as disillusionment with impersonal sex, fear of the new threat of AIDS, and premarital abstinence programs slowed the revolution. But by the end of the century, with the Internet and hook-up culture in full force, the pursuit of sexual pleasure seemed unbounded. Western sexual culture could not be more radically opposite to that of a mere century previous.

SEXUAL SCRIPTS

Accounting for such extreme variation, even within a single cultural tradition, would be impossible if human sexuality itself were not variable. Human sexuality is not simply either a male or female package given by God through nature, implanted prior to birth, "hard-wired into our DNA."[21] God may have originally created a straightforward male and female, but 1–2 percent of humans are born intersex, with some combination of male and female physical characteristics. Of those born with solely male or female anatomy, anywhere from 2–13 percent are not exclusively heterosexual in orientation. Of wholly heterosexual males or females, 100 percent experience sexual arousal in socially conditioned ways. Beneath the apparent innateness of sexual attraction lies profound learning; sexual arousal is not a purely natural physical and emotional response. The very experience of excitement that seems to originate from hidden inborn sources deep within us is in fact an acquired response, and it is only our insistence on the myth of naturalness that hides these social components from us. All humans are sexually socialized by internalizing their cultural beliefs and norms about sexuality.

According to Balswick and Balswick, sexuality "emerges as part of an interactive developmental process between biological and sociocultural factors,"[22] though the two factors are not equal in weight or function. "Bio-

---

21. For a Christian critique of the rigid sexual dimorphism that Western Christians assume—the belief that sexual bodies, orientations, and identities come in either one of two binary types—see Paris, *End of Sexual Identity*.

22. Balswick and Balswich, *Family*, 216. Balswick and Balswick present an elaborate

logical factors serve as necessary but not solely sufficient contributors to the formation of human sexuality, . . . (whereas) sociocultural factors serve as sufficient, but not necessary, contributors."[23] Put simply, sexuality can be entirely acquired, learned by internalizing a cultural sexual script. These sexual scripts define what in any particular culture constitutes a sexual situation, behavior, or sensation. They determine what images, actions, and forms are sexually attractive and arousing. They prescribe how to think about and act during sexual encounters. They instruct as to the what, where, when, why, how, how often, and with whom of sexual relations. For example, as we have seen, in the nineteenth century, the women men wanted did not want men. Today, the women men want want men. Even physical attractiveness is no longer enough; both men and women are now obliged to be both desirable and desiring as well. Desire desires desire.

As always, the best evidence for the social construction of sexuality, for the extent to which sexuality is learned, is historical and cross-cultural comparison. For example, looking back on sexuality within Western culture, as we have just done, reveals striking differences in definitions of sexual attractiveness. In ancient Greek art and sculpture, the smaller a man's penis, the more sexually appealing he was, whereas in modern porn, the bigger the better. The ideal body shape and manner of women has also veered from one extreme to another. The most desirable woman during the Renaissance, as readily evident in Renaissance art, had to be round and robust in body, with small breasts and large hips, and be matronly and nurturing in manner. Come the nineteenth century, as evident in its etiquette manuals, she needed to be thin and frail in body, with small breasts and small hips, and be feeble and disinterested in manner. Today's sex goddess, as evident in mass media portrayals, must be impossibly imbalanced in body, with large breasts and small hips, and be sleek and vigorous in manner. Some criteria, such as youth and health, full lips, shiny eyes, and elaborate hair, have remained constant over the centuries, but the discontinuities are more striking than the continuities.

Looking laterally at sexuality in contemporary non-Western cultures, the women men want in African cultures are similar in size to those of bygone Western Renaissance ideals.[24] There is also startling cross-cultural variation in which parts of the body are most sexualized. Helen Colton construes the hypothetical scenario of surprising a traditional woman in her bath to sug-

---

"Interactive Developmental Model of Sexual Development."

23. Ibid, 219.

24. In all cultures, the ideal female body signifies not just sexual desirability, but social status and child-bearing function as well, though at times by almost opposite criteria.

gest what part of her body she would "instinctively" reach to conceal. An Islamic woman would probably cover her face, a Laotian woman her breasts, a Chinese woman her feet, a Sumatran woman her knees, a Samoan woman her navel, and a Western woman her breasts with one arm and her genital area with the other.[25] A further, more familiar cross-cultural variation is in how much of the body is sexualized. At one extreme is the veiling practices of some women in the Muslim world that leave only their eyes to be seen behind their burkas. At the other extreme are the tribal societies of Southeast Asia for whom a cord that ties around a man's waist and holds up the head of his penis qualifies as public dress, compared to the sexual immodesty of going without it.[26] Of course, cross-cultural variations of sexual behaviors are likely even greater than those of sexual appearance alone. The Thonga of Southeast Africa are one of several societies for whom kissing is a revolting exchange of saliva and dirt, not the "naturally" erotic arousal Westerners experience it to be. Cross-cultural comparisons demonstrate that humans can be taught to feel aroused by a baffling variety of stimuli socially defined as sensual, and to feel either guilt or freedom in the process.

All these cultural sexual scripts are transcribed into the interpersonal and intrapsychic scripts of everyday individual life, the beliefs and assumptions about what males and females respectively think, feel, want, and more significantly, simply are.[27] They are used to assess ourselves as sexual beings, anticipate sexual engagement, respond to the other sexually, and evaluate our sexual experiences. Traditionally, they include the assumptions that women are undersexed and men are oversexed,[28] women are more interested in sensuality and men more in sexuality,[29] and women need a reason to have intercourse and men just need an opportunity. Historically, men have been understood as subjects of desire who take initiative, whereas women have been understood as objects of desire who monitor engagement. The consequence has been that men today engage in a non-relational sexuality that is "detached, objectified, and agentic,"[30] experiencing sex as primarily physical. In response, women have become alienated from their own body,

---

25. Colton, *Gift of Touch*.

26. A missionary once told me of a newly Christian tribe enthusiastically evangelizing a neighboring tribe and explaining to them that Christian morality called for all men to wear their penis cords at all times.

27. Regnerus and Uecker, *Premarital Sex in America*.

28. Most know that nymphomania is excessive sexual craving in a female, but few know that satyriasis is excessive sexual craving in a male, because a sex-driven female is considered worthy of a pathological label, whereas a sex-driven male is just normal.

29. This distinction is clearly built on a masculine conception of sexuality.

30. Levant and Brooks, *Men and Sex*.

and obsessed with its appearance, assessing it through the eyes of the male "gaze." These are some of the ways in which the ideas, images, and desires that stir in the privacy of our minds are rehearsed in the cultural language and scripts we acquire, whether enacted or not.[31] Little in sexual interaction, whether imagined or enacted, is truly novel or natural.

YES, YES . . . OH YES!

If it is true that in Western culture today desire desires desire, and that women from the nineteenth century on have been less sexually desirous than men, then tracing the recent course of female sexuality provides an instructive case study in the rise of the pleasure principle. Men have always wanted women, but women, for many good personal reasons and complicated sociocultural reasons, have not always wanted men. So how did men get women to want them again, or at least want sex as much as men do? Those two wants are not necessarily identical, and it may be that women rediscovered and heightened their desire on their own. Prior to the nineteenth century, women were considered to be at least equally if not more sexually passionate as men, and sexuality had been growing coarser by the century. "The eighteenth century in Europe, in terms of sheer crudity, was the bawdiest century of all, twentieth included. . . . (But) by the mid-nineteenth century, the passionate, orgasmic nature of women, which had been a given—regarded, indeed, as a threat—for thousands of years was missing, presumed dead."[32] Indeed, "most Victorian doctors considered sexual desire in a woman to be pathological and warned that female sexual excitement and indulgence could damage their reproductive organs."[33] In 1867, no less an authority than the surgeon general of the United States declared women to be asexual and devoid of desire or pleasure. For many it became a self-fulfilling prophecy. For some it did not.

In some doctor's offices, women were being treated for "hysteria," a malady of rather mysterious origins and unlimited symptoms; almost any ailment could fit the diagnosis. It dated back to ancient Greek gynecological treatises, and was named after the Greek word for the uterus, *hystera*.

---

31. For a more extensive Christian discussion of sexual scripts, see the excellent chapter in McMinn, *Sexuality and Holy Longing.*

32. Margolis, *O: The Intimate History of Orgasm,* 250 and 276. Among other manifestations, the eighteenth century produced the first work of pornography to be written in English, John Cleland's erotic novel *Fanny Hill, or the Memoirs of a Woman of Pleasure* (1748).

33. Margolis, *O,* 282.

The prominent second-century physician Galen considered hysteria to be a disease caused by sexual deprivation in particularly passionate women. In the nineteenth century, impatient physicians treated female patients with "pelvic massage"—straightforward manual stimulation of the genitals—until the woman experienced "hysterical paroxysm"—simple female orgasm. Physicians found the treatment rather tedious, but also quite profitable, as patients who experienced the new therapy demanded it frequently, and soon the ailment was considered fairly common among women. "Fainting rooms" were used for more privacy during home treatment. Alternate modalities were developed, such as hydrotherapy—gushing water massage—and, by the end of the nineteenth century, electromechanical vibrators, which shortened treatment significantly from hours down to minutes. The spread of home electricity brought the vibrator to the consumer market, and it became an essential home appliance sooner than the vacuum cleaner or the electric iron. Eventually it was generally, though reluctantly, acknowledged that all this was actually sexual, not medical. Women do have orgasms after all.[34]

Admitting the existence of female orgasm did not yet free women to pursue their own sexual pleasure. The mysteries and controversies surrounding female sexual pleasure and orgasm extended into the twentieth century. Debates still framed by male interests raged about whether female orgasm was seated in the clitoris or the vagina. Intent on keeping women away from masturbation, and committed to penile-vaginal intercourse, Freud argued, without evidence, that clitoral orgasm was purely an adolescent phenomenon. Mature women, he asserted, preferred vaginal orgasm.[35] But normal intercourse does not stimulate the clitoris sufficiently for most women to orgasm, leaving them feeling sexually inadequate and unsatisfied. Most women need some sort of direct clitoral stimulation. Seemingly lest women's sexual interests wander too far away from men's interests in penetrative intercourse, by the end of the twentieth century there was breathless scientific conjecture about the G-spot. It was reportedly a small, hypersensitive area behind the female pubic bone accessible through the anterior wall of the vagina that delivered the ultimate orgasm, and even female ejaculation.[36]

34. Full information can be found in Maines, *Technology of Orgasm*. Narratives of the same appeared in the 2009 Broadway play *In the Next Room (or The Vibrator Play)*, and the 2011 movie *Hysteria*.

35. Freud himself was sexually abstinent until marriage at age thirty, was a passionate and faithful lover for a few years, experienced long periods of low sexual desire by age thirty-five, became permanently disinterested and abstinent by age forty, and discovered in self-analysis at age forty-one that he really loved his mother and was jealous of his father. Nicholi, *Question of God*.

36. Recent studies suggest that the G-spot is the "legs" of the clitoris wrapping around the walls of the vagina, and that the vaginal orgasm is therefore still seated in

All this science of sex was plainly in the service of female pleasure, though it was just as plainly driven by a deeper male agenda. Liberal feminism sought full equality for women to be sexual subjects, not just sexual objects. Whereas one hundred and fifty years earlier, female orgasm had been medicalized as a pathology, by the turn of the twenty-first century it was anorgasmia, the inability to orgasm after ample sexual stimulation, that was cause for personal distress. In popular culture, the postfeminist *Sex and the City* television and film series glamorized the sexual escapades of four urbane women. *Girls Gone Wild* were everywhere on beaches and in bars. Cougars prowled as middle-aged men always had. Ariel Levy documented it all in *Female Chauvinist Pigs: Women and the Rise of Raunch Culture*.[37] The stunning reversal in just over a century from the social construction of female asexuality back to the social reconstruction of female hypersexuality was complete. The pleasure principle of sex reigned supreme.

THE SEXUAL ELEVATOR

Though current Western culture may be as sensate and hedonistic as any has been, sex cannot be reduced to mere physical pleasure. Unlike animals, human behavior is driven by meaning, not by simple stimulus-response alone, directed by the interpretation of stimuli and the meanings of response, not by physical sense inputs alone.[38] The essence of sex lies in its connotations, not its sensations. So when it is said that the brain is the largest sex organ, what is meant is that the disembodied cognitive constructs of mind and heart are more determinative of sexuality than bodies are. Sex is in truth more emotional, psychological, sociocultural, and spiritual than physical. Sexual body apparatus and technique are largely inconsequential apart from the meaning and relationship their engagement expresses. Sex is one of the most meaning-rich experiences in life, and its potential meanings range from pleasure to promise to procreation to power, from all that is best in humans to all that is worst. Sex therapist Wendy Maltz has developed a useful hierarchy of the meanings of sex that assumes that sexual energy is a neutral force that be-

---

the clitoris. An outstanding documentary entitled *In Search of the G Spot* is available from the Canadian Broadcast Corporation at http://www.cbc.ca/doczone/episode/in-search-of-the-g-spot.html.

37. Levy, *Female Chauvinist Pigs*. The movement took a darker turn with the release by James of the erotic—and many would say pornographic—novel for women, *Fifty Shades of Grey*. Despite, or perhaps because of its BDSM themes (bondage/discipline sadism/masochism), it became the fastest-selling paperback of all time worldwide.

38. This is a fundamental tenet of symbolic interactionism, one theoretical perspective within sociology.

comes connecting and integrating or disconnecting and disintegrating based on its intent and consequences.[39] Marital sexual intercourse can range from the agony of marital rape to the ecstasy of "one flesh," potentially even within the same marriage. Different episodes between the same husband and wife can have dramatically different dynamics. Maltz identifies three levels of positive interaction and three levels of negative interaction that are like riding an elevator up or down from the lobby on the ground floor.

Table 1

The Maltz Hierarchy of Sexual Interaction	
Level +3	Authentic Sexual Intimacy
Level +2	Making Love
Level +1	Role Fulfillment
Ground 0	
Level -1	Impersonal Interaction
Level -2	Abusive Interaction
Level -3	Violent Interaction

The first level going down the elevator, Impersonal Interaction, objectifies the other in a self-focused, self-gratifying pursuit of pleasure, with the effect of prostituting the spouse. As C. S. Lewis put it, "We use a most unfortunate idiom when we say of a lustful man prowling the streets, that he 'wants a woman.' Strictly speaking, a woman is just what he does not want. He wants a pleasure for which a woman happens to be the necessary piece of apparatus."[40] Impersonal marital sex occurs when the self fails to be present as a whole person, and fails to engage the other as a whole person. Being emotionally closed, there is then no regard for the psychological well-being of self or other, and the interaction ends up being at someone's expense. The second negative level, Abusive Interaction, moves from unintentionally misusing one's spouse to intentionally abusing him or her. This is the deliberate exercise of domination and control through psychological coercion, the conscious exploitation and humiliation of one spouse by the other. Forcing intercourse becomes marital rape, or refusing intercourse becomes marital sabotage. The perpetrator, acting out of a sense of entitlement or impunity, denies the damage to the self-esteem of the victim. At the third and lowest negative level, Violent Interaction, the psychological

39. Maltz, "Maltz Hierarchy."
40. Lewis, *Four Loves*, 87.

turns physical, wherein sex is used purposefully as a physical expression of rage and hostility, and sex organs are used as weapons or targets. Absolute control ensues, and "eventually, sexual experience is merely a sideline to an act of murder." Such a descent into the lower underground levels of sexuality is never taken willingly by two people together, but is traumatically and tragically imposed by one spouse on the other.

The first level going up the sexual elevator from the ground floor lobby is marital Role Fulfillment, a positive value, but minimally so. It constitutes a perfunctory fulfillment of cultural custom or religious duty according to socially sanctioned scripts, and the mutual respect and appreciation that doing so delivers. When the couple is trying to conceive, it takes on a special meaning. When it is merely sex drive reduction and release, it is physically satisfying without being personally fulfilling. It is like the stereotypically sexually frustrated husband pleading, "Look, I'm more than just a pair of ears, you know. I'm a whole person with deep needs." But the sexual repertoire tends to be limited, and the communication minimal. At the second positive level, Making Love, pleasure is again primary, this time as a mutual focus on pleasure for self and pleasing the other. This erotic re-creational co-experience is an exploratory and experimental form of play[41] and a celebration of the body, such as melodramatically portrayed in steamy movies and romance novels. There is a subtle danger here that sex play can easily devolve into sex work by the desire or pressure to become "good lovers." Instead of remaining one of the purest forms of spontaneous creativity, sex then becomes something formulaic and "methodical." When it becomes performance oriented and goal oriented, such as simultaneous or multiple orgasms, it becomes something to "work at." Technical manuals[42] are consulted, study and practice are scheduled. Making love by the book becomes a chore involving technical competence, skill development, a quest for mastery, a drive for success, a fear of failure. Yet working at sex does not work, because learning techniques makes one a good technician, not a good lover.

The highest level of positive sexuality, what Maltz refers to as the "roof garden level," is Authentic Sexual Intimacy. Both authenticity and intimacy connote complete openness and honesty in every dimension of the self, resulting in one of the deepest connections possible between two humans. At the same time, through this merging of selves, each ironically gains one of the deepest possible senses of his or her wholeness, as neither self is lost in the other. They share a sense of freedom, knowing they can go wherever

41. In *The Christian at Play*, Robert Johnston includes the sexual love in the Song of Songs as one component of the Hebraic model of play.

42. Sonia Borg and Sadie Allison may be the current leading pop culture generators of such.

they want, together, as one and yet two, as union without loss of uniqueness. Authentic sexual intimacy goes beyond interpersonal communication to interpersonal communion,[43] both a literal reunion and a re-enactment of mutuality in intercourse: approach, entrance/reception, full union, withdrawal. This merging is a profoundly spiritual connection, consisting paradoxically of both a deep reverence for one another's body, as well as an ecstasy that is by definition an out-of-body experience. Perhaps it is best described as a liminal experience, half way between two states of consciousness. It is far beyond sex as pleasure, commodity, or performance. Notably for our point here, it is unquestionably more relational than physical.

Chesterton asserted that "every man who knocks on the door of a brothel is looking for God." Many others have also observed a significant similarity between embodied sexuality and disembodied spirituality.[44] Both represent the human longing for completion in the other,[45] sexually in the complementary other, spiritually in the ultimate other. Sexual intercourse returns two separated humans to the "one flesh" of creation as much as any human experience can. The complementary sex completes us in unmatched and self-affirming, yet limited and temporary ways. Despite this urge to merge sexually, the final reality of human singularity is that when the sexual act is over, the two bodies must detach and the two souls be alone again, still imprisoned inside their own skin. This existential loneliness after sexual intercourse can be most profound, because the holy sexual longing for completion is only representative of a higher holy longing.[46] "The tragedy of sexual intercourse is the perpetual virginity of the soul," Yeats lamented. It is a reminder that there are places of the soul where only God can go, or as St. Augustine confessed, "God, you have made us for yourself, and our hearts are restless until they find their rest in you." We remain finite, incomplete creatures, and in the end sex alone is not enough. Short of "final reconciliation with God,"[47] even sexual union leaves us mourning incompleteness.[48]

---

43. In *What Is a Person?* Christian Smith ranks interpersonal communion as the highest of thirty human capacities.

44. Rob Bell recently provided a characteristically postmodern pop culture rumination on the similarities in *Sex God: Exploring the Endless Connections between Sexuality and Spirituality*.

45. Nelson and Longfellow, *Sexuality and the Sacred*.

46. McMinn, *Sexuality and Holy Longing*.

47. Allender and Longman, *Intimate Allies*, 213.

48. Ron Rolheiser provides a moving exposition of Judges 11, where Jephthah's daughter requests time, before he sacrifices her, to go into the desert to bewail the fact that she is to die a virgin, incomplete, unconsummated. Rolheiser, "Ultimately, We All Sleep By Ourselves," 10.

The Maltz hierarchy of sexual interaction suggests that the self-focused, self-serving pleasure of impersonal interaction is a disconnecting and disintegrating first-level negative, while the other-focused mutual pleasure of making love is a connecting and integrating second-level positive. What is clear is that, of the many disparate motivations for sex—releasing tension, having children, showing love, ending an argument, demonstrating commitment, degrading self or other, proving masculinity or femininity, seeking revenge, and so on—giving and receiving physical pleasure is seemingly not the highest motivation. "Sex speaks of spiritual realities far more profound than mere pleasure."[49]

ANATOMY, CHEMISTRY, AND MYSTERY

Peter Gardella has argued that it was actually spiritual realities, not culture, that led Christians to embrace sexual pleasure. In *Innocent Ecstasy: How Christianity Gave America an Ethic of Sexual Pleasure*, Gardella described how Christianity cooperated with the sexual ethic emerging in popular culture at the turn of the twentieth century, which experienced sex as innocent (without guilt) and ecstatic (taking us beyond self-consciousness). The struggle to overcome original sin and the highly emotional character of conversion played out in the salvific pleasures of sex. "Neither the gift of tongues nor female orgasm comes to the inhibited except through faith."[50] Yet Gardella could only document a correlation between Christianity and the new sexual ethic, and despite his book's title, he failed to provide any direct causal connection whereby Christianity might have led to the pleasure ethic, instead of more likely following it.

One measure of the cultural turn to physical pleasure as the primary purpose of sexuality is the explosion of sex manuals that occurred later in the 1970s as part of the sexual revolution. The Bible of that movement was *The Joy of Sex* (1972), in which Alex Comfort mocked prudish, clinical approaches to the mechanics of sex. Unexpectedly, Christians did not resist this movement as much as they simply made it their own, and a stream of Christian sex manuals followed. Unlike Comfort's approach, and minus the images, their often excruciatingly detailed scripts for sex implied that while everything about men and women was "natural," there was nothing "natural" about sexual intercourse. Its proper techniques had to be taught painstakingly, with

---

49. Thomas, *Sacred Marriage*, 209. The Roman Catholic rationale for prohibiting birth control is an especially profound spiritual principle. See John Paul II, *Theology of the Body*.

50. Gardella, *Innocent Ecstasy*, 82.

special emphasis on the critical importance of the first intercourse, presumably on the wedding night, and the precise steps necessary to achieve orgasm for the female, preferably through intercourse. Their focus on body apparatus and activities, and the need for knowledge, romance, and novelty, was otherwise undifferentiated from secular sex manuals. So it was that Ed and Gaye Wheat's title, *Intended for Pleasure*, proclaimed what would have been heresy to Christians of the early church, or to Christians a mere century previous.[51] But so successful were these manuals that Tim and Beverly LaHaye's *The Act of Marriage* was named by *Christianity Today* as the twenty-eighth most influential evangelical book of the second half of the twentieth century.[52] Evidently, theology alone was impotent in bed, and Christians concluded that God would not create in women the reproductively unnecessary capacity for orgasm—unique among female mammals[53]—if sex were not mostly about pleasure. "It would be easy to argue that sex manuals are just one more cog in the evangelical wheel to imitate and appropriate secular culture for its own ends."[54] The recent growth of websites devoted to marketing sex toys to Christians simply strengthens that argument.

Yet it is not as if Christians have reduced sex to physical pleasure alone. While increasingly accentuating pleasure in concert with culture, current Christian delight in marital sexuality is undergirded by ever more celebrated theological affirmations. Sex is now upheld as part of the creational order before the fall, originally unsullied by sin, as good and natural as eating and sleeping. Sex is a social/relational dimension of the image of God in humans, reflecting the differentiated complementarity, relationality, and unity of the Trinity. Sex is sacred, "set apart" for marriage for the purpose of binding wife and husband together by freeing them to give their bodies to each other. Sex is sacramental, as physical as the bread and wine of Communion and the water of baptism, creating a relational sanctuary in which God's love for us is literally "sensed."[55] Sex is procreational, enabling man and woman to participate in creation and care for their offspring together

---

51. The title of Douglas Rosenau book makes much the same claim: *A Celebration of Sex: A Guide to Enjoying God's Gift of Married Sexual Pleasure*.

52. "Top 50 Books."

53. The research is not wholly conclusive on female orgasm, but unlike most female mammals, women are clearly interested in sex even during days they are not fertile, and long past childbearing age. The human female is also the only mammalian female to develop breasts prior to first pregnancy. See Hrdy, *Mother Nature*.

54. DeRogatis, "What Would Jesus Do?," 133.

55. Boulton and Boulton provide an especially poignant exposition of this in "Sacramental Sex."

in family. Even while appropriating the cultural pleasure principle, sex for Christians is something more.[56]

The Scripture passages about sex most commonly cited are markedly more about relationship than about pleasure. "The Bible depicts sexuality as an attribute not of the individual but of the relationship,"[57] a combustible chemistry that happens between two people, not within either alone, commensurate with all other aspects of their relationship. The first earthling had no meaningful sexuality until a physically complementary other was drawn from the human. Sexuality was not in and for the first individual, but emerged only when human relationship became possible, when the two who had been one could become one flesh again. Proverbs 5:18-20 describes being enraptured, exhilarated, and ravished by sexual pleasure, but only in long, faithful relationship: "Rejoice in the wife of your youth. . . . May her breasts satisfy you at all times; may you be intoxicated always by her love. Why should you be intoxicated, my son, by another woman and embrace the bosom of an adulteress?" Though the Song of Solomon affirms and celebrates sexual love, it is far more than a blushingly erotic poem[58] that emphatically gives the woman voice to express her own desire. Initially drawn by sweet but superficial sexual attraction, the lovers dissolve the many barriers between them and, in their complete vulnerability to each other, create a sanctuary for each other.[59] Paul's instructions on marital sex in 1 Corinthians 7:3-5 focus on mutual rights and responsibilities, mutual authority over each other's bodies, and mutual avoidance of depriving the other for long—all principles of relationship, not calls for pleasure.

There is now evident in Christian circles a renewed emphasis on the relational character of sexuality, seemingly as a corrective to Christian accommodation to the cultural primacy of pleasure in sex. It is as if full permission to experience the full extent of the five senses in sex has been achieved, and it is time to remind ourselves that sex is more than sensational. When sex is isolated from relationship, it "loses its sense of consequence and responsibility. It becomes 'autonomous,' to be valued only for its own sake, therefore frivolous, therefore destructive—even of itself. Those who speak of sex as 'recreation,' thinking to claim for it 'a new place,' only acknowledge its displacement from Creation."[60] Failing to engage the whole

---

56. The balance struck by Smedes in *Sex for Christians* remains one of the best.

57. Miles, *Redemption of Love*, 187.

58. Perhaps the most graphic sections are 2:3-17 and 4:1-7.

59. Miles devotes a whole chapter to giving a beautiful exposition of the Song in *The Redemption of Love*.

60. Wirzba, *Art of the Commonplace*, 112.

person is likely to "lead some spouses toward engulfment and others toward disengagement. In either case, the relationship is kept at a superficial level. Lacking the ability to create person-centered connection, spouses either try to fill that emotional deficit through frequent sex for reassurance or little sex to stay safely disengaged."[61]

Dale Kuehne fears that both the love and intimacy of relationship are endangered by the obsession with sensual pleasure in what he terms the "iWorld." He "contrasts the long-established 'tWorld,' in which traditional morality reigned, with the present-day 'iWorld,' in which the immediate desires of the individual have been deemed paramount. He maintains that both fail to deliver the benefits of the proposed 'rWorld,' in which a larger web of healthy and nourishing social relationships provides the most personally fulfilling context for sexuality and relational well-being."[62] Notably, all three positive levels of sexuality in the Maltz hierarchy contribute to relational well-being, not just the highest. The ecstatic communion or oneness characteristic of peak sexual experience is an exceptional occurrence, and Christians have been guilty of placing terrible, tyrannizing pressure on themselves by holding it up as normative. Even the ordinary role fulfillment of unremarkable sex at the lowest positive level still contributes to relational well-being and carries rich theological meaning. It is only when sex becomes an individualistic, impersonal, self-focused, self-gratifying pursuit of physical pleasure that it becomes non-relational, negative, and less than God intended.

In sum, and generalizing to the extreme, the ancient Hebrew conception of sexuality and motivation for sexual engagement was primarily family centered and procreation driven. Yet from the biblical text as a whole it can be argued that God intended sex to be primarily person centered and relationship driven. Today in Western culture, sex is portrayed and pursued primarily as body centered and pleasure driven. Both the Hebrew and biblical ideals differ from this modern ideal in that they are other centered and meaning driven. Of course, just because one sexual ideal is predominant in a particular era does not suggest that other dimensions of sex are absent, only that some dimensions are foregrounded. Nor does a predominant cultural ideal suggest that every private sexual encounter is characterized by that ethic. For example, it is not as if person-centered, relationship-driven marital sex was completely foreign to Hebrew culture. Isaac was personally and relationally comforted by sex with his wife Rebekah after the death of his mother (Gen 24:67). It is not as if Hebrew marital sex was never body

61. Balswick and Balswick, *Model for Marriage*, 166.
62. Kuehne, *Sex and the iWorld*, back cover.

centered and pleasure driven either. King Abimelech caught Isaac fondling Rebekah in an unmistakably non-sisterly fashion for no apparent reason other than bodily pleasure (Gen 26:8). Similarly, it is not as if body-centered, pleasure-driven sex is contrary to the biblical ethic, the Song of Solomon being the best evidence.

However, it does appear from the biblical text that body-centered, pleasure-driven sexuality is most easily led astray morally. Such sex "has enough combustive force to incinerate conscience, vows, family commitments, religious devotion, and anything else in its path."[63] Had David's sexuality in the moment he saw Bathsheba bathing remained person centered and relationship driven, he likely would not have as readily become sexually wayward. From the warning in Proverbs not to "lust in your heart after her beauty or let her captivate you with her eyes" (Prov 6:25, NIV) to Jesus' warning that "everyone who looks at a woman with lust has already committed adultery with her in his heart" (Matt 5:28), lust is consistently presented in the terms of body-centered, pleasure-driven sexuality. Within the context of a marriage, body-centered, pleasure-driven sex may be sanctified by mutually giving it that very meaning occasionally, but as a cultural sexual ideal and ethic, it appears more prone to promiscuity. And body-centered, pleasure-driven marital sex is prone to impersonality to the extent that it loses sight of the relational other, ceases to function as a coupling dynamic, and becomes a form of mutual masturbation instead. However pleasurable sex may be, severed from relationship, meaning, and person, it becomes pornographic and animal before long.

Body-centered, pleasure-driven sex alone therefore falls short of the full purpose and potential of sex, seeking pleasure without communion. Other-centered, meaning-driven sex in general, and person-centered, relationship-driven sex in particular nurtures relational well-being, not just personal well-being. Remarkably, however innocently ecstatic sex may be, several of its purely physical aspects remain anatomically and chemically relational. For example, humans are the only species who most commonly copulate face to face with full body contact. Compared to pheromones, which are secreted chemicals acting outside the body to attract others, oxytocin is the "love hormone" released within the brain during orgasmic sexual intercourse, which functions as a bonding agent in both men and women, causing them to want each other more than anyone else. In the end, the body itself is an instrument of relationship.

Like many evangelicals, James Dobson surrendered to the cynical cultural script of male non-relational sexuality when he concluded that "men

63. Yancey, "Holy Sex."

are not very discriminating in regard to the person living within an exciting body. . . . He is attracted by her body itself."[64] In contrast, C. S. Lewis upheld a higher Christian ideal of relational sexuality: "Now Eros makes a man really want, not a woman, but one particular woman. In some mysterious but quite indisputable fashion the lover desires the Beloved herself, not the pleasure she can give."[65] In truth, the assertion that sex is "intended for pleasure" overstates Christian understanding of its primary purpose, though happily, God clearly intended sex to be pleasurable. Biblically, sex is principally a seal and celebration of relationship. This "absolute yearning of one human body for another particular body, and its indifference to substitutes, is one of life's major mysteries."[66] Sexual desire borne of love and intimacy wants the mind, heart, and body of a particular person, even while what is desired remains ultimately inexpressible and inexplicable. Beyond the anatomy of pleasure and the chemistry of relationship lies the mystery of sex.

64. Dobson, *What Wives Wish*, 115.

65. Lewis, *Four Loves*, 88.

66. Jean Iris Murdoch, quoted from http://www.great-quotes.com/quote/782530.

Mandate 8

Conflict

Should conflict in marriage
be understood as relational weakness?

FROM THE HOLY TRINITY of marriage—love, intimacy, and sex—we turn now to the holy terror of marriage—conflict. From basking in the joys of marriage, we turn to struggling with one of the sorrows of marriage, the clash that occurs when two wills driven by opposing interests collide. Marriages are frequently troubled by stresses such as separation, health, or finances, but never more painfully than by conflict. Depending on the issue, holy matrimony can descend gradually or quickly into unholy acrimony, mutual affection can turn slowly or suddenly into mutual antagonism. No marriage is truly totally free of conflict. If it is, or claims to be, then it is likely that "they haven't been married very long; they don't talk to each other very much; one spouse has all the power and the other has none; or they are in denial."[1] For a current Western marriage of any significant duration and honesty, happily ever after was once upon a time, and the ongoing challenge is how to live after happily ever after has dissipated.[2] Short of extreme mitigating factors such as a complete surrender of self by one spouse to the other, or a marriage of clones,[3] some conflict is inevitable.

1. Balswick and Balswick, *Model for Marriage*, 118.

2. A contemporary fairy tale suggests that single living can be as "happy" as marriage: Once upon a time a man asked a woman, "Will you marry me?" She said "No." And they lived happily ever after.

3. The maxim "If two people agree on everything, one of them is unnecessary"

Pondering marital conflict calls up questions about its causes, character, and consequences. The antecedents of marital conflict can be either personal or interpersonal. One spouse may simply blame their personal unhappiness on the other spouse in what psychologists alternately describe as projection, transference, or displacement. The unhappy spouse may feel that the marital relationship is miserable, when in truth he or she is merely bringing to the relationship his or her own personal misery resulting from factors that have nothing to do with the marriage. Or one spouse may simply have more interpersonal power than the other, and the conflicts they experience are not so much about the particular personal or situational issue as about challenging and defending the power imbalance between them. As for the character of marital conflict, in the opening line of *Anna Karenina* Tolstoy opined that "All happy families resemble one another, but each unhappy family is unhappy in its own way."[4] From more systematic study of marriage, Coontz begged to differ. "Leo Tolstoy once remarked that all happy families are alike, while every unhappy family is unhappy in its own way. But the more I study the history of marriage, the more I think the opposite is true. Most unhappy marriages in history share common patterns, leaving their tear-stained—and sometimes bloodstained—records across the ages. But each happy successful marriage seems to be happy in its own way. And for most of human history, successful marriages have not been happy in *our* way."[5]

The consequences of marital conflict are also both personal and interpersonal. Regardless of the content or course of conflict, the fact of its existence is at least disappointing, and when persistent, disheartening. Whether expressed or not, chronic aggravation evolves into low-grade anger, while acute aggravation explodes into high-grade anger. When its passion is spent, anger fades into apathy, which is an indifference and disaffection that no longer cares enough to protest, much less contend. The end point is an alienation that renders a spouse no longer fully present. Anger still wants and hopes. Alienation no longer does.

At least as heartbreakingly, conflict can take an alternate, more immediately destructive course, and descend into spousal abuse. Not all intimate-partner violence is only either personal or interpersonal. Some, such as gender-based violence, is systemic, and symptomatic of the historic macro-conflict between the genders. For example, patriarchal terrorism

---

applies.

4. Tolstoy, *Anna Karenina*, 1.

5. Coontz, *Marriage, a History*, 20.

must be distinguished from common couple violence.[6] Patriarchal terrorism, including wife battery, is systematic male violence that is deliberate, goal oriented, and coercive, and readily escalates when deemed necessary.[7] Common couple violence, in contrast, is less gendered and more explosive, the occasional outburst of violence that occurs when an argument gets "out of hand"[8] and either a wife or, far more frequently, a husband "snaps."

> Domestic violence is a leading cause of injury and death to women worldwide. Nearly one in four women around the globe is physically or sexually abused in her lifetime, and gender violence causes more death and disability among women aged 15 to 44 than cancer, malaria, traffic accidents or war. Regrettably, the church is not immune to this problem. Numerous studies suggest that incident rates among active churchgoers are nearly the same as those among the general populace.[9]

Indeed, van Leeuwen reports that "although eighty percent of sexual abuse and family violence occurs in alcoholic families, *the next highest incidence of both incest and physical abuse takes place in intact, highly religious homes.*"[10] Heggen suggests that such behavior is facilitated by popular Christian beliefs that God intends for men to control and women to submit, that because of a woman's role in the fall women are morally inferior to men, that marriages must be preserved at all costs, that suffering is a Christian virtue, and that Christians must promptly forgive those who sin against them.[11]

Though much domestic violence was condoned for much of Judeo-Christian Western history,[12] it is now condemned by both Christians and

6. Johnson, "Patriarchal Terrorism and Common Couple Violence."

7. In addition to simple domestic violence, cross-cultural practices of patriarchal terrorism have included sex-selective abortion and infanticide in Asia, honor killings in the Middle East, widow burning (suttee) in India, foot binding in China, witch burning in Europe, and female genital mutilation in Africa.

8. The idiom in this case could more accurately be reversed into an argument that gets "into hand."

9. Kroeger and Nason-Clark, *No Place for Abuse*, back cover.

10. Van Leeuwen, *Gender and Grace*, 170. Emphasis original. To refine the data, the lowest rate of domestic violence occurs among church-attending evangelical Christians. The highest rate occurs among non-church-attending evangelical Christians. Reported in Stafford, "Can This Institution Be Saved?"

11. Heggen, *Sexual Abuse in Christian Homes and Churches*.

12. Phyllis Trible identifies five narratives of rape, brutality, murder, human sacrifice, and widespread abuse of women in the Old Testament that she labels the "texts of terror" (Gen 16:1–16; Gen 21:9–21; Judg 11:29–40; Judg 19:1–30; 2 Sam 13:1–22). All are depicted callously, receive tacit approval from other characters in the stories and the narrator of the book, and seemingly serve no commendable purpose, remaining

Western culture alike. The second wave of the women's movement was the first to decry spousal abuse a generation ago, and though they had not led public censure of it, Christians were then not slow to denounce it as well. Such violence and abuse are, by current reading of the biblical text, unbiblical. But it is not the extremes of patriarchal terrorism or even common couple violence that are our primary concern here. Rather, our focus is the common couple conflict that too often leads to common couple violence. Couples who on Christian principle would never violate one another physically nevertheless are troubled by conflicts whose dynamics and toxic emotional effects cause them to question the strength of their marriage. If Christians have surrendered to culture in this regard, it is in the uneasy sense that the ordinary conflict in everyday marriage is evidence of relational weakness, and that despite its inevitability conflict is a failing that automatically degrades and destabilizes marriage. Simplistic appropriations of biblical concepts contribute to this sense. Christian emphasis on oneness in marriage makes conflict intolerable, as does marriage modeled on the Trinity, because no conflict exists within the Trinity. Facile applications of "do not let the sun go down on your anger" (Eph 4:26) are reduced to "never go to bed angry," implying that all conflict can be resolved in short order, and anger whisked away at will with little more than an attitude adjustment.

But marital conflict is not simple squabbling, bickering, or even fighting, with all its attendant agitations.[13] It cannot be entirely prevented by moral resolve, moderated by moral exhortation, or dispelled by moral admonition alone. If it is power that is exercised in conflict, what is power, how does it differ from authority, and where does it come from? Other than "I know it when I feel it," what exactly is marital conflict, what are the various kinds, and where does it come from? What types or stages of marriage are most vulnerable to conflict? How do spouses cope with it? What about the resultant anger? Addressing these questions again engages social theory more than social history.

---

unassimilated with the rest of the text. Trible, *Texts of Terror*.

13. Though they were not married to each other, Lady Astor and Winston Churchill exemplify the kind of caustic wit that can characterize marital spats. Lady Astor reportedly said to Churchill: "Winston, if you were my husband, I'd poison your tea," to which he is said to have replied, "Nancy, if you were my wife, I'd drink it." On another occasion, Lady Astor, an advocate of temperance, reportedly reprimanded Churchill saying, "Winston, you're drunk!," to which he replied, "Yes, and you Nancy are ugly, but tomorrow I shall be sober." But on yet another occasion when she was giving a costume ball and he asked her what disguise she would recommend for him, she reportedly suggested, "Why don't you come sober, Mr. Prime Minister?" No reply from Churchill is recorded.

THE LEGITIMACY OF CONTROL

To understand marital conflict adequately requires a grasp of concepts that cluster around interpersonal power, the mere mention of which tends to make many Christians rather uneasy. Their ambivalence about power varies with the level at which it is perceived to be operative. At the micro, individual level, they beam about power in their personal life, especially the power of God in their life and the enablement they feel to live a self-controlled, virtuous, and effective life. At the macro, societal level, they revere the greater, even cosmic struggle between good and evil, convinced that good will triumph in the end, and are committed to doing their part toward that end. In between, at the meso level of interpersonal and institutional power, they have long been apprehensive, perhaps disconcerted by the interpersonal and institutional abuse perpetrated by some churches, and persuaded that power corrupts. Though interpersonal power smacks to them of bullying, it has recently been redeemed by the concept of empowerment. As discussed in Mandate 4, the contemporary cant of psychologized marital relations, now intoned by our theological models as well, includes their obligation to be empowering; spouses are to facilitate the realization of each other's full potential as persons.

In more morally neutral sociological conception,[14] power is one form of domination, which is defined as the exercise of partial to total control over others. Domination is the capacity to produce intended effects on the thoughts, behavior, or emotions of another person, the ability to get another person to do what you want them to do. Submission is yielding to the control of another. Domination may be conscious or unconscious, intended or unintended; a dominator may not even be aware of the control they have.[15] It may also be achieved or ascribed, in that it can be merited through ability and effort, or granted without being earned or chosen. Achieving the status of husband and wife has traditionally also ascribed to each the status of superordinate and subordinate respectively.

Power is an illegitimate form of domination because it is based on coercion, and consists of the ability to carry out one's own will despite resistance. Conversely, authority is the legitimate form of domination because it is based on consent, and consists of the acceptance that the person making

14. The following definitions and distinctions are drawn from the work of the classical sociologist Max Weber. Unfortunately, contemporary use of the term "domination" carries negative moral connotations that Weber's use does not. Weber, *Economy and Society*.

15. When personal counselors address control issues, they include problematic conscious or unconscious control of self, others, and environment.

a demand or binding decision has the right to do so. Power is the ability to control another person against their will, and at times without their knowledge or understanding. It relies finally on the threat or use of force, and ultimately on physical force. In contrast, authority is control granted by the person subject to it, and thus elicits informed, voluntary compliance because it is seen as justified, valid, and fair. This legitimacy of authority can be derived from multiple sources, including state laws, social norms, or religious injunctions. At bottom, authority reveals more about the person granting it than the person to whom it is granted, because the legitimacy of authority, like beauty, rests mostly in the eye of the beholder. So it is that a civilian taking the life of an officer on the street is considered a murderer, whereas an officer taking the life of a civilian in a prison chamber is considered an executioner. So it is also that patriarchal terrorism for some is honor killing for others.

The difference between power and authority within families is most evident in parenting. Power will physically remove a kicking and screaming infant from the room, but authority will send a child from the room. The difference is that the child has developed the cognitive capacity to grant legitimacy in a way that the infant has not, enabling the parent to control them differently. Parents who have the respect of their children have authority (legitimate domination). Parents who do not have the respect of their children are left with power (illegitimate domination), and therefore resort to economic or physical coercion and force through reward and punishment. Authority is thereby supplanted by power, which in the last resort is physical and all too easily leads to abuse.[16] Just because a husband and wife are closer together in age and maturity does not ensure that power and authority are more equally distributed in marriage. Either may dominate or control the other. Nevertheless, husbands have traditionally had more power because of greater economic and physical clout. They have also traditionally had more authority because of traditional gender norms and, in Christian circles, biblical interpretations of male headship and female submission. When a wife is deemed to have inordinate influence, her husband is said to be hen-pecked, but there is no equivalent cultural notion of a wife being rooster-pecked. The most common measures of marital power and authority are who makes the most important decisions and who accommodates the other the least. Unilaterally making decisions about finances, or steadfastly refusing to do the dishes, and getting away with it, are examples

---

16. Few parents and children at this stage of life take into account the reversal of power and authority that will occur in the old age of the parent.

of power. Accepting responsibility for making decisions about finances, or delegating the doing of dishes, are examples of authority.

Economic and physical muscle are relatively obvious sources of interpersonal power, but there is more to marital power than that. Both are components of the resource theory of marital power, which hypothesizes that whichever spouse has the most resources has the most power.[17] Economic resources include education, income, and occupation, whereas physical resources include all the varied uses to which superior strength can be put. Other personal physical resources include domestic homemaking and house repair skills, and even attractive physical appearance can serve as a resource. Affective resources include emotional nurture, support, and protection, as well the love and sexual engagement that can be offered to or withheld from a spouse for manipulative purposes. Cognitive resources include an analytic and verbal ability to give persuasive explanations, as well as superior general or special knowledge and sound judgment. When one spouse is significantly more insightful and articulate than the other, a power imbalance is immediately present. Indeed, it may be more important that spouses be better matched in intelligence than in personality or temperament, to the extent that cognitive tools may be more determinative of their interaction. All these personal resources can be used to coerce a spouse through rewards for compliance or punishment for non-compliance. Remarkably, in a show of the power of social facts, all these personal resources of power can be neutralized and overridden by social statuses and roles, the clearest example being how traditional gender norms simply hand authority to husbands regardless of personal resources or even interest.

An alternate approach to marital conflict is based on the character of exchange relationships instead of on personal resources. In power-dependence theory, power is defined as the potential cost that one person can induce another to accept, while dependence is defined as the potential cost that a person is willing to tolerate within a relationship.[18] In an exchange relationship such as marriage, the power of Alice over Bob is a function of Bob's dependence on Alice. Alice may also in turn be dependent on Bob in other ways that may then create a balance of power. Therefore even in balanced relationships, power exists, albeit in a kind of equilibrium. Power-dependence theory is built on the older and broader social principle of least interest, which posits that the person with the least interest in a social exchange has the most power in it and over it.[19] Therefore the person with

17. Blood and Wolfe, *Husbands and Wives*, 1960.

18. Emerson, "Power-Dependence Relations."

19. The principle of least interest was first articulated by Simmel in "The Philosophy

the least interest in a courtship or marriage, or an argument in either, has the most power in it by virtue of their greater willingness to walk away from it. The person who is more devoted to it, invested in it, dependent on it, and ready to sacrifice for it is in fact the one most disadvantaged by their interest. The social dynamics of relational exchange seem here to trump personal virtue, as caring more ironically hands power to the person who cares less. Needless to say, this again has historically disadvantaged women, because they have been socialized to want marital relationship more, and socially situated to depend on it more, and therefore have been less willing to walk away from it. Of course, they have always countered such macro-manipulation with a micro-manipulation of their own, such as supposed least interest in sex.[20]

INNOCENT INCOMPATIBILITY

Whether balanced or not, interpersonal power is constantly present in marital relationships, though normally lying dormant or latent. The relative power of each spouse only comes to the fore and is manifest in situations of conflict, at which point power is brought to bear on a particular issue. As we have seen, interpersonal power is derived from personal resources, dependency, and interest.[21] Interpersonal conflict, however, is based on issues. At the simplest level, conflict is a difference of opinion about some issue. More fully, conflict is a struggle between two interdependent persons who perceive some incompatible goals or scarcity of rewards. In a conflict, the more one spouse gets, the less the other can have. If she wants to live in the city and he wants to live on the farm, they are in conflict, whether it is ever aired or not. Notably, this is not a communication problem that can be solved by greater clarity, nor a moral problem that can be solved by greater virtue. It is an interpersonal problem that can only be resolved by changing personal wants, or managed by regulating personal wants. Conflict resolution is certainly preferable to conflict management, but it is not always possible. Taking up residence in a small town will not solve this conflict.

---

of Money," and first applied to marriage by Waller and Hill, *The Family: A Dynamic Interpretation*.

20. Reidmann and Lamanna, *Marriage & Families*, 286.

21. Recall also that, in Weber's conception, power as illegitimate domination is amoral in the sense that control has been taken, not given by the person subject to it, which would have transformed control into authority. Power is not inherently evil, and can be used for great good when guided by love.

An all-or-nothing conflict such as this is a zero-sum conflict, in which the plus of one spouse is nullified by the minus of the other, resulting in a net gain or loss of nothing. Residing in a small town would turn it into a lose-lose situation, when what is desired is a win-win situation. That can only happen if, rather than a zero-sum conflict, it becomes a mixed-motive conflict instead, in which each spouse still wants to compete for getting what they desire, but also wants to cooperate for the sake of the relationship. A second dichotomy of marital conflict is situation-based conflict versus person-based conflict. Conflict is sometimes a situational state of marriage based on circumstance, sometimes a relational trait of marriage based on personality. Situational conflict calls for changing a situation or set of behaviors, whereas person-based conflict calls for changing a whole aspect of personality. This of course is enormously difficult to do, and sometimes obliges one spouse to accept and adjust to what cannot be changed in the other. Beyond situational conflict and interpersonal conflict lies systemic conflict, such as patriarchy, which is even more difficult to change.[22] A third dichotomy of conflict is non-basic conflict versus basic conflict. Non-basic conflict occurs within the "rules" or roles of a marriage upon which both spouses have agreed, such as who determines place of residence, or frequency of sex. Basic conflict is when the rules or roles themselves are contested, and there is no agreement on who decides who decides.

Common areas of marital conflict include finances, parenting, intimacy, sex, employment, gender roles, friends and family, and even what constitutes spiritual vitality and maturity. However, identifying what couples commonly fight about does not explain why they fight. At the most innocuous level, situational conflict can occur because some behaviors get defined as undesirable due to partner dissimilarity of preferences, when they are in no way personally inadequate, immature, or immoral. The hackneyed bathroom disputes are illustrative: toilet seat up or down, toilet paper unrolling from the top or bottom, toothpaste tube squeezed or rolled. Interpersonal conflicts of greater consequence can arise from discrepant values, such as patterns or rates of consumption, which can produce feelings of guilt or defiance in the face of the other's disapproval. Sometimes conflicting values result from focusing attention on different levels in certain situations, such as one spouse wanting to tip a server generously to show personal gratitude, and the other refusing to tip servers to protest the social system

22. Any husband and wife committed to an egalitarian marriage can choose to defy the dictates of a patriarchal society in which they may live, but they cannot choose to dismantle the social system in which they live. Any husband and wife committed to a complementarian marriage and living in a patriarchal social system will experience no overt conflict from the social system, because they have granted authority to it.

of obligatory gratuity. Forms of attachment to each other can also be interpersonally problematic, with disagreement on whether their relationship should be dependent, codependent, independent, or interdependent, as discussed in Mandate 4. One spouse may see the marriage as a partnership, as two attached individuals with separate identities, while the other spouse may see the marriage as a couple, a single unit with merged identities. Over time, the respective spouses my change and grow as individuals in different directions and at different speeds, producing lower self-esteem in one, and leading to negative coping strategies. Commitment to the relationship, instead of to the person, as we shall see in Mandate 10, then becomes crucial. Two fundamental concerns appear to underlie all marital conflict, whether situational, interpersonal, or systemic. Perceived threat involves a perception that one's partner is being hostile, and blaming or controlling the self. Perceived neglect involves a perception that one's partner is failing to make desired contributions to the relationship.[23]

As unhappy an experience as marital conflict is, conflict is nevertheless as morally neutral as the underlying power it exposes. Conflict is neither inherently good nor bad,[24] and is capable of producing potentially either good or bad relational results. Conflict becomes destructive when viewed as an either-or, win-lose, zero-sum situation instead of an opportunity to reach solutions together. It becomes more destructive when explicit or implicit agreements are overridden by power. It becomes most destructive when there is a breakdown of trust such that one spouse no longer assumes the honesty, loyalty, and good will of the other, and the relationship is thereby actually damaged, not just strained and pained. Yet conflict can become constructive when it provides opportunity for spouses to clarify their similarities and dissimilarities, to identify areas of their relationship that need attention, and to promote greater personal and marital growth. They may learn how to agree to disagree and live with the difference, viewing it as the uniqueness and enrichment of their partnership. They may learn how to "bar-gain" in such a way that neither one gains at the expense of the other, the purpose being to gain maximum joint profit, not personal profit. Most admirably, they may learn how to give agreement as a gift. Letting the other have their way is then not giving in and going against one's own will, but rather saying "I want to do this because you want to," and meaning it. There are few higher expressions of maturity than to give agreement as a gift of

---

23. Sanford, "Perceived Threat and Perceived Neglect."

24. If the issue of a particular conflict is some moral failing such as violence or abuse, conflict is good.

love without strings attached, without resentment or depression, and without demanding pity, gratitude, or admiration.

Ruth Graham was known to be possessed of greater frankness than her more famous and more diplomatic husband, Billy. One of her columns in *Christianity Today* was on marriage, and entitled "Needed: Incompatibility."[25] She recounted how "I once knew a man who refused to let his wife disagree with him on anything. Now, every man *needs* to be disagreed with occasionally. This poor man's personality, his ego, and even his judgment suffered." She then added the following anecdote:

> Three of us were lunching one day while our husbands relaxed over what, for me would have been hard work: a game of golf.
> "Would you two like to know the secret of our happy marriage?" our older companion asked.
> Forks in mid-air, we waited.
> "Because," and the mischievous eyes brimmed with laughter, "we never do anything together."

Graham's ends her column with "All I can say is, 'Three cheers for incompatibility!'"

POWER STRUGGLE

The recent social history of systemic power and conflict in marriage can be summarized briefly.[26] As little as two hundred years ago, marriages in Western culture were owner-property marriages, in which the wife was the property owned by the husband. He had sole control of all their economic resources, normative final authority in decision making, and social permission to use physical force if necessary. She had no independent or legal status as a person. This model evolved into the head-complement marriage, in which the wife gained more decision-making power but still gave final deference to him. The rise of companionate marriage gave her more relational resources of power in what is now known as traditional marriage. Senior partner–junior partner marriage emerged when wives entered the labor force and achieved some economic independence to go along with their rising social status. By the turn of the millennium, equal partner marriage was more normative, with equal authority, equal career commitment, and role interchangeability, though most marriages remain neo-traditional

25. Graham, "Needed: Incompatibility," 25.

26. The following series is from Scanzoni and Scanzoni, *Men, Women, and Change.* Though it was offered as a typology of marriage, it can serve equally well as a historical development sequence.

or quasi-egalitarian in actual function. Economic resources and gender roles have been the primary factors in bringing about greater symmetry in marital power, with its attendant effects on marital conflict.[27]

Interpersonal power and conflict are also central to the typology of contemporary marriage utilized in Mandate 6 to highlight differences in intimacy.[28] In traditional marriage, power is unequal because of asymmetrical economic resources and gender roles, as just noted. Therefore overt conflict is minimal, because both agree on how it will be settled, quickly.[29] In extrinsic marriage, the power is equal because husband and wife actually function quite separately. The conflict is limited because they do not actually bump into each other very often. In empty shell marriage, power and conflict are seldom issues because they are too disengaged for it to arise. In pseudo-intimate marriage, power is avoided as each attempts to be as accommodating as possible. Conflict is denied, lest it shatter their illusion of intimacy. In negative exchange marriage, power is contested and conflict is constant. As described previously, this is marriage as a series of hostility rituals between two conflict-habituated individuals who find fault-finding and fighting rewarding, even when it is unproductive. Both spouses take an uncompromising approach to conflict, and thus the same issues come up over and over, with no new insights. Both are more concerned about triumphing than about dealing effectively with the issues, more concerned with winning the battle than ending the war. In intimate marriage, both husband and wife put effort into maintaining a balance of power and managing conflicts.

It is one thing to observe the distribution of power and the frequency of conflict in various types of marriage, but quite another to claim that all marriages have a predictable period of interpersonal conflict. Stage theories are bolder claims than typologies. The interdisciplinary Christian scholar James Olthuis has offered a developmental stage theory of marriage in Western culture, already introduced in Mandate 6, which has as its pivotal point a marital power struggle.[30]

---

27. For a similar but more detailed analysis of the same trajectory over the same time period that focuses on the emergence of modern political and economic organizations instead of modern marriage, see Jackson, *Destined for Equality*.

28. Kersten and Kersten, *Marriage and the Family*.

29. The story is told of a bride and groom going home from their wedding in horse and buggy. The horse acts up, and the husband says, "That's once." The horse acts up again, and the husband says, "That's twice." When the horse acts up a third time, the new husband gets out of the buggy, pulls out his rifle, and shoots the horse. The new wife cries out in protest. The husband says, "That's once."

30. Olthuis, *Keeping Our Troth*.

Stage 1: Romance

Contemporary Western marriages begin in the ecstasy and mystery of passion, the sublime impetus to relationship that is nevertheless insufficient to sustain marriage. The imaging operative in courtship, discussed in Mandate 1, in which each spouse is motivated to present themselves as lovable, carries over into marriage for a while. Only as intimacy waxes and imaging wanes does the potential for conflict grow proportionally. As knowledge of each other deepens, so does the potential for interpersonal conflict, and the need to get grounded in reality.

Stage 2: Power Struggle

When fundamental differences are inevitably fully exposed, each spouse's identity is threatened and ego is broken.[31] "Small resentments take root. Slowly we retreat behind barriers and nurse our resentments,"[32] leading to games of denial and deceit, a dance of being in step, but out of touch. Both are driven by fear and weakness. Problematic emotional dovetailing between the two spouses, such as a pleaser and resister, a dominator and submitter, or a martyr and manipulator, exacerbate the state of affairs. Sometimes a truce is struck, accompanied by apprehensive exhortations to try a little harder and to give a little more, knowing that the character of their relationship, or the relationship, itself is at stake.[33] Soon the truce breaks, exposing a growing inner desperation, and it becomes decision time. They can settle for less, the reasonable coexistence with minimum pain of an empty-shell marriage. They can live in unspoken acceptance, the emotional and reflective numbness and absence of ideals or perceived options of a pseudo-intimate marriage. They can separate or divorce. Or they can struggle for growth. Olthuis insists that a marriage can fixate or equilibrate at any stage for life, and that a marriage can stay in an unresolved power struggle for its entire duration.

Stage 3: Shifting Gears

In revived hope of renegotiating, but in danger of simply retrenching, this is an honest looking inward on self and owning responsibility, instead of projecting onto the other. It requires demasking core fears, hurts, and motives, and owning up to the anger that derives from those fears, hurts, and frustrations. Distancing or differentiation is necessary to gain space for

31. Mason, *Mystery of Marriage.*
32. Olthuis, *Keeping Our Troth,* 61.
33. Dan Hill's song "Can't We Try" (*Dan Hill,* 1987) captures this fragile state well.

rapprochement. Then, meeting in the middle, "no longer do we use intimacy to make up for a lack of identity, but neither do we fear that intimacy will destroy identity."[34] This opening and owning of self must of course be mutual, because if one partner pleads innocence the process is stymied.

Stage 4: Mutuality

Arriving at "at-one-ment" means husband and wife have achieved belonging without possessiveness, forgiving without blaming, and caring without controlling. Theirs is now a complete vulnerability without insecurity, complete intimacy without fear. The change of heart in Stage 3 is now evident in changed ways of relating. Com-passion and com-promise are palpable in their patterns of communication, their meanings of sexual intercourse, and the context, duration, and management of their conflicts.

Stage 5: Co-Creativity

The joy of mutuality in marriage overflows into sharing with and caring for others in a manner expressed by Clapp's vision of marriage as mission base discussed in Mandate 3. Freed from enmeshment and empowered to serve, each spouse sends the other out into the world beyond the marriage to interconnect with all God's creatures. "In the Spirit of Christ we may rise above the domination/submission/alienation syndrome that has invaded creation and taken us hostage, even in our own families and marriages."[35]

Rick and Kay Warren, he of Saddleback Church and *Purpose-Driven Life* fame, skipped the romance stage of marriage altogether, and atypically began their marriage in a power struggle. "Other than their Baptist faith and their commitment to evangelism, Rick and Kay seemed to have little in common; their tastes and personalities were so starkly different."[36] Having each "heard from God"[37] separately that they were to marry the other, Rick proposed to Kay on their second date and she accepted, sealing it with their first kiss. During the following year when they were apart on separate summer missionary internships and then in different schools, it was clear to both that he was in love and she was not. Shortly before the wedding, Kay told Rick of having been sexually molested as a young child, subsequently

34. Olthuis, *Keeping Our Troth*, 101.

35. Ibid., 140.

36. Sheler, *Prophet of Purpose*, 71.

37. Rick explained how he receives divine guidance as follows. "When I say God said something to me, that's inspiration. It's thought. . . . God can certainly put a thought in my mind without him having to say it aloud. I have never heard God say something aloud, ever" (ibid., 75).

becoming "alternately fascinated and repelled by anything sexual," including addiction to pornography, and now being "totally messed up."

On their wedding day, they "were virtual strangers who were about to descend into marital hell. 'I remember standing in the back of the church,' Kay recalls, 'waiting to walk down the aisle, going, 'Okay, God, those feelings that you said you'd bring? It would sure be nice if you'd bring those feelings sometime soon.'"[38] The honeymoon was a disaster, sexuality was "a huge deal," and they were both dying inside. Over the next while, they argued and fought over money, sex, and in-laws as they sank deeper and deeper into a dark pit, their marriage in shambles. Kay saw no hope, and consigned herself to a lifetime of misery, divorce being out of the question. Rick was eventually hospitalized. "I was so sick from the stress. I was angry. It was like, 'Wait a minute. I saved myself for this?' I was just flat-out angry at God and felt cheated, and Kay thought she was going crazy."[39] They eventually sought marriage counseling and were able to shift gears, and have continued to go to counseling unashamedly over the years whenever they feel in need of a "tune-up." Kay recounts that "neither of us really knew how to handle conflict very well. So (counseling) at least opened the door to begin talking about the problems and the struggles and our differences."[40] Perhaps they got married because God told them to—it is easy to say so. Perhaps it was their principles that got married and they each came along—it is easy to do so. But intimacy and mutuality did not come without a fight.

ASSERTIVENESS AND COOPERATION

Having good grounds to fear the negative outcomes of conflict, but unable to avoid it, resolve it, or manage it, many couples frequently resort to denying it. As a defense mechanism that tampers with their cognitive reality, denial successfully wards off emotional pain, but when used extensively, also distorts their lived reality. Various methods of denying conflict actually alter the marital relationship. To rationalize conflict is to block out of consciousness and conversation the true nature of the issue, and instead frame it falsely and justify it. The resultant explanation is logical and convincing, but spurious, as it does not identify the true causal factors that are too painful to acknowledge. To displace conflict is to shift feelings onto someone or something else, venting frustrations on someone other than their source. Kicking the dog only transfers pain to the innocent. To escape conflict is

38. Ibid., 82.
39. Ibid., 83.
40. Ibid., 84.

to depart psychologically or even physically from the relationship, and immerse one's self in work, recreation, or ministry instead. With conflict out of sight, it is effectively out of mind, and its pain alleviated.

Of course, denying marital conflict is not just unproductive, but counterproductive, as it spawns negative consequences of its own beyond festering resentment and bitterness. Undesirable substitutes such as over- or under-eating may occur, as may other otherwise inexplicable physical illnesses. Depression is often understood as anger turned subconsciously inward, and deemed more socially acceptable than displaying anger toward a spouse. Passive aggression denies being angry, but retaliates indirectly through tactics such as sabotaging the other's activities. Sorrows may be drowned in substance abuse. Most insidiously, denying conflict can lead to interpersonal distance and disengagement, the creeping mental and emotional indifference that culminates in parallel lives and mere coexistence.

Conflict usually cannot be denied indefinitely, and some kind of coping strategy is enacted sooner or later in more realistic hopes of achieving conflict management rather than idealistic hopes of conflict resolution. Balswick and Balswick identify four styles of situational conflict management based on degrees of assertiveness and cooperation, each evidencing different levels of concern for self, other, and relationship.[41]

1. The Avoidance of Withdrawers: Low assertiveness and low cooperation shows little concern for self, other, or relationship.

2. The Accommodation of Yielders: Low assertiveness and high cooperation shows little concern for self, high concern for other, and moderate concern for relationship.

3. The Competition of Winners: High assertiveness and low cooperation shows high concern for self, but little concern for other or relationship.

4. The Collaboration of Resolvers: High assertiveness and high cooperation shows balanced concern for self and other, and high concern for relationship.[42]

---

41. Balswick and Balswick, *Model for Marriage* and *Family*.

42. Balswick and Balswick's model actually identifies five styles, but the fifth, the Compromise of Compromisers, is the midpoint of the four others, less distinct and helpful, and therefore is not included here.

Table 2

Balswick and Balswick's Styles of Conflict Management			
		Cooperation (concern for other)	
	High	*Low*	*High*
Assertiveness (concern for self)		Competition/Winners	Collaboration/Resolvers
	Low	Avoidance/Withdrawers	Accommodation/Yielders

How any given marital conflict will be managed depends not just on the situation, but the preferred style of each spouse, with multiple combustible combinations possible. A marriage between a Resolver and a Withdrawer, for example, exemplifies the classic demand-withdraw, cat-and-mouse pattern that occurs between husband and wife, and wife and husband with equal frequency.[43] Each spouse's personal style, likely learned in their family of origin, may reinforce the differing style of the other, and thus perpetuate the problematic imbalance in the relationship. The pairing of a Winner with a Yielder, for example, gives the false impression that the marriage is free of conflict, whereas the pairing of a Winner with another Winner is an alternate description of a conflict-habituated marriage, and so on.

Balswick and Balswick contend that the Collaboration of Resolvers is the most biblical style of conflict management, because it offers maximum satisfaction to each spouse. "Intensely committed to the relationship, resolvers work hard toward a win-win situation."[44] The danger is that they will be too relentless and almost force their spouse into an avoidant Withdrawer stance or an accommodating Yelder stance. "The disadvantage is that collaboration takes a lot of time, effort, and emotional energy. It also affords a (spouse) who is verbally skilled the advantage."[45] Yet Balswick and Balswick also decribe how Jesus practiced each style of conflict management at different times. Jesus occasionally avoided conflict with the Pharisees by withdrawing (Matt 12:14–15), he accomodated like a yielder when he did not resist arrest (Matt 26:50–53), he competed like a winner in clearing the temple of money changers (Matt 21:12–13), and he collaborated like a resolver in his long-term commitment to his disciples. Personal maturity is demonstrated in the ability and willingness to use more than one style, and to discern which style is most appropriate for a particular situation. Marital well-being is dependent on it.

43. Papp, "Demand-Withdraw Patterns of Marital Conflict."
44. Balswick and Balswick, *Model for Marriage*, 130.
45. Balswick and Balswick, *Family*, 266.

ANGER AND ANGST

Just as interpersonal power is unavoidable and interpersonal conflict is inevitable in marriage, so too anger is inescapable. All three are surely unpleasant, but Christians are also prone to viewing all three as ungodly. Yet they are not inherently evil, as the biblical directive to "Be angry but do not sin" (Eph 4:26) makes anger's moral neutrality clear. Anger is conventionally understood as a second-order or derived emotion. People become angry only because of something prior, such as first becoming frustrated because their goals have been blocked, or hurt because their feelings have been offended, or afraid because their well-being is threatened.[46] Each of these emotions is in their own right morally neutral. People also become justifiably angry in response to someone else's sin that has no direct effect on them. Jesus' cleansing of the temple, or our indignation at social injustice, are examples of justified anger. Yet just as power and conflict can become problematic in the way they are lived out, so too can anger when it is misdirected, disproportional, mistimed, disingenuous, or disrespectful. As Aristotle put it, "Anyone can become angry—that is easy. But to be angry with the right person, to the right degree, at the right time, for the right purpose, and in the right way—that is not easy."[47] Feeling anger does not entitle someone to abuse another any more than feeling attraction entitles someone to rape another. Ephesians gives further direction: "Do not make room for the devil. . . . Let no evil talk come out of your mouths, but only what is useful for building up, as there is need, so that your words may give grace to those who hear. . . . Put away from you all bitterness and wrath and anger[48] and wrangling and slander, together with all malice, and be kind to one another, tenderhearted, forgiving one another, as God in Christ has forgiven you" (4:27, 29, 31–32).

In his memoir, the son of Francis and Edith Schaeffer describes how his hot-tempered father and pious mother of L'Abri fame competed with each other for success in ministry. "Each was such a powerful force that they sometimes seemed to eclipse the other. Dad was abusive at times, but my mother was in no way intimidated. In fact, she seemed to relish her martyr status."[49] From when he was seven years of age and on, Franky's mother would tell him that his father demanded sexual intercourse every night.

46. Oliver and Oliver, "Marital Anger and Highly Conflicted Couples."

47. Quoted from http://www.great-quotes.com/quote/22465.

48. Though Paul has just indicated that anger is not a sin, it nevertheless at some point needs to be put away, presumably by dealing with it and its first order roots, not merely suppressing it.

49. Schaeffer, *Crazy for God*, 104.

When L'Abri was at its zenith in 1968, "on some days, Mom was hiding bruises on her arms; on other days, she was flirting shamelessly with Roger, a handsome 'sensitive poet' from San Francisco, twenty years younger than her. This was the source of my parents' biggest fights. . . . Dad was reduced to glaring fury by these activities."[50] Frank Schaeffer's humorous, controversial, and stinging novel, *Portofino*, casts further aspersions on the marriage of his parents.[51] He himself is a controversial figure,[52] with a marriage of his own that was at times hellish, by his own making and admission.

The marriages of Billy and Ruth Graham, Rick and Kay Warren, and Francis and Edith Schaeffer suggest that marital conflict of all types and levels is common, even among evangelical royalty. Their high social status and social capital within the Christian subculture may be what gives them permission to admit otherwise carefully guarded secret struggles, just as it is prerequisite for biographies and exposes to be written about them in the first place. After all, Christians tend to tell only the success stories of winners, those of high status who have triumphed over conflict, not the unsuccessful stories of losers, those of low status who have lived in life-long conflict-habituated marriages, or those whose marriages conflict has terminated. Dennis and Vicki Covington, for example, are two Christian commoners left to pen their own autobiography, a shockingly raw and brave account of how their marriage and bottomless love for each other endured chronic mutual alcoholism and multiple mutual sexual affairs of which they were both aware.[53] Who is to say whose experience is anomalous and whose is the norm?

Much of the angst surrounding marital power and conflict is a consequence of misunderstanding their respective natures and sources, combined with the unrealistic expectation of evading them. In itself, conflict is not a moral problem, relational failure, or marital weakness, though it undoubtedly presents a relational challenge. Even happily married couples engage in cycles of reciprocal negativity.[54] When the issue of a particular conflict is some moral failing present in the marriage, conflict is in truth often the

---

50. Ibid., 216. Edith, author of the well-received *What Is a Family?*, has acknowledged that Francis threw more than one flower pot in the house.

51. More than a novel, Schaeffer's *Portofino* is a *roman á clef*, a novel that has the extra-literary interest of portraying well-known real people more or less thinly disguised as fictional characters.

52. Os Guinness lived with the Schaeffers for three years and was close to Frank for six. In his review of *Crazy for God*, Guinness criticizes Frank's portrait of his parents as "cruel, distorted, and self-serving," though Guinness defends the family behavior of Edith more than that of Francis. Guinness, "Fathers and Sons."

53. Covington and Covington, *Cleaving*.

54. See for example Gottman et al., *Mathematics of Marriage*.

only means of achieving a greater marital good. Indeed, failure to confront moral failure, such as deceit, is itself a moral problem when all prerequisites for doing so, such as safety, are present. Conflict is in fact better evidence of the intensity of a marriage than of its quality, and does not automatically degrade or destabilize it. The measure of a strong marriage is not how much situational, interpersonal, or even systemic conflict occurs, but how effectively it is resolved and, when irresolvable, how well it is managed. Yet due to our ideals of intimate harmony and happiness, Western culture perceives all marital conflict as a sign and beginning of the end. The naïve notion that marriage can and ought to be free of power and conflict, combined with a rampant aversion to the hard work of relational challenge, has facilitated the culture of divorce. As soon as conflict arises, the marriage is said to be not working and, as conflict persists, to be suffering from irreconcilable differences. The end result is acceptance of, even preference for, divorce as a method of problem solving.

Their protests notwithstanding, Christian couples tend to be little different than non-Christian couples in this regard, except perhaps in pretense. They are just as prone to judge the ordinary conflict of everyday marriage as evidence of relational weakness, and just as liable to see and use it as a fatal flaw of marriage. While some may dispute that this constitutes surrender to the cultural mandate of conflict-free marriage because marital conflict is equally biblically taboo, the social history of this Christian view of conflict in marriage coincides with the cultural view. Doubly motivated by both their culture and their reading of their sacred text, contemporary Western Christians appear more inclined to deny marital conflict, though no more able to avoid it, and left without conceptual tools to understand it or relational tools to live with it. The cultural is once again conflated with the biblical, stranding the Christian couple to cope with conflict however they can. Culture has done them no favors. Christianity has done little more.

Mandate 9

Dissolution

Should marital dissolution be understood as personal failure?

CONFLICT TROUBLES MARRIAGE, BUT does not necessarily destabilize or end marriage. Though marital quality and marital stability are undoubtedly correlated, and even causally related in the sense that conflict can contribute to instability, they remain separate dynamics of marriage. As we have seen in Mandate 8, a conflict-habituated marriage is not necessarily an unstable marriage, or even a bad, weak, or unhappy marriage. Neither is a conflict-minimal marriage necessarily a good, strong, happy, or stable marriage. The extent to which marital quality is correlated with marital stability, or the extent to which quality predicts the statistical probability of stability, is controlled by culture. For example, when the cultural norm is to view marriage as a commitment to a social institution, marital quality becomes much less predictive of marital stability, and is potentially altogether irrelevant. If there are social structural supports in place to hold a marriage together from the outside regardless of what is happening inside, marriages will remain intact and enduring. However, when the cultural norm is to view marriage as a commitment to the other person, marital quality becomes highly predictive of marital stability. In the absence of external social structural supports, the internal dynamics of a marriage will determine its fate. When a culture commits itself above all to keeping marriages intact regardless of the cost to persons in them, it can do so. Likewise, when a culture commits itself above all to the quality of life experienced by persons in marriages, especially when they themselves are the judge of it, there will be a cost to the institution of marriage. As the renowned anthropologist Margaret Mead put it, "There is no society in the world where people have stayed married without enormous community pressure to do so."[1]

With external constraints on Western marriage shrinking in recent centuries, and internal expectations expanding, as chronicled throughout this book, it is no wonder that marriages are dissolving at alarmingly high rates. Many people now enter marriage with high hopes but low expectations of permanence, and the uncertainties now engulfing marriage then become a self-fulfilling prophecy. Once committed, those determined enough to find a way to exit marriage have always done so, depending on the external constraints they have had to overcome. In certain historical eras and political jurisdictions, if a spouse wanted to retain public respectability in the process of uncoupling and had the means to do so, an annulment was arranged. This was a civil or religious declaration favored by the Catholic Church that the marriage was invalid in the first place because of illegalities, fraud, mental incompetence, or lack of sexual consummation, and therefore never existed. Where and when and for whom annulment was not a viable option, desertion was often the only recourse for uncoupling. In what has been termed "poor person's divorce," one spouse would simply abandon the other and have no further contact, leaving the spouse left against her or his will in great hardship. When it became possible to uncouple and still retain public face, separation became the most feasible means. This informal or formal mutual agreement to remain married but no longer live together could serve as a "time out," a trial divorce, or a life-long finality.

Eventually, divorce, which is the legal termination of a marriage, became equally available to all, but even that had to await the evolution of divorce law to the point of no-fault divorce before it was standardized as the most common marital exit strategy. Today, the ease and prevalence of divorce mocks marriage, as increasingly partners are renting, not buying. Wedding chapels in Las Vegas hotel casinos suggest that marriage for some is little more than a game of chance. For some celebrities, marriage is no more than public posturing and profiteering, not really promising.[2] Despite a recent leveling off and even decline of divorce rates, divorce threatens marriage more than any social trend other than cohabitation and the

---

1. Quoted in Gushee, "Crumbling Institution," 45.

2. A high-profile example is reality starlet Kim Kardashian filing for divorce from NBA player Kris Humphries after a lavish, star-studded, televised wedding and seventy-two days of marriage. Humphries sought an annulment based on fraud, claiming that Kardashian had no intention of proceeding with the marriage, and that the wedding was a contrivance for the benefit of her show and to make money.

looser "friends with benefits." No current trend in intimate partner coupling is as pronounced as the growing preference for the Velcro of cohabitation instead of the glue of marriage, disregarding the formalities of marriage altogether.[3] The increase in cohabitation is likely the largest reason for the decrease in divorce—hardly good news for the institution of marriage. But then, there are no statistics for the rates at which marital relationships of any positive quality have effectively ended without legal termination of the marriage throughout history.

Over the last half-century, rates of marital dissolution have climbed to where approximately half of Western marriages now end in divorce. Social scientists have employed multiple ways of measuring and tabulating divorce rates, but despite their appearance as hard facts, social statistics are also socially constructed and interpreted. Our purpose here is not to identify who is doing the statistical accounting, dissect what exact measures they are taking, critique how they are interpreting their data, question the agenda being served, or even concern ourselves with one particular Western nation. Of concern here is that the rates of marital dissolution are high, and that the rates for Christians are evidently not significantly lower than national averages, despite strong biblical disapproval of divorce. In America, for example, the Barna Research Group reports that "when evangelicals and non-evangelical born again Christians are combined into an aggregate class of born again adults, their divorce figure is statistically identical to that of non-born again adults: 32% versus 33%, respectively."[4] In this regard, Christians are as paradoxical as the soft patriarchs described in the second chapter, who espouse a complementarian theology of gender yet practice egalitarian relationships in daily living. National versus Christian rates of premarital sex is another aspect of coupling in which the ideals of Christian beliefs are incongruous with social norms, while the realities of Christian practices are not. As with the rates of divorce, the causes, processes, and effects of divorce are not unique for Christians either. Like others, Christians endure Bohannan's six stations of divorce: emotional divorce, legal divorce, economic divorce,

---

3. In the 1965 global hit musical *Fiddler on the Roof*, set in 1905, everyone's goal is marriage, with the only disputes being who should marry whom and who should decide. In the climax of the 2000 global hit musical *Mama Mia!*, the young couple halts their own wedding ceremony and rejects marriage in favour of living their dream of traveling the world together.

4. Barna Group, "New Marriage and Divorce Statistics." Based on surprisingly limited data sources of his own, Bradley Wright disputes such statistics in *Christians Are Hate-Filled Hypocrites . . . and Other Lies You've Been Told.*

co-parental divorce, community divorce, and psychic divorce.[5] Like others, Christians suffer the effects of divorce, which may be mixed for the divorcing couple, but are almost always almost completely negative for their children, except when the marriage is severely conflicted and family life is abusive.[6] "A divorce is like an amputation; you survive, but there's less of you."[7]

Like others, Christians also divorce for reasons ranging from the personal to the cultural. The myriad causes of divorce infect a Christian marriage as much as any other, with perhaps none more foundational than the individualism addressed in Mandate 2. Beyond what any other culture has dared to condone, Western culture has advanced the individual's right to choose their course of action based on self-interest. With that right comes the responsibility to own the consequences. When what the individual chooses fails, the culture of individualism is as quick to blame the individual as it was to empower the individual in the first place. When a contemporary Western marriage fails, the man and woman who chose it and inhabited it are held accountable for its demise and dissolution. Christians tend to concur with individualistic rights and responsibilities, viewing marital breakdown as primarily a failure of personal character and will, and in the end, evidence of spiritual failure or simple sin.

For example, Lauren Winner is a hip, young evangelical scholar who has brought much new perspective and hope to conservative Christians. Her breakout memoir, *Girl Meets God: On the Path to a Spiritual Life*,[8] recounted her courtship with Christ and commitment to Christian faith. Her *Real Sex: The Naked Truth about Chastity*[9] brought sexual realism and responsibility to a generation of young Christian adults. Her *Still: Notes on a Mid-Faith Crisis*[10] reflects on her spiritual desolation wrought in part by the dissolution of her discontented six-year marriage. "Winner blames mostly herself for the divorce, what she calls a 'spectacular, grave, costly failure,' and the source of her unhappiness seems mysterious even to herself."[11] She is typical of many divorced Christians in this attribution and assessment, and especially of many not-divorced Christians who observe them. She and they

5. Bohannan, *Divorce and After*.

6. The classic study is Wallerstein, Blakeslee, and Lewis, *Unexpected Legacy of Divorce*. A more recent study is Marquardt, *Between Two Worlds: The Inner Lives of Children of Divorce*.

7. Margaret Atwood, quoted in *Time*, March 19, 1973.

8. Winner, *Girl Meets God*.

9. Winner, *Real Sex*.

10. Winner, *Still*.

11. Beaty, "Girl Meets Grace," 62.

are not entirely wrong, but neither are they entirely right. A more complete and helpful assessment of marital dissolution requires an understanding of both the biblical perspectives and social causes of divorce. Explanations for divorce at both the macro and micro levels are likewise useful, indeed necessary. Christian assessments and interventions suggest that Western Christians seem again to have for the most part surrendered to culture.

WHAT GOD HAS JOINED

The most recent round of debate about the permissibility of divorce for Christians reached its peak while divorce rates were peaking amid the culture wars and family values debates in the last quarter of the twentieth century, as noted in Mandate 3. The debate about divorce was more or less preceded by the debate about gender, and in turn overtaken by the debate about same-sex marriage in the current century. Christians seeking to trace a chronology of what they feel is a cultural assault on traditional marriage draw a straight determinative line from first rethinking gender, to then rethinking divorce, to now rethinking same-sex marriage, to soon rethinking polygamy. What some Christians see as godly liberation, equality, and grace, others see as a slippery slope to ungodly ruin. Of course, slippery slope arguments are fallacious because they involve the fallacy of hasty conclusion, failing to understand the complexity of factors and the independence of issues. A conclusion reached and position taken on one marital issue does not automatically set off a causal chain reaction of conclusions on other issues that inevitably lead to devastation. It is entirely possible to be an egalitarian without being a polygamist; indeed, the former would preclude the latter. While it is true that the sequence of rethinking these martial issues has resulted in a consistently greater openness, that alone does not make those conclusions biblically erroneous or morally regressive. Relative openness is as much a comment on the past as on the present and future. Such greater openness toward divorce is pertinent to our concerns here because it impacts judgments about the kind of failure divorce constitutes.

That divorce constitutes a failure of some sort is not generally disputed among Christians, nor is God's disapproval of it. "I hate divorce, says the Lord, the God of Israel, and covering one's garment with violence, says the Lord of hosts" (Mal 2:16).[12] God clearly intended marriage to be life-long, and divorce is at least a consequence of human brokenness and depravity. According to Jesus, Moses allowed divorce because of the hardness of hearts

12. The disproportionate attention and energy given by the Christian subculture to the first half of the verse is astonishing.

(Matt 19:8), leaving unspecified whether that meant the hearts of the couple divorcing or the heart of the whole society. Yet Jesus did not condemn the woman at the well for her failed marriages, but offered her redemption and a new beginning (John 4). What is disputed among Christians is what God allows or permits. Competing views were set forth in one of the classic multiple-views books, *Divorce and Remarriage: Four Christian Views*.[13] The positions taken were that God permits 1) no divorce and no remarriage, 2) divorce but no remarriage, 3) divorce and remarriage for reasons of adultery and desertion, or 4) divorce and remarriage under a variety of circumstances such as "spiritual separation," abuse, and irreconcilable differences. Over the course of the last century, the majority view has shifted from the first, most restrictive view to the fourth, most open view.

So, "what does the Bible say about divorce?"[14] David Instone-Brewer, a senior research fellow in rabbinics and the New Testament, is a leading evangelical scholar on divorce who reads the relevant texts like a first-century Jew would have read them.[15] In general, Instone-Brewer finds that "both Jesus and Paul condemned divorce without valid grounds and discouraged divorce even for valid grounds; that both Jesus and Paul affirmed the Old Testament grounds for divorce; and that the Old Testament allowed divorce for adultery and for neglect or abuse."[16] Exegetically then, divorce is only allowed for adultery (in Deut 24:1, affirmed by Jesus in Matt 19), emotional and physical neglect (in Exod 21:10–11, affirmed by Paul in 1 Cor 7), and abandonment and abuse (included in neglect, as affirmed in 1 Cor 7).[17] Such a literal list of "clear and consistent rules for divorce"[18] always runs the risk of legalistic commitment to an institution. Some more theological approaches resist reduction to such legalism. For example, Anderson and Guernsey argue that Jesus' statement that "what God has joined together, let no one separate" (Matt 19:6) removed both marriage and divorce from the status of being under a law. They insist that "there can be no 'rules' by which

---

13. House, *Divorce and Remarriage*.

14. Certainly more than it does about dating!

15. For example, the question put to Jesus by the Pharisees in Matthew 19:3, "Is it lawful to divorce a wife for any cause?," turns out to be a reference to a specific current dispute between the Hillelite rabbis and the Shammaite rabbis about the liberal interpretation of "any cause" divorce based on Deuteronomy 24:1. In his reply, Jesus did not condemn "divorce for any cause," but rather condemned the newly-invented, permissive "any cause" divorce for offenses such as a burnt meal or new wrinkles on a wife's face. See Instone-Brewer, *Divorce and Remarriage in the Church*.

16. Instone-Brewer, *Divorce and Remarriage in the Bible*, back cover.

17. Instone-Brewer, "What God Has Joined."

18. Ibid., 29.

marriage can be dissolved, any more than there are marriages which can be sanctified before God by observing certain legalities."[19] God's regard for a marriage or divorce cannot be equated or conflated with the presence or absence of human love or will, or with the institutional decrees or legalities of church or state. "To create a 'law of marriage' that would deny God the authority and power to put a marriage to death and to raise the persons to new life through repentance and forgiveness"[20] is theologically problematic. It may well be that in some cases "dissolution by divorce is a recognition of the fact that God has already brought the marriage under the judgment of nonexistence. . . . [W]here God puts asunder as a judgment against sin and disorder . . . let not (humans) uphold a law against God."[21]

Debates about the biblical permissibility and grounds of divorce have recently been superseded by the larger question of marriage itself. "When people think of couples on the verge of breakup they ask, 'Can this marriage be saved?' There's a bigger question, however: 'Can marriage be saved?'"[22] At the societal level, high divorce rates are taken by some Christians as just one of several cultural assaults on the social institution of marriage. Together these social forces have led to what Christian commentators from sociologist David Popenoe to moral philosopher David Gushee describe as a social disestablishment of marriage, most precisely termed the deinstitutionalization of marriage. Gushee identifies what he describes as recent social revolutions that have cracked the pillars of the cathedral of marriage:[23] 1) the sexual revolution that separated sex from marriage, 2) the contraception and abortion revolutions that turned the focus of marriage away from children and even more toward intimacy, 3) the illegitimacy revolution [sic] that produces ever higher percentages of children being born outside of marriages, 4) the cohabitation revolution that has increased couple instability and shortened couple life expectancy, 5) the reproductive technology revolution that has further separated childbearing from marriage, and 6) the gay rights revolution that has altered the very definition of marriage. All these revolutions together may be crumbling the cathedral of marriage, but they are also contributing to divorce. Therefore Gushee lists another revolution: 7) the divorce revolution that has emerged as an alternative cathedral, a new social institution characterized by serial monogamy and constantly blending families. Christian judgments of divorce such as this clearly make

19. Anderson and Guernsey, *On Being Family*, 101.

20. Ibid., 103.

21. Ibid., 100, 104.

22. Stafford, "Can This Institution Be Saved?"

23. Gushee, *Getting Marriage Right* and "Crumbling Institution."

divorce morally problematic. The consensus of social-scientific research shows that the effects of divorce are personally and socially problematic as well. Why then are couples divorcing at such high rates?

THE CONDITIONS OF CHOICE

The causes of divorce are multiple and multi-leveled, and care must be taken to clarify what we mean by "cause." As with most social variables, most of what are identified as causes of divorce are only contributing factors, factors that make divorce more likely. They are not necessary factors that must be present for a divorce to occur, nor are they sufficient factors that inexorably bring about divorce all by themselves.[24] Bloodstained history shows that even the most horrific spousal abuse is not sufficient for divorce. No internal factor of divorce is sufficient to overcome external factors determined to keep marriages intact. At the same time, there are internal factors such as love, will, and belief that will keep a marriage intact in the absence of external factors doing so, or even in the face of external factors bent on tearing it apart. Furthermore, what are often considered causes of divorce are actually only correlates of divorce.[25] Divorce rates may rise or fall at the same time as another variable such as income, but that does not prove that different levels of income cause different rates of divorce, or vice versa. A third variable such as education may have contributed to the rise or fall of both divorce and income. As is often said, "correlation is not cause," though correlation is a necessary, yet not sufficient, condition for cause. If two variables are not at least correlated, then one cannot be having any kind of causal effect on the other. But there are multiple factors at multiple levels that are correlated with divorce and are understood to be contributing factors or "causes," because they precede divorce and seem to influence its likelihood.

The factors of divorce can be categorized in various ways. For the purpose of overviewing them here, two micro-level categories and two macro-level categories serve best. At the micro level, the personal factors of the individuals divorcing involve both their personal lifestyle and the reasons they give for divorcing. At the macro level, the collective factors of patterns of divorce include both demographic and sociocultural variables. Personal

---

24. Sufficient factors may not be necessary factors, because a combination of two other factors may bring about divorce as well. The strongest sense of cause is a factor that is both necessary and sufficient, but those occur mostly in physical science, not in social science.

25. Other competing terms of preference include origins, sources, determinants, or predictors of divorce.

lifestyle factors refer to choices the couple makes, such as the age at which they marry. The younger the age at marriage, the higher is the statistical probability of divorce because of emotional immaturity, financial insecurity, incomplete identity formation, and undeveloped coping skills. Premarital pregnancy robs a couple of the opportunity to get to know each other and adjust to marriage as a twosome, brings immediate extra stress and responsibility, and inhibits the acquisition of education or income that would stabilize the marriage, especially among adolescents. Premarital cohabitation increases the overall statistical probability of divorce, but the relationship between the two is extremely complex, with further variables such as cohabitation history involved. There is also likely an "adverse selectivity" process occurring in cohabitation, in which people who choose to cohabit are systematically different from those who choose to marry without first cohabiting. In other words, cohabitation may not itself increase likelihood of divorce as much as couples who choose to cohabit are already those more likely to divorce.[26] Intergenerational transmission is another factor, with children of divorced parents at a higher risk of divorcing themselves,[27] presumably because of greater cynicism about marriage, and greater acceptance of divorce as a method of problem solving. No doubt the interplay of individual characteristics within the marriage, the relational skills and attitudes of each spouse, and the emotional climate of a marriage remain primary determinants of its stability.

The second set of micro-level factors is the reasons couples give for divorcing, what they themselves identify as the cause of or grounds for their divorce. The reasons given in courts as legal grounds for divorce may differ from the biblical grounds given by Christians to justify their divorce, which in turn may differ from the personal accounts given to intimates and themselves in an attempt to make sense of it. People do not always understand the reasons for their own behavior. Given the intimacy ethic of contemporary Western marriage, divorcing Christian couples today are most likely to claim emotional neglect or abuse, because irreconcilable differences are noticeably absent from the list of biblically valid grounds.[28] Otherwise, rea-

---

26. There are also significant differences between persons who cohabit once and then marry their partner (for whom divorce rates are not significantly different than non-cohabiters) and persons who are serial cohabiters prior to marriage.

27. They also marry at lower rates.

28. Christian broadcaster Pat Robertson said a man would be morally justified to divorce his wife with Alzheimer's disease in order to marry another woman. Moore considered this "a repudiation of the gospel of Jesus Christ" (Moore, "Pat Robertson Repudiates the Gospel"). Many years earlier, Robertson had said that any woman who votes for no-fault divorce is like a turkey voting for Thanksgiving.

sons given typically include poor communication, constant conflict, infidelity, emotional or physical abuse, addictions and substance abuse, financial ineptitude, unsatisfactory sex, lack of commitment, few shared values and interests, perceived inequality and inequity, disinterest and disrespect, and simple boredom. Notably, many of these self-reported causes seem likely to be effects of some prior cause. The various causes huddle together under one of two umbrellas, either irreconcilable differences or a sense of satiation that occurs when a stimulus no longer stimulates because of repeated exposure. Significantly, the conditions of marriage cited as reasons for divorce may not differ from the same conditions of other marriages that do not divorce, so that again, true cause remains in question. Strikingly, these marital conditions frequently occur long before divorce, often predating the marriage itself.[29] Why they at some point become "causes" of divorce remains unclear.

The first set of macro-level factors of divorce, demographic factors, may not explain personal choice as well, but they do predict it better, and are often cited as the statistical predictors of risk. People with higher education have had lower divorce rates for the last century, perhaps because they also therefore delayed marriage longer, were better equipped to handle marital challenges, and had higher incomes. Higher income avoids the financial stresses that destabilize marriage. Higher employment status also lowers divorce rates, as lower employment status and unemployment also cause marital stress. Divorce also varies by race and ethnicity, with Afro-Americans facing the highest risk, due partially to also facing the greatest poverty. Since all major religions discourage divorce, religious couples in general are less likely to divorce, and the more seriously they take their faith, the even less likely they are to divorce.[30] Religious similarity is a form of couple compatibility, and a source of institutional support, while religious dissimilarity increases risk of divorce. As predictive of divorce as demographic factors are, they are also hardly visible, highly interactive, and constantly in flux. They remain barely visible to the people who cope with the personal consequences of those factors on a daily basis. They leave the uneducated, poor, unemployed, black, irreligious couple in multiple jeopardy. They are shifting most recently to where the middle class is now evidencing the same weak and fragile marital patterns that have characterized the lower class, while marriage in the upper class appears to be getting even stronger.[31]

29. See Weisman, *Serious Doubts.*

30. Because their populations are overwhelmingly Catholic, Ireland did not legalize divorce until 1995; Chile until 2004.

31. This is the finding of a recent report with a hyperbolic and alarmist title, *When Marriage Disappears*, edited by Wilcox and Marquardt. It is the 2010 annual State of Our Unions report from two cooperating research and advocacy groups, the National

The second set of macro-level factors of divorce, sociocultural factors, is largely invisible to particular couples going through the self-absorbing pains of divorce. These are the societal and cultural mandates of marriage to which Christians and non-Christians alike surrender. It has been our task here to identify and critique them from our reading of the biblical text. Buying in to ideals of self-selection based on love, small isolated nuclear families, marriage as a primary calling, personal need fulfillment, romantic love, deep intimacy, ecstatic sex, and conflict-free marriage creates many fronts on which a couple may flounder.[32] When they fail to measure up to these cultural ideals, they become publicly defensive and privately defeated, and in one last ironic concession to cultural mandate, simply exit marriage. In a perverse sense, high rates of divorce and remarriage, or serial monogamy, are a backhanded compliment to our lofty ideals of and unrealistic hopes for marriage, or our human need for coupling. When we fail, we do not question our cultural beliefs; we simply assume we either misbehaved or chose the wrong person, or both, and try again.

As noted throughout all the cultural mandates of marriage we have examined, societal factors have pervasive and insidious effects on marriage, and divorce is certainly not immune. Increased social mobility severs social ties and strands couples as isolated social units. Even without mobility, lack of social integration does the same. The liberalization of divorce law generally and the advent of no-fault divorce in particular are both cause and effect of changing social norms. The rising status and economic independence of women enables them to divorce more readily, and be divorced more readily. As noted in Mandate 2, many functions previously performed by the family have been taken over by other institutions: hospitals, schools, police, media, and so on. Given the role that religion has played historically in stabilizing marriage, secularization is also unquestionably involved as one aspect of a general retreat from all social institutions. Sociocultural values such as classic Western individualism, materialism, and hedonism lurk behind many particular cultural mandates of marriage, and any particular marriage's end.

This is the proverbial water in which Western fish swim, whether joining a school or breaking from it. With all due respect to the grounds and accounts that divorcing couples give for divorcing, and the demographic factors that predict the statistical probability of divorce, the cultural factors

---

Marriage Project and the Center for Marriage and Families at the Institute for American Values. The report was summarized in Wilcox, "Marriage: Marginalized in the Middle."

32. Zsa Zsa Gabor, the Hollywood glamor queen, was likely unaware of the cultural insight she expressed when she declared that "Getting divorced just because you don't love a man is almost as silly as getting married just because you do." Quoted from http://www.notable-quotes.com/d/divorce_quotes.html.

that underlie them all are likely closer to the "causes" of divorce, and the largest contributing factors. The personal explanations that people give for their divorce actually flow from demographic and sociocultural factors. In other places and times, currently acceptable reasons such as irreconcilable differences would be deemed frivolous and immoral, but in Western context, they are deemed justifiable and sufficient. "Before people decide to divorce on particular grounds, a social and cultural climate has to exist that offers a legitimate framework for their reasons."[33] Personal reasons make sense only in societies that facilitate them culturally. For Christians to hold that divorce is simply a personal failure is to fail to understand that while individuals do make choices, they do not choose in conditions of their own choosing.[34] When their choice is congruent with their culture, it is unjust to judge it as simple personal failure. Nor will it do to label it crass "conformity to the world," when so much of the Christian thinking they were taught is likewise "conformed to the world."

MORAL HORIZONS

The best explanation of both individual divorce and societal divorce rates is cultural, not moral. Indeed, what is cultural soon enough becomes what is considered moral, and even scientific. Marital dissolution offers a fascinating case study of the reach of culture into not just individual human behavior, but moral and social-scientific explanations of human behavior as well. We have already seen this dynamic previously in Mandate 6, where the rise of intimacy culturally produced an intimacy ethic in marriage that in turn shaped a social-scientific typology of contemporary marriage.

The rise of marital dissolution is unquestionably due in large part to the historical shift in cultural values from prioritizing social order over personally perceived quality of life, to now prioritizing exactly the reverse. Notably, the biblical text was written in the former collectivistic cultural milieu, not in the current Western individualistic reversal, where personal quality of life is prioritized over social order. Declaring their independence, modern Western humans came to hold as self-evident truth that they were endowed by their creator with the inalienable right to pursue happiness. Whether an increase in the quality of life of individuals has actually been

---

33. Ambert, *Changing Families*, 359.

34. This is the common paraphrase of the maxim from Karl Marx: "Men make their own history, but not of their own free will; not under circumstances they themselves have chosen, but under the given and inherited circumstances with which they are directly confronted" (*Eighteenth Brumaire of Louis Bonaparte*).

achieved by privileging its pursuit is an entirely separate question, beyond the scope of our discussion here. As introduced in Mandate 2, individualism has persistently undermined marriage since at least the Enlightenment.[35] In their masterwork *Habits of the Heart*, Bellah and his colleagues defined individualism as "a belief that the individual has a primary reality, whereas society is a second-order, derived, or artificial construct."[36] Its core values are human dignity, autonomy, privacy, and self-development,[37] and it is manifest in two types in American life. Utilitarian individualism "sees human life as an effort by individuals to maximize their self-interest . . . (and) views society as arising from a contract that individuals enter into only in order to advance their self-interest."[38] Expressive individualism "holds that each person has a unique core of feeling and intuition that should unfold or be expressed if individuality is to be realized."[39] Conspicuously, utilitarian individualism has an affinity to a basically economic understanding of human existence, whereas expressive individualism shows affinities with the culture of psychotherapy.

Bellah's research team found that marriage has become a primary context for expressive individualism, built on the second of two modes of understanding marital love. Christians have traditionally favored love as obligation, whereas the middle-class mainstream has favored love as therapy. Love as obligation is a matter of will and action rather than feelings. Love as therapy is based on self-knowledge, driven by self-realization, and thereby commensurate with expressive individualism. For expressive selves, "love means the full exchange of feelings between authentic selves, not enduring commitment resting on binding obligations."[40] The two modes also occurred somewhat in historical sequence, as Celello later traced how the notion of marriage as work arose in the twentieth century in part as response to the rising divorce rate.[41] Marriage would require focused effort to achieve the self-realization and happiness it was intended

35. Though the ascendancy of individualism is conventionally located in modernity and the Enlightenment, the origins of individualism can, ironically, be traced back to the Christian doctrine that humans are created in the image of God, and endowed with personal dignity, value, and free will. The Protestant Reformation accelerated the rise of individualism.

36. Bellah et al., *Habits of the Heart*, 334. This belief is also known as ontological individualism.

37. Lukes, *Individualism*.

38. Bellah et al., *Habits of the Heart*, 336.

39. Ibid., 334.

40. Ibid., 102.

41. Celello, *Making Marriage Work*.

to deliver. Yet a century earlier marriage had been understood as duty, as a state of being and a service to the social order, in which unhappy couples were simply told to stick it out.

Two other later culture critics drew on Bellah's concepts to analyze divorce directly. Not writing from an explicitly Christian perspective, Whitehead documented the rise of expressive divorce in her definitive book *The Divorce Culture*. The psychological revolution of the second half of the twentieth century brought marriage into the domain of mental health, changed the locus of divorce from the outer social world to the inner world of the self, and redefined divorce as an individual experience. It had already redefined marriage, "once the realm of the fettered and obligated self, as a fertile realm for exploring the potential of the self, unfettered by roles and obligations. . . . Thus, the psychological revolution cast the sad business of marital dissolution into a new and more positive light."[42] Having contributed the notion of an inner life that could be described scientifically, the psychological revolution extended the ethic of expressive individualism into not just the ethic of marriage, but the ethic of divorce as well. "Its governing principle was that one's first obligation in the dissolution of marriage was to oneself."[43] Marriage counseling migrated from the church to the professional service sector, and psychotherapy functioned as a "personal happiness" business. Furthermore, Whitehead detected an affinity between the expressive ethic and the spirit of capitalism.

> Expressive divorce saw one's inner resources as a block of capital, to be developed and deployed to maximum advantage. The deeper logic of expressive divorce was the logic of capitalism. . . . In order to maximize profits, capital had to be mobile. . . . Relationships that are binding or permanent are risky investments. The most reliable form of investment thus becomes the investment in the self. . . . Marketplace values of choice, unfettered freedom, contingency, and dynamic change were the values of expressive divorce.[44]

Writing from an explicitly Christian perspective, Lee saw the same three overarching or undergirding cultural factors qua ethics in his analysis of divorce.[45] Already described in Mandate 3 as moral horizons, the moral discourses of individual rights, the consumer marketplace, and psychotherapy were equally formative of how Christians in his qualitative data

42. Whitehead, *Divorce Culture*, 54.
43. Ibid., 66.
44. Ibid., 76–77.
45. Lee, *Beyond Family Values.*

set reflected on divorce. Though they held to a biblical ideal of permanent matrimony, they spoke the same language of an independent bearer of rights, a self-interested consumer in the marketplace, and a therapeutic self in search of fulfillment. In a capitalist ethos, everything, including marriage, is commodified, and disposable. We learn to be consumers of not just material goods, but of ideas, experiences, and relationships. Consumption is viewed as personal right, and identity, and therapy. Marriage then becomes a market in which we commodify, package, and barter with our selves, exchanging the "goods" of status, appearance, abilities, personality, and interests. Needless to say, the consumer marriage that is a product of this culture is far from covenant marriage. If marriages are consumed at unprecedented rates in such a voracious and insatiable culture, it is not because the cup of marriage is half empty. The cup is twice as big as it needs to be. But then, as elaborated in Mandate 4, our culturally induced psychotherapeutic sensibilities tell us that our super-sized cup can be full, that we need and deserve it to be full, and that we will never be whole if we settle for less.

In his own inimitable way, Wendell Berry portrays the desolation of sexual capitalism in marriage.

> Failing, as they cannot help but fail, to be each other's all, the husband and wife become each other's only. The sacrament of sexual union . . . has now become a kind of marketplace in which husband and wife represent each other as sexual property. Competitiveness and jealousy, imperfectly sweetened and disguised by the illusions of courtship, now become governing principles, and they work to isolate the couple inside their marriage. Marriage becomes a capsule of sexual fate. . . . The protective capsule becomes a prison. It becomes a household of the living dead, each body a piece of incriminating evidence. Or a greenhouse excluding the neighbors and the weather for the sake of some alien and unnatural growth. The marriage shrinks to a dull vigil of duty and legality. Husband and wife become competitors necessarily, for their only freedom is to exploit each other or to escape. . . . The idea of fidelity is perverted beyond redemption by understanding it as a grim, literal duty enforced only by willpower. This is the "religious" insanity of making a victim of the body as a victory of the soul. Self-restraint that is so purely negative is self-hatred. And one cannot be good, anyhow, just by not being bad. To be faithful merely out of duty is to be blinded to the possibility of a better faithfulness for better reasons.[46]

---

46. Wirzba, *Art of the Commonplace*, 113–15.

Like the economic system of capitalism, a marketplace mentality in marital sex, and in marriage generally, carries the seeds of its own destruction.

EXCHANGE AND ATTRIBUTION

If these cultural values explain the primal impetus to marital dissolution at the macro level, then exchange theory attempts to explain the implicit cognitive processes of divorce at the micro level. As seen in Mandate 1, exchange theory goes a long way in explaining mate selection when entering marriage, and goes further in explaining mate deselection when exiting marriage. As a combination of economics and behaviorism, exchange theory begins with the premise that "interpersonal relationships are evaluated by those involved in terms of the costs and rewards they experience in the relationship."[47] Principles such as maximizing profit, ensuring reciprocity, and agreeing on distributive justice within the relationship follow. For example, relational equity is calculated by how much each spouse is putting into the marriage compared to how much each is getting out of it: inputs versus outcomes. If her input costs are four units and her outcome rewards are eight units, while his inputs are two and outcomes are four, they do not have an equal relationship, but they do have an equitable relationship. The issue is how her ratio of input costs to outcome rewards compares to his, not just whether her total amount of outcome rewards is more or less than his. But if she invests four to gain eight, while he invests two to gain six, they have an inequitable relationship, and she is disadvantaged, despite "getting more out of it." This "comparison level" between her ratio and his ratio quickly leads to a "comparison level of alternatives," in which the equity and total outcome rewards potentially available in a different relationship tantalize.

Exchange theory sounds at once both self-evidently true and uncomfortably unchristian. Despite its dark view of humans as cold-hearted, self-centered, profit-seeking calculators, exchange theory nevertheless makes sense and rings true to us, but only to us in contemporary Western culture who are already swimming in the sea of "methodological individualism,"[48] marketplace consumerism, and therapeutic self-fulfillment. Exchange theory, it turns out, is itself another cultural artifact, even while it denies the formative effects of culture on how people think. Contrary to exchange theory, humans are better conceived as enculturated beings, or "moral,

47. Hamon, "Social Exchange Theory and the Christian Faith," 19.

48. This is the insistence that all social phenomena are in principle explicable in ways that only involve the individual.

believing, narrating animals,"[49] not merely rationalistic calculators, unless their culture shapes them to be so. If and when it does, their belief in the morality of economism will indeed narrate their lives. Once again, the cultural becomes the moral, which in turn becomes the scientific; economism creates the offense of inequity that explains divorce. The reach of culture can seemingly never be overestimated or overstated. Yet the premise of exchange theory would be shattered if Christians would truly live out the Golden Rule authentically, because "do to others as you would have them do to you" (Matt 7:12) is an ethical imperative for each individual in relationship, not the establishment of a norm of reciprocity in relationships. It uses reciprocity only as a referent for choosing our behavior, and calls us to act accordingly, whether our behavior is reciprocated or not. The parables of the good Samaritan, the prodigal son, and the laborers in the vineyard also call Christians beyond equity and reciprocity. But most Western Christians in the throes of divorce instead find biblical grounds to require equity and reciprocity, and thereby surrender to their culture.

True to Western cultural form, moving from the macro-sociological to the micro-sociological to the psychological takes us a final step closer to understanding assessments of divorce. Attribution theory explains further the cognitive processes of our cultural and Christian patterns of reasoning about divorce. To make an attribution is to infer backwards to causes that explain human behavior, to infer the sources of why people act the way they do. One dichotomy of attributions is between dispositional attributions, which explain behavior based on some internal state or quality of the person on one hand, and situational attributions, which explain behavior based on external factors in the person's environment on the other. A second dichotomy is between stable, unchangeable factors of the source of behavior that are unchangeable features on one hand, and unstable factors of the source that are constantly in flux on the other. Success or failure in any endeavor then is seen as attributable to one of four possibilities produced by a matrix of locus of control (internal or external) and stability (stable or unstable). An individual spouse may attribute the success or failure of their marriage 1) to their own character (ability is internal and stable), 2) to the nature of marriage or the nature of their spouse (task difficulty is external and stable), 3) to their own will (effort is internal and unstable), or 4) to chance, fate, or destiny (luck is external and unstable).

49. Smith, *Moral, Believing Animals*, 118.

Table 3

Attributions for Success or Failure		
	Locus of Control	
	Internal *(dispositional)*	*External* *(situational)*
Stable	Ability	Task Difficulty
Degree of Stability		
Unstable	Effort	Luck

Western culture strongly inclines evaluators of behavior to make the internal dispositional attributions of ability and character or effort and will in assessing success or failure, downplaying external situational factors in the process. This bias is readily evident in the actors within a marriage, the husband and wife themselves, but even greater in the observers of a marriage.[50] The emotional consequence of an actor attributing failure to their own feeble ability is to despair and stop trying in the future. The emotional consequence of an actor attributing failure to their own poor effort is to feel guilt and shame and try harder in the future. Either way, the responsibility for failure rests entirely with the individual. But what if the task is actually too difficult? What if there are stable external factors such as unrealistic cultural expectations that doom the couple to failure?

The distinction between personal/private troubles and social/public issues is a central analytic construct of sociology.[51] For one person to be unemployed is a personal trouble. If that person is unemployed because she is uneducated, unskilled, lazy, irresponsible, and obnoxious, the problem is due to who she is as a person, and changing her personal qualities will solve the problem. However, if she is unemployed because of racial discrimination or runaway unemployment rates, the problem is due to the social system, and changing her personal qualities will not solve the problem. Likewise, one unhappy marriage that ends in divorce is a personal trouble for the couple involved, a private tragedy. Many unhappy marriages producing high divorce rates is a social issue begging for public analysis and action at the collective level of culture. Needless to say, in individualistic Western societies, most people interpret their problems as personal troubles, blaming themselves more readily than culture. They therefore attempt to

---

50. The "fundamental attribution error" is the tendency of observers to overestimate the importance of dispositional factors and to underestimate the importance of situational factors.

51. The distinction was made first and best by Mills in *The Sociological Imagination*.

solve their problems at the personal, private level, by attempting to align themselves better with their taken-for-granted culture, leaving that culture unquestioned, and free to coerce the next person equally. Granted, some blame everything on "the system," taking no personal responsibility, even when they ought. Western Christians, by dint of their cultural socialization, tend to interpret marriage problems as personal troubles, inadequacies, or failures, leaving unquestioned the demands and stresses placed on marriage by Western culture. Locating sin in and limiting sin to the individual human heart, they have little concept of social structural strain and institutional evil, and therefore go about earnestly trying to patch up broken individuals and relationships, rather than the broken culture that begins the breaking.

CHRISTIAN INTERVENTIONS

So it is no surprise that the predominant Christian response to the social/public issue of high divorce rates has largely been to address marital dissolution as if it were mostly a personal/private trouble. The first level of Christian intervention has been moral exhortation addressed to individuals and couples, making it clear that God hates divorce and therefore they should do their duty and stick it out. Unfortunately, increasing calls for greater personal moral responsibility on an issue that has become increasingly systemic are not helpful, at different times tantamount to swimming upstream, up the rapids, or up the waterfall. They may also be dangerous, such as Moore's call for "a fidelity that is cruciform. . . . Love is fidelity with a cross on your back. Love is drowning in your own blood. Love is screaming, 'My God, my God, why have you forsaken me.'"[52] This is the insistence that, in the end, a divorcing spouse could always have changed his or her attitude and behavior sufficiently to have saved the marriage, but chose not to do so. Therefore divorce is always in the end a personal failure of character and will of one or both partners. If a faithful religious martyr can choose to die rather than recant his or her faith, so too should a faithful Christian spouse choose to stay rather than recant their marital vow. Yet here again lurks the power of culture. In some cultures martyrdom makes sense, but divorce does not. In contemporary Western culture, martyrdom does not make sense, but divorce does. Again, choices make sense only in societies that facilitate them culturally.

The second level of Christian intervention has been marriage education programs for individuals and couples. These take the form of marriage preparation and enrichment materials and programs that provide greater

52. Moore, "Pat Robertson Repudiates the Gospel."

awareness of self and other, as well as teaching relational skills that together are intended to strengthen marriage and thereby prevent divorce. They are not unlike Christian premarital chastity programs in intent, and perhaps in success rates. The *Journal of Psychology and Theology* devoted a special issue to Christian marriage that featured seven leading Christian interventionists of marriage.[53] One of the psychologists acknowledged that "the primary threats to marriage today are sociological, not psychological,"[54] and added that "The proliferation of films, seminars, books and other resources on marriage within the Christian cultural milieu might well be analogous to rearranging deck chairs or showing movies on the Titanic! A more profound and pervasive systemic change within the Christian community is needed."[55] Another expert included in the special issue confessed elsewhere that "If I had to choose between education and changing the culture, I'd take the culture."[56]

A third level of Christian intervention has been proposed that does in fact address divorce as a social/public issue, though it is more focused on demographic factors than on sociocultural factors. Christian sociologist Mark Regnerus has argued[57] that because a) there are about three single women for every two single men among evangelical churchgoers, b) young women mature sooner than young men, c) women want marriage more than men, and d) men want sex more than women, young Christian women have been placed in a severely disadvantageous demographic position. Men have all the power of least interest. Young women are forced to agree to premarital sex in order to compete, and to accept any half-decent offer of marriage they can get. Meanwhile, young men can get sexual activity while delaying marriage at length without lessening their odds of eventually finding a woman they want to marry. Thus the effect of the unbalanced Christian sex ratio is producing both rampant premarital sex and bad marriages.[58]

As a solution to both problems, Regnerus advocates for earlier marriage within the context of a more supportive Christian community in order to ameliorate the negative effects of early marriage in Western culture. In effect, he calls for a return to traditional marriage in its traditional setting.

53. Ripley, "Current Issues in Christian Marriage." At the same time, the "father of Christian marriage ministries," Ray Mossholder, was divorcing his wife of forty-two years and planning to remarry shortly. Butcher, "'Father' of Christian Marriage Ministries."

54. Edwards, "It Takes a Village," 191.

55. Ibid., 190.

56. Scott Stanley quoted in Stafford, "Can This Institution Be Saved?," 54.

57. Regnerus, "Case for Early Marriage." See also Regnerus and Uecker, *Premarital Sex in America.*

58. This analysis resonates with Whitehead's in *Why There Are No Good Men Left*, discussed in Mandate 1.

"Though young marriers in our society have high rates of divorce, young-marrying societies, in which the average age at marriage is low, have low rates of divorce. Typically, countries with low average ages of marriage have other features—for example, high rates of childbearing, strongly institutionalized religion, extended families, and restrictive divorce laws—that keep the divorce rates low for people of all ages."[59] Regnerus is correct to observe that "When the *conditions* in which relationships develop change—as they have—it's foolish to expect that relationships won't change with them."[60] But the conditions to which he refers are mostly demographic, not cultural. He himself enthusiastically speaks the language of "the marriage economy" and the "market price of sex." Here we have a Christian sociologist proposing "market solutions" to the problems of premarital sex, declining marriage rates, and high divorce rates—a Christian social scientist thoroughly enculturated into, and surrendered to, economism. When the cultural conditions of explanations change, it is foolish to expect that even scientific explanations will not change with them.

Christians do well to combat marital dissolution through education programs. But they would do better to rethink their allegiance to and complicity with a Western cultural milieu that makes those programs necessary. They would do better to take the lead in *The Redemption of Love: Rescuing Marriage and Sexuality from the Economics of a Fallen World*.[61] Marital dissolution is not necessarily caused primarily by personal inadequacy or spiritual failure. Where Christians choose to lay blame is determined largely by how they are enculturated to read their Bible, through a lens that limits brokenness and sin to individuals, or a lens that can also comprehend the brokenness and sin of collectivities and cultures. Too often they fail or refuse to comprehend that it also takes a village to sustain or sabotage a marriage,[62] and that the malfunctions of a village contribute to the malfunctions of a marriage.

---

59. McDaniel and Tepperman, *Close Relations*, 280.

60. Regnerus, "Sex Economics 101," 27.

61. Miles, *Redemption of Love*.

62. Edwards, "It Takes a Village."

Mandate 10

Commitment

*Should marriage be a commitment
to an institution?*

HAVING TRACED THE CULTURAL mandates of marriage from the beginning
of a marriage in mate selection to the untimely end of a marriage in dissolution, and having examined the most definitive characteristics of a marriage
during its life course, we conclude by probing the essence of a marriage.
We are ready now, finally, to ask with greater capability what really are the
first questions of marriage. What is marriage at its core, and how does it fit
into society and the Christian life? How is marriage perceived by Western
culture, and by contemporary Christians in Western culture? Is marriage a
divine institution ordained by God or a socially constructed human institution? We frequently hear colloquial references to the institution of marriage,
sometimes as the butt of a joke. For example, Groucho Marx cracked that
"Marriage is a wonderful institution, but who wants to live in an institution?" and James Graham opined that "Love is blind, and marriage is the
institution for the blind." What is the institution of marriage, compared to a
marriage itself? Do we marry the institution as much as our spouse? What
is the nature of the relationship that we enter upon marrying? How and to
what do we commit ourselves in marriage?

Addressing these questions requires engaging sociological theory, social history, and Christian theology one more time, hopefully having gained
some comfort and confidence in doing so. We first encountered the concept
of marriage as a social institution in Mandate 2, where the differentiation

and specialization of social institutions brought about by modernity was described. Premodern societies did not distinguish between the economy, polity, religion, education, medicine, leisure, and family the way modern societies now do, leaving the family with much more specialized functions. Mandate 9 discussed the extent to which the social institution of marriage is now being threatened by declining rates of marriage, rising rates of cohabitation, and high rates of divorce. Some even talk of the deinstitutionalization of marriage. We are ready now in conclusion to grasp more fully what a social institution is, and how the particular social institution of marriage has evolved throughout Judeo-Christian history. We are ready now to return to the beginning of history in order to rethink the origins of marriage, before unpacking the foundational Christian concept of marriage as a covenant. Then we will be better prepared to assess what it is that Christians best commit themselves to in marriage. We will find that, beyond commitment to an institution or a person, as culture has successively cast marriage, Christian marriage is primarily a commitment to relational well-being.

BEING HUMAN TOGETHER

In the second chapter, we defined culture as a collective definition and interpretation of reality that produces a whole way of life, a whole design for living. No culture can exist without being grounded in a society, and every society has at least one culture, but culture and society are not the same thing. A society is a complex, all-encompassing system of interrelationships that connects people within a defined territory. In short, society is the actors, culture is the script. For any society to sustain itself, at least five basic social processes need to happen continuously. First, people must be born or recruited to replace those who die, in order to maintain the population of the society. Second, those new members of society must be taught the values and norms of that society, in order to understand the people with whom they will share life, and to interact meaningfully with them. Third, laws about what is permissible and what is not must be made and enforced, in order to prevent anarchy and preserve social order. Fourth, goods and services must be produced, distributed, and consumed, in order to equip people for living. Fifth, a collective interpretation of reality (a culture) must be established and maintained, in order to give members of the society an identity that unites them, and purposes that motivate them. Social institutions are the means by which all of these needs of society are met.[1]

1. Charon, *Ten Questions*.

As introduced in Mandate 2 regarding the institutional differentiation and specialization of the family, social institutions are the major spheres of social life that form around these five major challenges of collective living. For example, every society has to master nature to some extent in order to obtain food, shelter, and clothing, therefore it will develop some kind of an economy. Every society will have to regulate how its people live, therefore it will develop some form of politics and law. And every society will have to transmit its culture to the next generation, therefore it will develop some kind of family system. The five classic social institutions that exist in all societies are the economy, polity, religion, education, and family.[2] Each has its own history and values, and serves to instruct the members of that society about how they should "do" religion, family, and so on.

Social institutions are constructed and maintained by humans as they collectively decide how they will meet the challenges of everyday living. The number and particular characteristics of social institutions is not dictated in any detail by either nature or God. Presumably God intended, or at least knew, that human life would be organized by social institutions, but he did not specify which ones, or what form they should take. It could be argued that, in establishing the nation of Israel, God did set out some principles upon which he wanted an economy based, such as Sabbaths when humans were to rest, sabbaticals when the land was to rest, and years of Jubilee when there was to be some socioeconomic leveling. His original form of political governance for Israel was a theocracy, where he ruled directly through judges, but his children soon insisted on a monarchy, to his dismay and their regret.

But for the most part, the creation and formation of social institutions was left to human ingenuity, and they bear all the finiteness and fallenness of the humans that constructed them. Though essential to survival, social institutions are as capable of injustice and unrighteousness as individuals are. Sin does not reside only in individual human hearts, but also in the social structures and systems that individuals together create. The oppressive and dehumanizing economic social structure of slavery is a ready and still current example, and servile marriage is one form of slavery.[3] Because social institutions form around the challenges of collective living, those who are theologically curious speculate whether there would have been such problems in the world before sin entered the human experience and condition. Perhaps material possessions, power, and sex would not have been social

2. Some recently emergent social institutions are science, mass media, and healthcare.

3. The United Nations 1956 Supplementary Convention on the Abolition of Slavery, the Slave Trade, and Institutions and Practices Similar to Slavery augmented the 1926 Slavery Convention by acting to ban servile marriage, among other practices.

problems that needed to be managed by social structures before sin entered the world. Likewise, at the other end of history, heaven may be a return to pre-fall, pre-social institutional life. Perhaps social institutions are only temporary pragmatic necessities. Marriage, for one, seemingly is, because in Jesus' words, "in the resurrection they neither marry nor are given in marriage, but are like angels in heaven" (Matt 22:30).

Christians conventionally claim that marriage is not merely a human invention or social construction, but rather a sacred institution created and ordained by God in the Genesis creation narrative. The LORD God observed that "It is not good that the man should be alone; I will make him a helper as his partner" (Gen 2:18), and then proceeded to create the woman from the man. "Therefore a man leaves his father and his mother and clings to his wife, and they become one flesh" (Gen 2:24). This is taken as God's creation of the institution of marriage, the evidence that marriage was God's good idea from the beginning. God had already seen that the non-human creatures he created were good, and then pronounced that the male and female human creatures were "very good." Though the humans were as naked as the animals, unlike the animals, they were capable of shame because of their most unique human attribute of self-consciousness. Yet they were not ashamed, suggesting that their relationship, even in their own assessment, was also very good. Some posit that marriage is the only human social institution originally intended by God and begun in perfection, because all other human institutions only emerged after the fall. All other social institutions are therefore necessitated by sin, a response to sin, and borne in sin, but the idea of marriage, it is said, is purely divine. Humans and their cultures have merely institutionalized God's agenda and enacted it as marriage, with all manner of rights, privileges, and responsibilities attached thereto.

Of course, the words "marriage" and "institution" do not actually appear in Genesis 1–3, and the social institution of marriage to which Western Christians currently commit themselves is a construal of God's original intent inferred from the text. It requires a cognitive leap to conclude that the form of Christian marriage in Western societies in this third millennium is exactly what God had in mind in the beginning. It is more likely that, instead of immediately instituting social structures of society, God first had to teach the first human being what being human meant, and how one went about it. A normal child is born with all the capacities for full personhood, but will have to exercise and develop those capacities in order to realize full personhood.[4] In the same way, the first humans were formed with all those

4. Christian Smith has detailed the emergence of personhood as "the process of constituting a new entity with its own particular characteristics through the interactive combination of other, different entities that are necessary to create the new entity but

same capacities, but they had to be brought into them to actualize their full humanity. If we read the first chapters of Genesis without reference to human cultures and institutions—none would have yet existed—God can be seen to be busy teaching the first human beings what the essence of being human entailed. They were to be uniquely 1) responsible creatures, as implicit in caring for the earth; 2) symbol-using creatures, as implicit in naming the animals; 3) moral creatures, as implicit in the tree of good and evil; 4) self-conscious creatures, as implicit in their potential for shame of nakedness; and 5) social creatures, as implicit in God's observation that it was not good that they be alone.[5]

Just as the triune God is relational in character, so too are we humans who bear the image of God. In order to draw relationship out of his human creature, God took *ha adam*, "the [first] human," whose maleness to that point is presumably irrelevant and perhaps undetermined, and created a human female more suitable than any animal as a partner, "bone of my bones, flesh of my flesh" (Gen 2:21–23). Like the triune God, humans too can be partitioned into separate persons in relationship, but are ultimately one, exhibiting both unity and uniqueness. The first human would cleave to the second in such a way that the two would in some way become one flesh again, as they began. To cleave is to join together, in this case restoring the oneness of the original human earthling. The core human longing of separated persons will always be wholeness and completion, and becoming "one flesh" returns the human condition to its original state. In this sense, marriage reverses creation. In creation, God made possible a physically complementary (completing) relationship, by making two out of one. In marital relationship, God returns them to oneness, by making one out of two.[6]

In this interpretive light, there is something more profound being conveyed in the Genesis narrative than the founding of the institution of marriage. Humans are built to long for completion and wholeness in relationship with a human "other," just as their spirituality is a longing to be complete and whole again in relationship with the divine "wholly other." That this sparse description of the first human relationship should lead to, approximate, or much less be equivalent to contemporary Western notions of marriage is also a theological (human) deduction, not a divine directive

---

that do not contain the characteristics present in the new entity" (Smith, *What Is a Person?*, 25–26).

5. In both *What Is a Person?* and *Moral, Believing Animals*, Christian Smith has given a profoundly Christian account of the essence of human personhood without appealing to the authority of the biblical text. It is an exemplary model of how Christian thinking can contribute significantly to secular theoretical scholarship.

6. I am indebted to my colleague Ed Neufeld for this interpretive insight.

given by God. Of course, by the time Jesus and Paul comment on marriage with reference to Genesis, the text is further entangled in questions of culture (as the writing of the book of Genesis is itself), and we are left with the thorny hermeneutical questions regarding what God intended to be cultural or transcultural. What in the text is descriptive and indicative, telling us what will happen, compared to what is prescriptive and imperative, telling us what should happen?[7]

THE EVOLUTION OF MARRIAGE

As highlighted throughout this book, myriad cultural forms of marriage have evolved from that first human male-female relationship described in Genesis. But it has not been a random chaos of marital forms. The essential purpose of social institutions is to fend off disorder by establishing order, and while established order inherently resists change, institutions nevertheless can and do change, given sufficient time and social impetus. At times there can even be more than one order existing within a single social institution, in which case the contrasting orders compete to be taken as the most legitimate and authoritative. For example, the concept of marriage in a religious cult can compete with the concept of marriage in the cult's host society. In some eras and cultures, the concept of marriage seems contested by several perspectives, while in other eras and cultures a single perspective seems to predominate. In some eras and cultures, multiple perspectives of marriage challenge the dominant perspective, while in other eras and cultures a single perspective seems to predominate without challenge.

In seeking to comprehend the evolution of marriage in Western culture, it may be oversimplifying to identify historical stages through which it has passed, and we may do better to speak more cautiously of competing perspectives of marriage. Yet, while an evolutionary series of stages may be too tidy a conceptualization, there nonetheless remains a certain linearity or progression in the historical change. Whether they are stages of evolution of marriage or competing perspectives of marriage, the social institution of marriage has taken on four identifiable forms as follows.[8]

---

7. Webb, *Slaves, Women, and Homosexuals.* The definition of marriage employed here is a normative definition, what a marriage "should" be. There are other types of definitions of marriage and family, such as legal, structural, functional, and phenomenological. See White and Klein, *Family Theories.*

8. The following discussion is drawn from Witte, *From Sacrament to Contract* and "Meanings of Marriage."

Table 4

Witte's Historical Stages of Marriage						
Marriage as a	Natural Institution	→	Spiritual Association	→	Social Estate	→	Personal Contract

Marriage began in antiquity as a rather informal and private arrangement by today's standards, commencing with an official pronouncement of some sort, and leading to the couple practicing fidelity however the community defined it. It has always been understood by the Judeo-Christian tradition as a natural institution, that is, one that originates and is given in nature itself. Natural law, natural rights, and natural justice have in common the notion that some aspects of a good and proper life are self-evident in nature, and are therefore transcultural and universal. Inasmuch as Christians attribute nature to the will and hand of God, those natural aspects are also taken as God-given; it is God who is the source of and has authority over natural institutions. Reason, conscience, and custom are employed to discern the natural laws that make marriage what it "naturally" is. Many conclude by these means that homosexuality, incest, polygamy, and bestiality are unnatural violations of the nature of marriage, just as contraception, abortion, infanticide, and child abuse are violations of the natural marital functions of propagation and childrearing. This first form of marriage as a natural institution has been emphasized consistently throughout Christendom, but has never been the predominant view.

Roman Catholics and Protestants agree that marriage is a natural institution, but have differed on several other perspectives of marriage, primarily regarding its status as a sacrament. For Catholics, marriage is a spiritual association governed by the Church as one of its seven sacraments, or "divine mysteries." As the sacrament of matrimony, marriage is a visible sign of an invisible reality, as Augustine put it. Catholicism shifted the emphasis from the "naturalness" of marriage to its need for religious sanction. The Church claimed authority over marriage,[9] and it became subject to the creed, code, and canons of the religious community. It was viewed as a remedy for sexual sin, not a recipe for righteousness, because celibacy was held to be a higher spiritual state. This second form of marriage dominated Western society until the Protestant Reformation of the sixteenth century.

Protestants, in turn, shifted the emphasis in marriage from religious to social legitimation, with authority over it belonging to the state, not the

---

9. The Roman Catholic Church gained legal control of marriage through canon law in 1184.

church. Marriage came to be viewed as a social standing or class[10] governed by the secular state through civil law. Marriage was subject to special state laws of property and inheritance, and the expectations of the local community. Protestants rejected marriage as a sacrament, the spiritual superiority of clerical celibacy, and the prohibition of contraception and divorce. Whereas Catholics taught that God ordained marriage after the fall for the purpose of sexual relations and procreation, Protestants insisted that God ordained marriage before the fall for the primary purpose of companionship, and as the normal adult state. This third, Protestant form of marriage as a social standing shared dominance of Western society with the Catholic view of marriage as a spiritual association from the mid-sixteenth century until the mid-nineteenth century.

Though remnants of the conceptions of marriage as a natural institution, spiritual association, and social standing remain in current consciousness, marriage today is more likely to be viewed as a private interpersonal contract. The emphasis has shifted again from marriage as a sacrament or social standing to marriage as a voluntary union. A marriage in current culture in effect consists of little more than the mutual consent of the two persons involved, the little more being the perfunctory legalities that separate it from cohabitation. Authority over a marriage is now claimed by the couple that constitutes the marriage; marriage is governed by the voluntary wills and preferences of the couple. Prior to the Enlightenment, with its emphasis on rational individual liberty and autonomy, marriage was more of a social contract. A person contemplating getting married understood it to be in his or her rational self-interest to voluntarily give up the individual freedom she or he had in the state of nature in order to obtain the benefits of the institutionalized social order of marriage. But in the modern era, marriage is increasingly viewed as a private contract between two individuals. It is designed to maximize self-fulfillment, with only limited, superficial consent from society, in keeping with the increasingly contractual character of (post)modern society.[11]

In all, marriage at best is part natural institution, part spiritual association, part social standing, and part personal contract, irreducible to any one. It seemingly is best governed both externally by legal authority and internally by moral authority. What becomes evident from surveying the evolution of marriage from its beginnings in the first male-female relationship in the garden to its current cultural conception, is that the character of

10. Marriage was in fact a social estate, much like the medieval European social estates of the nobility, clergy, and commoners.

11. For further such analysis, see Witte and Ellison, *Covenant Marriage in Comparative Perspective*.

marriage has clearly not been dictated in detail directly by God. Nor has it been understood uniformly by God's people.

COVENANTS AND CONTRACTS

It is by now also conventional for Christians to emphasize the covenantal character of marriage,[12] precisely because it contrasts so sharply with the contractual model prevalent today. Both covenants and contracts are binding agreements, but a contract is a legally binding agreement, enforceable in a court of law. It is a promise to engage in or refrain from a specified action, and if the promise is broken, the law will provide recourse, even if not a remedy. Notably, contracts are ultimately driven by mistrust. Because we no longer trust another person's word, or handshake, we want to be able to bring the weight of the state against them if they break their word. Threat of punishment replaces trust. Careful calculations, specifications, qualifications, and reservations are spelled out in the typically rational terms of modernity. Such is the guarded character of how we now relate to each other in everyday life as suspicious strangers. As we shall see, a contract also differs from a covenant in that it is an exchange of promises between two or more parties.

Conversely, a covenant is a solemn one-way agreement whereby the covenanter is the only party bound by the promise, and consequently the only party that can break the covenant. Looking to the biblical texts, we see that covenant is the fundamental order of God's relation to creation, and to all creatures. God first covenanted with the earth, and then with specific persons (e.g., Abraham—Gen 15:18), people groups (e.g., Israel—Exod 19:5), and humanity in general (e.g., Noah—Gen 9:17) before finally making a new covenant through Jesus Christ (Matt 26:28). God's covenant with Israel is depicted as a marriage covenant in the story of Hosea and Gomer. The applicability of God's covenanting to human marriage is also implicit in Paul's analogical exhortation that husbands should love their wives the way Christ loves the church (Eph 5:23–32).

Balswick and Balswick have articulated a well-received theological model for marriage based on covenant (to love and be loved), grace (to forgive and be forgiven), empowerment (to serve and be served), and intimacy

---

12. For example, see Joseph, *Marriage as a Covenant Relationship*; and Chapman, *Covenant Marriage.* The sense in which we use "covenant marriage" here is more theological and social-psychological than the recent social movement to draft public policy that makes marriage religiously and legally more difficult to enter and exit. See Nock, *Covenant Marriage.*

(to know and be known).[13] These four stages constantly spiral inward, growing into ever-deepening levels of relationship. If they fail to grow, they do not merely stagnate, but reverse into their opposites. Covenant is then reduced to contract, grace reduced to law, empowering reduced to possessing, and intimacy reduced to distance. The Balswicks' elaboration of God's loving covenant, or covenant of love, applied to marriage is built on two dimensions: unilateral (one-way) commitment versus bilateral (two-way) commitment, and conditional commitment versus unconditional commitment. Four types of marriage result as follows.

Table 5

Balswick and Balswick's Types of Marital Commitments		
	Conditional	*Unconditional*
Unilateral	Modern Open	Initial Covenant
Bilateral	Contract	Mature Covenant

First, marital commitment that is bilateral and conditional is the classic contractual marriage, where partners strike a bargain, vowing to stay on the condition that each fulfills the specified terms of relationship. Second, marital commitment that is unilateral and conditional is the modern open marriage, where each reserves the right to walk away from the marriage whenever they choose, meaning whenever they feel their needs or interests are no longer being met. Third, marital commitment that is unilateral and unconditional is what the Balswicks term an initial covenant, where one partner makes a decision to enter binding relationship regardless of what the other chooses. Finally, marital commitment that is bilateral and unconditional is God's intent for marriage, a mature covenant, the joyous coincidence that each separately says to the other that they will love regardless of what the other chooses.

In addition to its theological significance, covenantal marriage has profound relational significance for a couple, contrasting sharply with the relational consequences of contractual marriage. Take for example the hypothetical modern-day Bo and Ruth compared to Sam and Della. Bo and Ruth know that their relationship will have an overarching character of its own apart from their individual identities, and are open and eager to see what it will become. They know that many people care about their marriage, and that because their marriage is important to others, others should have some say in it. Bo and Ruth know each other deeply because they each know

13. Balswick and Balswick, *Model for Marriage*, 38–47; idem, *Family*, 17–35.

who they are individually, and disclose who they are in a way that generates equally deep attachment. Their sexual intercourse expresses their desire for each other's whole person more than the other's body or their own pleasure. They value where they came from and what brought them together, yet realize that wisdom about marriage they glean from others will have to be adapted to the idiosyncrasies of their relationship.

Sam and Della are different. They see their marriage as two individuals combining their assets and liabilities into the best fit possible, as they themselves construct it. Seeing their marriage as their own, they resist the input of family and friends, insisting that they must make it on their own, in their own way. Sam and Della learn much about who they each are as persons by relating to the other, and grow individually because of it, feeling grateful for the intentional or unintentional role the other has played in their maturation. They have an instrumental view of sex as being about personal release, pleasure, and satisfaction, a physical celebration in which they feel most fully alive. They do not want to be bound or burdened by the past, or tyrannized by the future. When they encounter problems in their marriage, they seek input from expert others who advise them what to do to solve their problems. Bo and Ruth's marriage tends toward the covenantal end of the spectrum, Sam and Della's toward the contractual.[14]

Covenantal marriage produces vastly more positive meanings and dynamics that make possible all the rich potentialities of marriage.[15] Covenantal marriage is two people on a quest that is bigger than each person individually, or even both together, whereas contractual marriage is limited to the possibilities of the two individuals involved. Covenantal marriage is accountable to the community that supports and corrects it, whereas contractual marriage is each individual accountable only to him or herself. Covenantal marriage leads to intimacy with the other through the self; the self is the medium through which intimacy with the other is achieved, binding one to the other. Contractual marriage only seeks intimacy with the self through the other in its pursuit of self-fulfillment; the other is the medium through which intimacy with the self is achieved, actualizing the self. Sexual exchange in covenantal marriage is communion with the other, whereas sex in contractual marriage is ultimately a form of self-pleasuring. In covenantal marriage the past matters, as the relationship creates a unique history of what can only be understood as a story of growing complexity and trust, and cannot be captured or explained by any how-to formula. Contractual

14. Covenant and contract are best understood as the two poles of a conceptual continuum, with each real-life marriage being somewhere in between.

15. Clapp, *Families at the Crossroads*, 114–32.

marriage lives only in the present, concerned only about meeting terms from moment to moment. It assumes that good relationship is the result of employing the right techniques of relationship, and that marriage is like a machine whose breakdowns can be fixed by expert mechanics. In all, covenantal marriage and contractual marriage create two very different kinds of people, with contractual marriage fostering the union of interests, but covenantal marriage fostering the union of selves.

The two principal attributes of a covenant that are most salient to the institution of marriage are that covenants are both personal and relational, as were the first male and female humans. Unlike contracts, which can be struck between two impersonal legal entities or corporations, only individuals can covenant. Yet a covenant is not limited to that which occurs between two individuals. It is entirely possible for an individual to covenant with a group or community, as when members of a congregation agree to live and work together according to the precepts of their faith. For example, many Christian universities have a formal covenant of community life in addition to their statement of faith, with which all students, faculty, and staff agree to abide. But only the individual herself or himself can commit to a covenant.

Furthermore, relationship requires life, and the party with which a covenant is made must be a living entity. It is nonsensical to be in meaningful relationship with a non-living object, whether that object is material or immaterial. Non-living material objects, like rocks, are fixed in their being, and their non-variability makes the unconditional character of covenant meaningless, because they are incapable of changing themselves. We can be committed to a non-material object such as an idea (freedom), an activity (social activism), or a social institution (democracy), but we cannot be said to covenant with them. Like a contract, a covenant is a certain kind of commitment, limited to a certain kind of other, specifically a living, personal other. As such, the Christian covenant of marriage cannot be a commitment to the social institution of marriage.

ULTIMATE COMMITMENTS

Nevertheless, the traditional commitment of spouses has been to the social institution of marriage, the bond of holy matrimony, for better or worse, "till death do us part." Commitment in this sense is to something much bigger than the couple, the community, or even the church. In this view, to marry is to enter the ordinance of God, and be constrained to continue a line of action regardless of personal health or happiness. What matters most in this type of commitment is that the marriage remain structurally stable and intact, not that the personal relationship or individual experience within it be of a certain quality. According to this line of thinking, even if the marital bond should turn to bondage and become abusive, at least God's primary intent has been fulfilled. This kind of wedlock, for that is what it is, is unbreakable, indissoluble, indestructible. To its credit, it has produced social order and stability throughout history, holding at bay what otherwise might devolve into sexual chaos for adults and familial chaos for children. Social order is good, and our collective commitment to our social institutions, in this case marriage, is one way of achieving that good.

In contrast, the modern contractual commitment of spouses has been to the well-being of the persons involved in the marriage, to the self and/or other, "as long as we both shall love." Love in this sense means fidelity as long as we feel our respective needs and interests are being served, and we are each happy with ourselves and the other. Commitment becomes contingent on the condition of personal health and happiness, and in effect becomes commitment *to* individual health and happiness within the relationship. Given that attraction and satisfaction are notoriously unstable personal states, this type of open and voluntary commitment is fragile, subject to the ebb and flow of unruly emotions. When the object of commitment, either self or spouse, is variable, commitment itself becomes variable. In the end, the health and happiness of the other spouse is rarely sufficiently enduring to keep such a marriage intact, and this kind of commitment is exposed as being primarily to self and remedying one's own ill health and unhappiness. Consequently, modern freedom and autonomy has produced a culture of divorce, as elaborated in Mandate 9. To its credit, such individualistic commitment has fostered a self-fulfillment that institutional commitments alone could never deliver. And self-fulfillment is also good.

A third type of commitment, more congruent with the biblical concept of covenant, is commitment not to the institution of marriage nor to ensuring the well-being of the persons involved, but to the well-being of the marital relationship itself. As we have seen, covenant requires persons in relationship; in essence, a covenant *is* a relationship. Commitment to a social institution is too impersonal to qualify as covenant. Commitment to personal well-being is too vulnerable to being merely self-serving, and too precarious because people change in myriad ways. Marriage in this third view is a commitment to nurture and protect a relationship, not to enter an institution, or to pursue health and happiness through interpersonal need fulfillment. The best locus of commitment is not the object of the institution, the self, or the other, but the relationship itself, in the context of being true to God, other, and self. One measure of such commitment to relational well-being is the ability of each spouse to do whatever in their best judgment is best for the relationship, even when self or other is pained in the process. It is saying that "I choose this unpleasant line of action that you or I would prefer to avoid, because I think it is best for our relationship." Given that God's fundamental way of being is relational within the Trinity and with humanity, and that we who are made in God's image are likewise fundamentally relational, marriage as commitment to relational well-being is the fundamental good.

The three types of commitment outlined here are not simplistically separate; they overlap and interplay. For example, commitment to relationship alone is ultimately no different than commitment to institution alone, because commitment to relationship, by definition, will never do anything to break relationship, just as commitment to institution will never do anything to break a marriage. But there are times when a relationship is so broken and dysfunctional that it can never be well, and the best thing for it is to be dissolved. For instance, when spouses have become pathologically codependent on each other, and cannot break that pathology on their own, perhaps breaking the relationship is the only way forward. Granted, we are all broken people, and a fully functioning marriage will always be holding two broken people together. Nonetheless, there are circumstances when the marital relationship itself is also broken beyond repair, and the individuals in it can only regain their own health through the termination of the relationship. That can only happen if marriage is something other than wedlock.

Of course, it is always preferable that individual spouses themselves are whole and healthy enough to be able to seek the well-being of the relationship. It takes a sturdy, robust sense of self to contribute to a healthy relationship, and a relationship can only be as healthy as its weakest member. We can only love the other as wholly as we love ourselves, and a surrendered self, a self already abdicated, has nothing with which to nurture the well-being of a relationship, as noted in Mandate 5. To sacrifice the self within reason is to say "I am something, and I give it to you." To abdicate the self beyond reason is to say "I am nothing; I make no difference." Paradoxically, while healthy relationships require healthy selves, they also heal selves. It is always preferable that personal brokenness be lessened in and by relationship. Indeed, that is one of the best functions of marital relationship. Nevertheless, marriage is first and foremost a commitment to the well-being of the relationship, because only a healthy relationship can serve the individuals, community, and God.

One aspect of the tension between self and society is that we no longer believe in the permanency of the individual, yet we still believe in the permanency of marriage. Marriage is now envisioned as a dynamic relationship between two individuals constantly in flux, not a fixed and static state locked into place at a wedding. Knowing that the evolution of self now nurtured by culture cannot be forced volitionally, nor denied relationally, we now marry expecting that our spouse will very likely change very significantly during the course of the marriage. If the personal change of both spouses is in the same direction at the same pace and at the same time, a richly rewarding mutual journey ensues. But given the vagaries of the modern self, that is unlikely and not always even possible, and when absent, necessitates a renegotiation of relationship. The only other options then are arrested development or marital dissolution. But—and here is the point—even growing difference need not and should not lessen commitment to relationship. Spouses can always love, care, respect, and share with each other regardless of whether their original interpersonal fit or even liking endures. Unexpectedly, they often over time then discover a new, renegotiated fit and liking that renovates, regenerates, and rejuvenates their relationship. What God requires and rewards is faithful presence in relationship,[16] even when one cannot always be fully present in relationship because of emergent differences.

Balswick and Balswick have suggested that biblical marital commitment is equally to all three types of commitment delineated here. "Covenant love goes way beyond loyalty to marriage as an institution and far surpasses a self-fulfillment motif. It is a promise to sacrifice for the sake of relationship. Commitment to the institution results in legalism; commitment to personal fulfillment results in hedonism; commitment that embraces all three (institution, person, and relationship) is a commitment to caring for the needs of each spouse, nourishing the relationship itself and upholding the institution of marriage."[17] Clearly there is much good in all three types of commitment, and much biblical warrant for each. But marriage as commitment to an institution is problematic in that its status as a holy or social institution is thorny, its impersonal nature renders covenanting sterile, and its inflexibility can produce personal and interpersonal pathos. Marriage as a commitment to personal well-being is problematic in that it is a form of self-absorption, it is contractual versus covenantal in character, and it is totally unpredictable in its outcomes. Marriage as commitment to relational well-being would appear to be most effectual and biblical, incorporating aspects of institution and personal well-being, being built on covenant, and remaining flexible. Christian marriage may well contain elements of all three commitments, but commitment to relational well-being is primary.

---

16. In *To Change the World*, James Davison Hunter reflects on a theology of faithful presence as the optimal mode of being Christian in the world.

17. Balswick and Balswick, *Model for Marriage*, 42.

The final mandate of marriage we have examined here turns on one of the most profound dualities of human social life: its simultaneously individual and collective character. Historically, Western culture has viewed marriage as a commitment to a social institution, and most Christians surrendered to it. In a complete about face, current Western culture views marriage as commitment to the individual, meaning to personal well-being, and many Christians are complicit with it. While commitment to marriage as an institution is not necessarily improper, it is nevertheless incomplete, deficient, and ultimately misguided, as is commitment to personal well-being in marriage. A biblical marriage is one primarily committed to relational well-being, buttressed by secondary commitments to institution and personal well-being.

Reclaiming Christian Marriage

CULTURE AND CHRISTIANITY

IN THE END, CONTEMPLATING marriage is just one case study of the interplay between culture and Christianity in general, one site of engagement that represents what happens on every front in every realm of life. Christianity has had an enormously formative role in Western culture at large that still lingers long after secularization has wiped away social memory of Christianity's seminal influence. Many of the most foundational values of current Western culture have originated in Christian theology and worldview, even if not explicitly in the biblical text. As noted in the second chapter, fully developed values of individualism, egalitarianism, democracy, and human rights are not found in the biblical text, but the theological or worldview bases from which they derive are.[1] Nevertheless, our focus has been on the reverse. Our focus has been on how culture shapes how we read the Bible, and what we say the Bible says about whatever our topic of interest may be. This is more urgently important for Christians in a post-Christian culture, where the gulf between culture and Christianity is growing rapidly, and conflating the two is becoming ever more problematic.

Niebuhr's *Christ and Culture* was written in mid-twentieth century, and it informed most thinking on the interplay between culture and Christianity for the balance of the century.[2] His categories of Christ against culture, Christ of culture, Christ above culture, Christ and culture in paradox, and Christ the transformer of culture served as the basis for conceptualizing Christian engagement with culture at a time when the assumption of a strong Christian presence in Western culture was still valid. But come the new century and millennium, when Niebuhr's favored Christian transfor-

---

1. Max Weber's *The Protestant Ethic and the Spirit of Capitalism* is a sociological classic that traces the formative effects of Reformational Calvinist theology on our current economic system.

2. Niebuhr, *Christ and Culture*.

mation of culture was manifestly less plausible, his typology needed to be reconsidered and updated. Carter offered a post-Christendom revision that no longer assumed that Western culture was Christian.[3] In the same vein, Crouch[4] delineated how some Christians condemn culture and attempt a fundamentalist withdrawal from it. Other Christians critique culture by passing judgment on its values and worldview. Still others copy culture by forming a parallel subculture that mostly mimics broader culture. Many simply mindlessly consume culture. According to Crouch, in contrast to these inadequate approaches, the call of God to us, indeed the image of God in us, compels Christians to create and cultivate culture, to be gardeners like the first Great Gardener. Could Christians create and cultivate a new subculture of marriage? Should they?

It bears repeating that cultural conceptions of marriage are not all necessarily undesirable and contra-Christian. There is much to bless and little to banish in self-selection, need fulfillment, romantic love, dyadic intimacy, and sexual pleasure in marriage. The point is simply that marriages not realizing these values, or not even devoting themselves to maximizing these values, are not thereby contravening the biblical text. They are simply being countercultural in the context of contemporary Western culture. When thoroughly socialized into Western culture, spouses in such marriages will probably experience themselves and their marriage as defective and deficient, yet they are not by biblical standards. It may be in their personal best interests, given their enculturation, to counsel them in the "best practices" of their culture, but these are the concessions and compromises of unavoidably living in a culture, not the call of God. It is imperative that we let go of what is not explicitly and essentially biblical *as Christian*, even when we may want to retain it as cultural. In those dimensions where cultural imperatives of marriage are in essence or function pathological, such as consumerist underpinnings that too often belie Christian claims to covenant marriage, then as Krishnamurti put it, "It is no measure of health to be well-adjusted to a profoundly sick society."[5]

---

3. Carter, *Rethinking Christ and Culture*. Carter's categories are Christ separating from culture, Christ legitimating culture, Christ humanizing culture, and Christ transforming culture.

4. Crouch, *Culture Making*.

5. Quoted from http://www.great-quotes.com/quote/173723.

SOCIAL REALITY

Contemplating cultural mandates that shape Christian marriage commonly creates at least two effects, a sense of both illumination and liberation. We come away from the exercise seeing marriage differently, seeing it as a socially constructed human institution, not as a structure independent of human will. Marriage may be a divine institution created by God, but whatever God's original intent and parameters for it were, humans have clearly taken it and made of it what we will. This is what is meant by the sociological phrase "the social construction of reality," which is the understanding that society is creatively invented and actively produced by human beings, not something given to us.[6] Comprehending this fully potentially frees us from its tyranny. If marriage as we know it has been socially constructed by culture, Christians can then also deconstruct it and reconstruct it as we will, in greater accord with what we understand the biblical text to say about it. The problem addressed by this book is that Christians have mistaken cultural mandates of marriage as biblical, instead of carefully and conscientiously deconstructing and reconstructing them. Christians could conceivably "change the world" regarding marriage, but we have taken the easy way out, and not just surrendered to culture, but sacralized it in order to sweeten our surrender.

Even if contemporary Christians can no longer change Western culture as a whole, having lost foremost control of it in a post-Christendom world, we can still choose to conduct our own marriages in a more authentically Christian manner, as countercultural as that may now be. This is what is known as cultivating the "sociological imagination," which is the acquired ability to link the micro and the macro levels of social reality, to connect biography and history, as we have done throughout this book. It enables us "to take into account how individuals, in the welter of their daily experience, often become falsely conscious of their social positions."[7] Without a sociological imagination, we are less able to see how we have been shaped by our social location in time and place, and hence less able to understand with vivid awareness the relationship between our personal experience and the wider social context. That is possible only when we pull away from focusing on our immediate personal circumstances and experience, when we "think ourselves away" in order to place ourselves in our broader cultural milieu. Like radar, a sociological imagination enables us to see through the smokescreen, fog, or night of culture.

6. Berger and Luckmann, *Social Construction of Reality*.
7. Mills, *Sociological Imagination*, 5.

Like all social-scientific endeavors, the sociological imagination seeks to comprehend social reality as accurately, precisely, and fully as possible. This is a daunting prerequisite for engaging social reality beneficially that too many Christians unwisely rush past. They are impatient with the "merely" descriptive *is* of life that is social science, and are eager to get on with the prescriptive *ought* of moral theology. Or they assume they have sufficient description of reality from their reading of the biblical text, and therefore have no need of empirical measures of reality before they get on with advocacy. Like Sunday school preschoolers, the implicit mentality of this disposition is "Jesus is the answer. What is the question?" They then often embarrass and hinder the cause of the gospel with their naiveté, presumption, and polemics, resorting to excessively and at times exclusively individualistic and moralistic approaches to personal and social problems. As the saying goes, "If the only tool you have is a hammer, everything looks like a nail." As Gaede put it, "Western Christians do not know how to think Christianly about most subjects. They reduce Christianity to a matter of morality, and assume that to think biblically about a social issue is to engage in social ethics. To engage in a Christian understanding of the social sciences requires a much grander concept of God than is currently held by many Christians."[8] If they want their prescriptions for social reality to be taken seriously, Christians must earn the right to be heard by first doing their homework and demonstrating that they have adequate descriptions of reality. Good descriptions temper hasty and trite prescriptions. Truly understanding the causes and consequences of social behavior is necessary in order to practice social ethics well. In a sense, the task of social ethics begins only where the task of social science ends.

As we have seen in Mandate 3, descriptions of marriage and prescriptions for marriage are complicated by the fact that prescriptive values of marriage are also social facts that can be observed, described, and explained. As demonstrated throughout this book, sociology describes the prescriptions of both culture and Christianity regarding marriage, at the same time that it describes the actual cultural and Christian practice of marriage. In both cases, both the ideal and the real are social facts that are external to and coercive of the individual. For example, cultural and Christian ideals of premarital sex and divorce are divergent ethics drawn from discrepant values, yet the reality of cultural and Christian practice of premarital sex and divorce is similar. Meanwhile, cultural and Christian ideals of need fulfillment and intimacy are similar, as is their pursuit in reality. We have been interested in describing marital ideals and examining their congruence with

8. Gaede, *Where Gods May Dwell*, 93–94.

the biblical text, but have been more interested in marital reality as it is lived out in kitchens and bedrooms and church pews relative to those ideals. Nevertheless, though the first principles of social science are to be empirical and value free, superior descriptions implicitly and inevitably suggest prescriptions, especially the descriptions of the kind of critical sociology we have employed here.[9] Having described the conflation of cultural and Christian mandates of marriage, we can allow ourselves some tentative, speculative prescriptions in closing.

CREATIVE TENSIONS

We have critically examined how contemporary Western culture mandates that marriage be formed, connected, valued, pursued, characterized, focused, energized, troubled, ended, and perceived—virtually every aspect of marriage. Each mandate has concluded that Christians have, without biblical warrant and however sweetly, surrendered to culture on the particular aspect of marriage examined. Even more uncomfortably, each mandate has left us in a quandary, unsure of a way forward. Arriving at and lingering in these dilemmas has been deliberate, lest these deliberations succumb to being another prescriptive, how-to, self-help handbook on marriage. Upon closer examination, each endpoint has constituted a tension between rival conceptions of, or incongruent approaches to, the particular mandate of marriage. Yet these tensions need not be as unsettling or immobilizing as they may have been experienced. If embraced with Christian resolve, these tensions can be creative and activating. They can serve as the impetus to collaborative conversations among people of faith that revision the broad contours of more authentically Christian marriage. They too can illuminate and liberate, inspire and empower.[10] Toward that end, brief preliminary reflections on these creative tensions are humbly offered here as a start toward reconstructing marriage and creating a new Christian culture of marriage.

Mandate 1: Mate Selection. There is little chance of or merit in returning entirely from a cultural system in which marriage partners select themselves based on love to a cultural system in which partners are arranged by others based on kinship practicalities, such as practiced in biblical times. A much tighter total cultural ethos is required to hold arranged marriages

9. Sociology contains and reflects three different systems of knowledge: scientistic knowledge, interpretive knowledge, and critical knowledge. See Habermas, *Knowledge and Human Interests.*

10. I am indebted to colleagues Scott Monsma for observing that the mandates tended to end in creative tensions, and Valerie Hiebert for suggesting ways forward.

together, and make them work. Nevertheless, a middle way forward in which premarital couples consult their community more is very possible and commendable. The decision to marry should not be made alone. Giving premarital couples a more honest idea of what marriage really is, facilitated most effectively by parents being more transparent about their own marriages, would also help greatly.

Mandate 2: Connectedness. Premodern collectivistic cultures had as many shortcomings as modern individualistic cultures, and as much as some might wish it were otherwise, modernity's disconnecting effects on marriage can likewise not be readily reversed. The marriage unit needs to be respected as a unit, but its disembeddedness from community in modernity strains the marriage and deprives the community. Here is a real opportunity for the church to offer a middle way forward, to be a real community and actually share life together, not just talk about life together. It should also send its marriages out into the wider community beyond church programs to be a faithful presence there as well, and be strengthened for doing so.

Mandate 3: Calling. Though marriage and family is a holy calling, to make it an idol to which all else must bow is not biblical. The family is not the highest calling in life. Likewise, to make an idol of kingdom work to which all else must bow is equally misguided and potentially destructive. Both remain means of loving God and neighbor, but neither are legitimately ultimate ends in themselves. Neither should investment in family be the extent of one's kingdom work. The most God-honoring way forward is not for Christians to idolize their families on one hand, nor to sacrifice their families *to* kingdom work on the other, but to ensure that their families sacrifice *for* kingdom work.

Mandate 4: Need Fulfillment. Marital partners today meet many of each other's personal and relational needs quite admirably. However, that is a mandate of Western therapeutic culture, not the biblical text, whose silence on the issue may simply reflect its own cultural ethos. In a milieu in which we relate to many more others much differently, notions of spousal all-sufficiency, or even primacy, create more personal and marital problems than they remedy. Husbands, wives, and marriages would be healthier and stronger for transparently not expecting, demanding, or pursuing such notions. Another way forward is already being demonstrated by the younger generation, among whom it is no longer unheard of that the primary wedding party attendant of a bride or groom is a cross-sex friend.

Mandate 5: Love. Romantic love is an unadulterated joy in marriage, but is as likely to undermine a marriage as underline it, as likely to weaken marriage by its fickleness as strengthen marriage by its passion. Its euphoria erects a straw house where a stone house is needed, yet while Christians preach love, they tend to celebrate being in love disproportionate to its actual role in robust marriage. As a way forward, we must regain the truth that just as true happiness is a byproduct of pursuing something meaningful other than happiness, and just as the best therapy is more meaningful engagement with the world, not more self-indulgence, so also true romance is an adventure, not a feeling, and true love is giving, not getting.

Mandate 6: Intimacy. Like need fulfillment, Western culture places high demands on marriage for intimacy, while the biblical text is virtually silent on the matter. Again, it is only in a therapeutic culture that intimacy is framed as a need that must be fulfilled. General biblical principles of the need for and practice of the self in relationship are applicable, but stop well short of the Western culture of narcissism.[11] Though mutual self-disclosure can be volunteered at any time, true intimacy, like "quality time" with children, cannot be manufactured at will, but requires full faithful presence over time. If expectations early in marriage are not modest, they can lead to premature disillusionment.

Mandate 7: Sex. Whether sex is primarily for the purpose of pleasure or relationship is a question that cannot and need not always be answered. Yet while reducing sex to physical pleasure is unbiblical, expecting it to be unfailingly ecstatic communion is also disillusioning. The spiritual oneness of sex is not always felt or realized in the moment, but only in the rhythms of ongoing relationship, and it is just as unwise and unbiblical to expect or demand too much of sex in the moment as too little. Whenever we focus on one part of marriage, we implicitly diminish the whole, and the whole of a marriage is reflected in its sexual engagement more than what sexual engagement contributes to the whole.

Mandate 8: Conflict. Western culture encourages married couples to flee from conflict either by winning it, denying it, or breaking up because of it, whereas the biblical text assumes conflict and is constantly building the virtues required to process and manage it. We would do best to follow the biblical approach. We need a more transparent and positive approach to conflict, recognizing the opportunity for growth that it constitutes and benefiting from the energy it generates. One practical way to do so would be to encourage spouses to discuss with each other their respective sources of interpersonal power and patterns of interpersonal conflict at a time when they are not mired in a conflict.

11. Lasch, *Culture of Narcissism.*

Mandate 9: Dissolution. Divorce is both a personal failure and a community failure. Christian communities need to shoulder their share of the responsibility by not just responding with "support" when a couple is in crisis, but by being aware of its potential before it happens, and by not washing their hands of it after it happens. Blaming the couple alone is unfair and unhelpful. As a poignant, symbolic expression of our solidarity and equal status in the family of God, churches could seat brothers and sisters in Christ mixed together, instead of as couples and singles. How unimaginable that seems because of the impracticalities of child supervision, hosting visitors, and so on is a measure of how surrendered we are to our culture.

Mandate 10: Commitment. Historically, both cultural and Christian marital commitments have been to the social institution of marriage. Today, culture has largely abandoned the institution and fostered commitment to the self or other in marriage. Sensing the fragility of commitment to the person, Christians have sided weakly with the emptying institution in hopes of filling it up. They should rather avoid both ditches by committing themselves to the well-being of their relationships. Institutions and persons predate and postdate any given marriage. What a particular marriage creates is a new living entity that would otherwise not exist, an agentic relationship that acts back on its co-creators and acts out on its world, something to be treasured, nurtured, and empowered.

FULLER WAYS FORWARD

Overall, instead of sweetly surrendering to cultural mandates of marriage, Christians ought to re-examine them thoroughly, resist them where they are more or less than what a culturally informed reading of the biblical text mandates, and reclaim for themselves the freedom to forge their marriage in the transcendent God alone. The Christian marriages that might then emerge would not be beholden to the current cultural and Christian ideals that in their excess are deeply disheartening and make defeated liars of us all. Despite how relatively little the biblical text says about marriage, Christians have created a whole discourse on marriage that we claim is biblical, but is little more than an enculturated extrapolation from the Bible. This Christian conflation of culture and the biblical text creates winners and losers in its own image, as many of the latter as the former, that disgraces and dishonors as many marriages as it graces and honors. We have not only surrendered to cultural mandates such as primacy, need fulfillment, and intimacy, but accentuated them further by sacralizing them. It is no wonder that we then suffer from lack of transparency about the real state of our marriages, and that this lack of transparency exacerbates the problems of marriage. We need more, and more honest conversations about the empirical realities of Christian marriage, not the philosophical ideals of Christian marriage,[12] recognizing that mutual, collective problems require mutual, collective solutions. We need less moralizing and more mercy.

Gaining freedom *from* tyrannical marital ideals, we may also then gain freedom *for* marriage to become useful for something beyond itself. It is bewildering to hear the family extolled time and again as the cornerstone of society, when the form of family practiced in Western culture stands so completely apart from society, turned inward on itself. If self-transcendence, not self-realization, is the highest achievement of a person, then marital transcendence, not marital realization, is the highest achievement of a marriage. Self-absorption is as self-defeating in marriage as in individuals. Many narcissistic Christian marriages need to be told flatly to "Get over yourself; it's not all about you." Turning outward contributes to the health of both a marriage and its community, yet such emphasis has been painfully lacking in the evangelical subculture. Christian marriage needs a better balance between attending to the internal needs of its constituents and the external needs of its community. If marriages cared more for their community, perhaps communities would care more for their marriages.

Finally, we need more marital love that is not silent and passive, but speaks and acts what it thinks and feels, love that is not just lodged safely in hearts and minds, but is expressed riskily in open communication and active caring. We need more generous marital love that does not calculate equity or reciprocity. We need more consistent practice of basic Christian virtues toward each other, more fruit of the Spirit—love, joy, peace, patience, kindness, goodness, faithfulness, gentleness, and self-control (Gal 5:22–23). Biblically and relationally, there is relatively little that is unique to marriage relationships, and we are unwise to make of marriage such a wholly other state of being. Perhaps therein lies the error of asking what the supreme or ultimate goal of marriage is. Perhaps that is the wrong question, no more useful than the question of the "chief end of man," because marriage is just another state of being human. Do we as readily or usefully inquire about the supreme or ultimate goal of being single? Both are simply stations or locations in life; neither are primarily a means to an end. Other than sex and childrearing, marriage does not call for a radically separate Christian agenda.

---

12. Characteristically, Marx put it rather colorfully: "Philosophy stands in the same relation to the study of the actual world as masturbation to sexual love" (*German Ideology*, 103).

FINAL THOUGHTS

In their update of trends in American marriage in the new century and millennium, Amato and his colleagues[13] explicated two major competing perspectives in social-scientific literature on marriage: marital decline[14] and marital resilience.[15] They trace the evolution of marriage from what Burgess termed "institutional marriage"[16] at the beginning of the twentieth century, to "companionate marriage" at mid-century, to what Cherlin termed "individualistic marriage"[17] at the end of the century. Their own description of marriage at the outset of this century is "alone together," which they locate on middle ground between marital decline and marital resilience. Based on their extensive data analysis, they conclude that "It remains an open question whether marital quality has improved, declined, or remained constant in recent decades."[18] More to our point here, "marriage is an adaptable institution, and in accommodating the vast changes that have occurred in society over the recent past, it has become a less cohesive, yet less confining arrangement."[19]

Christian faith has itself been forced to accommodate to the vast changes in modern Western society, quite apart from and beyond what Christians may think about marriage. Modernity has forced religion as a social institution to disengage from other social institutions, to compete for authority and legitimacy in a pluralistic world, to become ever more rational in response to science, and to accept relegation to the private realm of life.[20] Modern Christians hold beliefs, whereas premodern Christians were held by beliefs.[21] In debates about secularization, some argue that the chosen beliefs of modernity are more tenuous, whereas the given beliefs of premodernity were more secure.[22] Others argue that now choosing our beliefs makes them more meaningful and valuable to us.[23] The same could be said for our cultural values; it is one thing to actively hold them, and another

13. Amato et al., *Alone Together*.

14. See for example Wilson, *Marriage Problem*.

15. See for example Coontz, *Marriage, a History*.

16. Burgess, Locke, and Thomes, *Family*.

17. Cherlin, "Deinstitutionalization of American Marriage."

18. Amato et al., *Alone Together*, 32.

19. Ibid., back cover.

20. McGuire, *Religion*.

21. Geertz, *Interpretation of Cultures*. One effect has been the rise of modern apologetics.

22. See for example Berger, *Sacred Canopy*.

23. See for example Bellah, *Beyond Belief*.

to be passively held by them, never having pondered them or their alternatives. And yes, the same could be said for marriage; it is one thing to hold a marital relationship, quite another to be held by a marital relationship. Who is to say that perceiving no choice in the character and permanence of marriage is a qualitatively superior condition and experience than perceiving choice? Perhaps choosing anew every morning increases the meaning and value of marriage, and our inclination to nurture the relationship in all circumstances, thereby developing virtue greater than dogged duty. Perhaps what is decline in some forms and by some measures is resilience in other forms and by other measures.

Nevertheless, most evangelicals evidently hold to the marital decline perspective, and their professionals have responded by generating multifarious marriage intervention programs, social-scientific "techniques" that are themselves products of modern Western culture.[24] For example, in the relentless push of cultural globalization, an award-winning *Intimate Marriage Curriculum Kit*[25] has been prepared for potential export from the Global North to the puzzled but compliant Global South. But positing decline requires some historico-cultural point of reference, and it remains unclear what that point should be. What is clear, however, is that marriage is resilient, having adapted to all cultures, which in turn have informed the Christian understandings of marriage within them. If our analysis here has held any merit, it is equally clear that cultural mandates of marriage have not just informed contemporary Western Christian understandings of marriage, but that we have thrown ourselves into the arms of culture, passionately embraced it, and sweetly surrendered.

If culture is not the lover itself, then it is at least the bed of lovers. As a social construction, it is impossible to keep the marriage bed pure (Heb 13:4), just as it is impossible to disembed marriage from culture. Therefore a confrontational Christ against culture approach that simply condemns culture and attempts complete withdrawal is both naïve and unhelpful. Yet as we lie in the bed we have made, we best not rest easy or fall asleep in a cozy Christ of culture manner that simply legitimizes, copies, or consumes culture. Christian marriages are best served by being taught to be restless with their culture, first and at least in their thinking, not by being taught to conform more closely to their culture. They are best served by living collaboratively in the creative tensions of a Christian community that transforms

---

24. The classic analysis here is that of the French Christian sociologist and theologian Jacques Ellul in *The Technological Society*.

25. Allender and Longman, *Intimate Marriage Curriculum Kit*.

culture as much as possible, or creates and cultivates a new subculture where necessary and possible.

Christians should be given the quintessential themes of the biblical text pertinent to marriage and a parsimonious theology of marriage—no less, but no more—filtered as vigorously as possible for cultural biases. The biblical text is not a detailed marriage manual. It is a mysterious love story, and love does not yield gracefully to formula. Christian marriages should then be given the freedom to write their own love story, letting it play out as it will relative to their culture, because the biblical imperative is to love fully—no less, but no more. In sum, Christians would benefit from looser, more graceful and inclusive definitions of successful marriage. The current tighter cultural definitions are excessively restrictive, anxiety producing, and counterproductive for average Christians, the large majority of whom are tormented by the ideals that tyrannize them, and by the all-too-common disjunction between image and experience. In the end, we do not help marriages by tightening the screws or raising the bar, just as we do not help by softening the bed and making it more inviting. That only places more marriages at risk. Only by gaining greater cultural awareness can Christian marriages remain proportionally pure and free to celebrate love and life.

Bibliography

Acevedo, Bianica P., and Arthur Aron. "Does a Long-Term Relationship Kill Romantic Love?" *Review of General Psychology* 13/1 (March 2009) 59–65.

Adams, Bert N. *The Family: A Sociological Interpretation.* 5th ed. Fort Worth, TX: Harcourt Brace, 1995.

Allen, Charlotte. "The Patriarchal Bargain." *First Things* (March 2005) 41–43. Online: http://www.firstthings.com/article/2007/01/the-patriarchal-bargain-24.

Allender, Dan B., and Tremper Longman III. *Intimate Allies.* Wheaton, IL: Tyndale House, 1995.

———. *Intimate Marriage Curriculum Kit.* Downers Grove, IL: InterVarsity, 2006.

Amato, Paul R., Alan Booth, David R. Johnson, and Stacy J. Rogers. *Alone Together: How Marriage in America Is Changing.* Cambridge, MA: Harvard University Press, 2007.

Ambert, Anne-Marie. *Changing Families: Relationships in Context.* 2nd Canadian ed. Toronto: Pearson Canada, 2012.

Anderson, Ray S., and Dennis B. Guernsey. *On Being Family: A Social Theology of the Family.* Grand Rapids: Eerdmans, 1985.

Atwood, Margaret. "On the Streets, Love." In *The Circle Game*, 24–25. 3rd ed. Toronto: Anansi, 1978.

Bailey, Beth L. *From Front Porch to Back Seat: Courtship in Twentieth-Century America.* Baltimore: Johns Hopkins University Press, 1989.

Balch, David L., and Carolyn Osiek, editors. *Early Christian Families in Context: An Interdisciplinary Dialogue.* Grand Rapids: Eerdmans, 2003.

Balswick, Jack O. "The Psychological Captivity of Evangelicalism." In *Religious Sociology: Interfaces and Boundaries*, edited by William H. Swatos, 141–52. New York: Greenwood, 1987.

Balswick, Jack O., and Judith K. Balswick. *The Family: A Christian Perspective on the Contemporary Home.* 3rd ed. Grand Rapids: Baker, 2007.

———. *A Model for Marriage: Covenant, Grace, Empowerment, and Intimacy.* Downers Grove, IL: IVP Academic, 2006.

Balswick, Jack O., Pamela King, and Kevin Reimer. *The Reciprocating Self: A Theological Model of Human Development.* Downers Grove, IL: InterVarsity, 2005.

Barna Group. "New Marriage and Divorce Statistics Released." March 31, 2008. Online: http://www.barna.org/family-kids-articles/42-new-marriage-and-divorce-statistics-released.

Bibliography

Beaty, Katelyn. "Girl Meets Grace: Lauren Winner's New Reflection on Her Divorce and Desolation." *Christianity Today*, January 23, 2012. Online: http://www.christianitytoday.com/ct/2012/january/review-still-lauren-winner.html.

Beck, Ulrich, and Elisabeth Beck-Gernsheim. "Families in a Runaway World." In *The Blackwell Companion to the Sociology of Families*, edited by Jacqueline Scott, Judith Treas, and Martin Richards, 499–514. Malden, MA: Blackwell, 2007.

Bell, Rob. *Sex God: Exploring the Endless Connections between Sexuality and Spirituality*. Grand Rapids: Zondervan, 2007.

Bellah, Robert N. *Beyond Belief: Essays on Religion in a Post-Traditionalist World*. Berkeley: University of California Press, 1991.

Bellah, Robert N., Richard Madsen, William M. Sullivan, Ann Swidler, and Steven M. Tipton. *Habits of the Heart: Individualism and Commitment in American Life*. New York: Harper & Row, 1985.

Berger, Bridgette, and Peter L. Berger. *The War Over the Family: Capturing the Middle Ground*. Garden City, NY: Doubleday/Anchor, 1983.

Berger, Peter L. *The Sacred Canopy: Elements of a Sociological Theory of Religion*. Garden City, NY: Doubleday, 1967.

———, and Thomas Luckmann. *The Social Construction of Reality: A Treatise in the Sociology of Knowledge*. Garden City, NY: Doubleday, 1966.

Bisagno, John R. *Love Is Something You Do*. Houston: Lucid, 2010.

Block, Daniel Isaac. "Marriage and Family in Ancient Israel." In *Marriage and Family in the Biblical World*, edited by Ken. M. Campbell, 33–102. Downers Grove, IL: InterVarsity, 2003.

Blood, R. O., Jr., and D. M. Wolfe. *Husbands and Wives: Dynamics of Married Living*. New York: Free Press, 1960.

Bohannan, P. *Divorce and After: An Analysis of the Emotional and Social Problems of Divorce*. Garden City, NY: Anchor, 1970.

Boulton, Elizabeth Myer, and Matthew Myer Boulton. "Sacramental Sex: Divine Love and Human Intimacy." *Christian Century* 128/6 (2011) 28.

Bouma-Prediger, Steven, and Brian Walsh. *Beyond Homelessness: Christian Faith in a Culture of Displacement*. Grand Rapids: Eerdmans, 2008.

Brennan, Dan. *Sacred Unions, Sacred Passions: Engaging the Mystery of Friendship between Men and Women*. Elgin, IL: Faith Dance, 2010.

Browning, Don. S. *Marriage and Modernization: How Globalization Threatens Marriage and What to Do About It*. Grand Rapids: Eerdmans, 2003.

Brueggemann, Walter. *The Covenanted Self: Explorations in Law and Covenant*. Minneapolis: Fortress, 1999.

Burge, Christopher L., and Pamela Toussaint. *His Rules: God's Practical Road Map for Becoming and Attracting Mr. or Mrs. Right*. Colorado Springs: Waterbrook, 2005.

Burgess, Ernest W., Harvey J. Locke, and Mary Margaret Thomes, *The Family: From Institution to Companionship*. New York: American Book Co., 1963.

Butcher, Andy. "'Father' of Christian Marriage Ministries Says He Plans to Divorce." *Charisma and Christian Life*, March 27, 2002, 22–26.

Campbell, Ken M., editor. *Marriage and Family in the Biblical World*. Downers Grove, IL: InterVarsity, 2003.

Carter, Craig A. *Rethinking Christ and Culture: A Post-Christendom Perspective*. Grand Rapids: Brazos, 2006.

Celello, Kristin. *Making Marriage Work: A History of Marriage and Divorce in Twentieth-Century United States*. Chapel Hill: University of North Carolina Press, 2012.

Chapman, Gary. *Covenant Marriage: Building Communication and Intimacy*. Nashville: Broadman and Holman, 2003.

———. *The Five Love Languages: The Secret to Love that Lasts*. Chicago: Moody, 2009.

Charles, Tyler. "(Almost) Everyone's Doing It." *Relevant Magazine*, September/October 2011, 65–69. Online: http://www.relevantmagazine.com/life/relationships/almost-everyones-doing-it.

Charon, Joel M. *Ten Questions: A Sociological Perspective*. 6th ed. Belmont, CA: Wadsworth, 2006.

Cherlin, Andrew. "The Deinstitutionalization of American Marriage." *Journal of Marriage and Family* 66 (2004) 848–61.

Cianci, R., and P. A. Gambrel. "Maslow's Hierarchy of Needs: Does It Apply in a Collectivist Culture?" *Journal of Applied Management and Entrepreneurship* 8/2 (2003) 143–61.

Clapp, Rodney. *Families at the Crossroads: Beyond Traditional and Modern Options*. Downers Grove, IL: InterVarsity, 2006.

———. "From Family Values to Family Virtues." In *Border Crossings: Christian Trespasses on Popular Culture and Public Affairs*, 110–25. Grand Rapids: Brazos, 2000.

Clark, Jeramy. *I Gave Dating a Chance: A Biblical Perspective to Balance the Extremes*. Colorado Springs: Waterbrook, 2000.

Clinton, Hillary Rodham. *It Takes a Village: And Other Lessons Children Teach Us*. New York: Simon & Schuster, 1996.

Colton, Helen. *The Gift of Touch: How Physical Contact Improves Communication, Pleasure, and Health*. New York: Putnam, 1983.

Coontz, Stephanie. *Marriage, a History: From Obedience to Intimacy, or How Love Conquered Marriage*. New York: Viking, 2005.

Covington, Dennis, and Vicki Covington. *Cleaving: The Story of a Marriage*. New York: North Point, 1999.

Cowen-Fletcher, Jane. *It Takes a Village*. New York: Scholastic, 1995.

Crabb, Larry J. *Basic Principles of Biblical Counseling*. Grand Rapids: Zondervan, 1975.

———. *Effective Biblical Counseling*. Grand Rapids: Zondervan, 1977.

———. *The Marriage Builder: A Blueprint for Couples and Counselors*. Grand Rapids: Zondervan, 1992.

———. *Men and Women: Enjoying the Difference*. Grand Rapids: Zondervan, 1991.

———. *Understanding People: Why We Long for Relationship*. Grand Rapids: Zondervan, 1987.

Croft, Scott. "Biblical Dating: How It's Different from Modern Dating." *Boundless*, March 23, 2012. Online: http://www.boundless.org/2005/articles/a0001401.cfm.

Crouch, Andy. *Culture Making: Recovering Our Creative Calling*. Downers Grove, IL: InterVarsity, 2008.

Crow, Graham, and Catherine Maclean. "Families and Local Communities." In *The Blackwell Companion to the Sociology of Families*, edited by Jacqueline Scott, Judith Treas, and Martin Richards, 69–83. Malden, MA: Blackwell, 2007.

Curtis, Brent, and John Eldredge. *The Sacred Romance: Drawing Closer to the Heart of God*. Nashville: T. Nelson, 1997.

Danesi, Marcel. *The Encyclopedic Dictionary of Semiotics, Media, and Communication.* Toronto: University of Toronto Press, 2000.

Davis, Rebecca L. *More Perfect Unions: The American Search for Marital Bliss.* Cambridge, MA: Harvard University Press, 2010.

Dean, Kenda Creasy. *Practicing Passion: Youth and the Quest for a Passionate Church.* Grand Rapids: Eerdmans, 2004.

DeRogatis, Amy. "What Would Jesus Do?: Sexuality and Salvation in Protestant Sex Manuals," *Church History* 74/1 (2005) 97–137.

Dick, Kirby, and Amy Ziering, directors. *Derrida.* Jane Doe Films, 2002.

DiMarco, Hayley, and Michael DiMarco. *Marriable: Taking the Desperate Out of Dating.* Grand Rapids: Revell, 2005.

Dobson, James. *What Wives Wish Their Husbands Knew about Women.* Wheaton, IL: Tyndale House, 1975.

Doriani, D. "The Puritans, Sex, and Pleasure." In *Christian Perspectives on Sexuality and Gender*, edited by A. Thatcher and E. Stuart, 33–51. Grand Rapids: Eerdmans, 1999.

Doyle, Laura. *The Surrendered Wife: A Practical Guide to Finding Intimacy, Passion, and Peace with a Man.* New York: Fireside, 2001.

————. *The Surrendered Wife: A Woman's Spiritual Guide to True Intimacy with a Man.* Costa Mesa, CA: St. Monday, 2000.

Drigotas, S. M., and C. E. Rusbult. "Should I Stay or Should I Go?: An Interdependence Model of Break-Ups." *Journal of Personality and Social Psychology* 62 (1992) 62–87.

Driscoll, Mark, and Grace Driscoll. *Real Marriage: The Truth about Sex, Friendship, and Life Together.* Nashville: T. Nelson, 2012.

Dunker, Marilee P. *Days of Glory, Seasons of Night.* Grand Rapids: Zondervan, 1984.

Durkheim, Emile. *The Division of Labor in Society.* 1895. Reprint. New York: Free Press, 1964.

Eagar, Rob. *Dating with Pure Passion: More than Rules, More than Courtship, More than a Formula.* Eugene, OR: Harvest House, 2005.

Edwards, Keith J. "It Takes a Village to Save a Marriage." *Journal of Psychology and Theology* 31/3 (2003) 188–95.

Egan, R. Danielle, and Stephen D. Papson. "You Either Get It or You Don't: Conversion Experiences and *The Dr. Phil Show.*" *Journal of Religion and Popular Culture* 10 (Summer 2005). Online: http://www.usask.ca/relst/jrpc/art10-drphil-print.html.

Eldredge, John. *Wild at Heart: Discovering the Secret of a Man's Soul.* Nashville: T. Nelson, 2010.

Eliot, T. S. *Murder in the Cathedral.* New York: Harcourt Brace Jovanovich, 1963.

Ellul, Jacques. *The Technological Society.* Translated by John Wilkinson. New York: Vintage, 1964.

Emerson, Richard M. "Power-Dependence Relations." In *Social Theory: Roots and Branches*, edited by Peter Kivisto, 304–15. New York: Oxford University Press, 2008.

England, Paula. "The Decline of the Date and the Rise of the College Hook Up." In *Family in Transition*, edited by Arlene S. Skolnick and Jerome H. Skolnick, 151–62. 14th ed. Boston: Allyn & Bacon, 2006.

Erikson, Erik. *Childhood and Society.* New York: Norton, 1993.

Evans, Rachel Held. *A Year of Biblical Womanhood: How a Liberated Woman Found Herself Sitting on Her Roof, Covering Her Head, and Calling Her Husband Master.* Nashville: T. Nelson, 2012.

Farrel, Bill, and Pam Farrel. *Men Are Like Waffles, Women Are Like Spaghetti: Understanding and Delighting in Your Differences.* Eugene, OR: Harvest House, 2007.

Fay, L. "Turning Down the Temperature: Handling One of Marriage's Most Explosive Crises." *The Family Therapy Networker* 18 (1994) 83–90.

"Featured Filmmaker: Alex Kendrick." November 20, 2006. Online: http://www. christiancinema.com/catalog/newsdesk_info.php?newsdesk_id=279.

Fein, Ellen, and Sherrie Schneider. *All the Rules: Time-Tested Secrets for Capturing the Heart of Mr. Right.* New York: Warner, 2007.

———. *The Rules: Time-Tested Secrets for Capturing the Heart of Mr. Right.* New York: Warner, 1995.

Fischer, Robert B. *God Did It, But How?* 2nd ed. Ipswich, MA: American Scientific Affiliation, 1997.

Fishburn, Janet. *Confronting the Idolatry of Family: A New Vision for the Household of God.* Nashville: Abingdon, 1991.

Foucault, Michel. *The History of Sexuality.* Vol. 1, *An Introduction.* New York: Vintage, 1980.

Fowler, Marian. *In a Gilded Cage.* Toronto: Vintage, 1993.

French, Marilyn. *Beyond Power: On Women, Men, and Morals.* London: Abacus, 1988.

Friedan, Betty. *The Feminine Mystique.* New York: Norton, 1963.

Gaede, S. D. *Where Gods May Dwell: On Understanding the Human Condition.* Grand Rapids: Zondervan, 1985.

Gallagher, Sally K. *Evangelical Identity and Gendered Family Life.* Newark: Rutgers University Press, 2003.

Gardella, Peter. *Innocent Ecstasy: How Christianity Gave America an Ethic of Sexual Pleasure.* New York: Oxford University Press, 1985.

Garland, David E., and Diana R. Garland. *Flawed Families of the Bible: How God's Grace Works Through Imperfect Relationships.* Grand Rapids, Brazos, 2007.

Gecas, Viktor, and Peter J. Burke, "Self and Identity." In *Sociological Perspectives on Social Psychology,* edited by Karen S. Cook, Gary Allan Fine, and James S. House, 41–67. Toronto: Allyn and Bacon, 1995.

Geertz, Clifford. *The Interpretation of Cultures: Selected Essays.* New York: Basic Books, 1973.

———. *Local Knowledge: Further Essays in Interpretive Anthropology.* New York: Basic Books, 1983.

George, Rosemary. *The Politics of Home: Postcolonial Relocations and Twentieth-Century Fiction.* Cambridge: Cambridge University Press, 1996.

Gibran, Kahlil. *The Prophet.* 1926. Reprint. Middlesex, UK: Senate, 2002.

Giddens, Anthony. *Modernity and Self-Identity: Self and Society in the Late Modern Age.* Stanford, CA: Stanford University Press, 1991.

———. *The Transformation of Intimacy: Sexuality, Love, and Eroticism in Modern Societies.* Stanford, CA: Stanford University Press, 1992.

Gilder, George F. *Sexual Suicide.* San Antonio: Quadrangle, 1973.

Gillis, John R. *A World of Their Own Making: Myth, Ritual, and the Quest for Family Values.* New York: Basic Books, 1996.

Goode, William J. *World Revolution and Family Patterns.* New York: Free Press, 1970.

Gottman, John M. *What Predicts Divorce: The Relationship Between Marital Processes and Marital Outcomes.* Hillsdale, NJ: Erlbaum, 1994.

Gottman, John M., James D. Murray, Catherine C. Swanson, Rebecca Tyson, and Kristin R. Swanson. *The Mathematics of Marriage: Dynamic Non-Linear Models*. Cambridge, MA: Bradford, 2005.

Goudzwaard, Bob. *Idols of Our Time*. Downers Grove, IL: InterVarsity, 1984.

Graham, Ruth. "Needed: Incompatibility." *Christianity Today* 25/16, September 1981.

Gray, John. *Men are from Mars, Women are from Venus: A Practical Guide for Improving Communication and Getting What You Want in Your Relationships*. New York: Harper Collins, 1992.

Greenwald, Rachel. *Find a Husband After 35: Using What I Learned at Harvard Business School*. New York: Ballantine, 2004.

Grossman, Jennifer. "Anarchy in Eros: Where the Men Went." *American Spectator* June/July 2003, 56–58.

Grudem, Wayne. *Biblical Foundations for Manhood and Womanhood*. Wheaton, IL: Crossway, 2002.

Gudorf, Christine. "The Graceful Pleasures: Why Sex Is Good for Marriage." In *Human Sexuality in the Catholic Tradition*, edited by Kieran Scott and Harold Daly Horell, 123–36. Lanham, MD: Rowman & Littlefield, 2007.

Guinness, Os. "Fathers and Sons: On Francis Schaeffer, Frank Schaeffer, and *Crazy for God*." *Books & Culture* 14/2 (March/April 2008) 32–34.

Gungor, Mark. *Laugh Your Way to a Better Marriage*. DVD. Laugh Your Way America, 2008.

Gushee, David P. "A Crumbling Institution: How Social Revolutions Cracked the Pillars of Marriage." *Christianity Today*, September 1, 2004, 42–45. Online: http://www.christianitytoday.com/ct/2004/september/14.42.html.

———. *Getting Marriage Right: Realistic Counsel for Saving and Strengthening Relationships*. Grand Rapids: Baker, 2004.

Habermas, Jürgen. *Knowledge and Human Interests*. Boston: Beacon, 1971.

Hamon, Reann R. "Social Exchange Theory and the Christian Faith: Is a Satisfactory Marriage Possible?" *Journal of Psychology and Christianity* 18/1 (1999) 19–27.

Hamon, Raeann R., and Bron B. Ingoldsby, editors. *Mate Selection Across Cultures*. Thousand Oaks, CA: Sage, 2003.

Harley, Willard F. *His Needs, Her Needs: Building an Affair-Proof Marriage*. Rev. ed. Grand Rapids: Revell, 2011.

Harris, Joshua. *Boy Meets Girl: Say Hello to Courtship*. Sisters, OR: Multnomah, 2000.

———. *I Kissed Dating Goodbye: A New Attitude toward Relationships and Romance*. Sisters, OR: Multnomah, 1997.

Heggen, Carolyn Holderread. *Sexual Abuse in Christian Homes and Churches*. Scottdale, PA: Herald, 1993.

Hess, Richard S., and M. Danny Carroll R., editors. *Family in the Bible: Exploring Customs, Culture, and Context*. Grand Rapids: Baker, 2003.

Hiebert, Dennis W. "Toward Adult Cross-Sex Friendship." *Journal of Psychology and Theology* 24/4 (1996) 271–83.

———. "Toward a Post-Postmodern Christian Concept of Self." *Didaskalia* 16 (2004) 1–24.

Hiebert, Paul G. *Anthropological Insights for Missionaries*. Grand Rapids: Baker, 1985.

Hrdy, Sarah Blaffer. *Mother Nature: Maternal Instincts and How They Shape the Human Species*. New York: Ballantine, 1999.

Hochschild, Arlie Russell. *The Managed Heart: Commercialization of Human Feeling.* Berkeley: University of California Press, 2004.

Horney, Karen. "The Problem of the Monogamous Ideal." In *Feminine Psychology.* New York: Norton, 1993.

House, H. Wayne, editor. *Divorce and Remarriage: Four Christian Views.* Downers Grove, IL: InterVarsity, 1990.

Hugo, Victor. *Les Misérables.* Translated by Norman Denny. London: Penguin, 1982.

Huitt, W. "Maslow's Hierarchy of Needs." *Educational Psychology Interactive.* Valdosta State University, 2007. Online: http://www.edpsycinteractive.org/topics/conation/maslow.html.

Hull, C. L. *Principles of Behavior: An Introduction to Behavior Theory.* New York: Appleton-Century-Crofts, 1943.

Hunter, James Davison. *Culture Wars: The Struggle to Control the Family, Art, Education, Law, and Politics in America.* New York: Basic Books, 1992.

————. *To Change the World: The Irony, Tragedy, and Possibility of Christianity in the Late Modern World.* New York: Oxford University Press, 2010.

Hunter, James Davison, and Alan Wolfe. *Is There a Culture War?: A Dialogue on Values and American Public Life.* Washington: Brookings Institution Press, 2006.

Hurley, James B. *Man and Woman in Biblical Perspective.* Grand Rapids: Zondervan, 1981.

Ingoldsby, Bron B. "Mate Selection and Marriage." In *Families in Multicultural Perspective,* edited by Bron B. Ingoldsby and Suzanna Smith, 143–45. New York: Guilford, 1995.

Instone-Brewer, David. *Divorce and Remarriage in the Bible: The Social and Literary Context.* Grand Rapids: William B. Eerdmans, 2002.

————. *Divorce and Remarriage in the Church: Biblical Solutions for Pastoral Realities.* Downers Grove, IL: InterVarsity, 2006.

————. "What God Has Joined." *Christianity Today,* October 5, 2007, 26–29. Online: http://www.christianitytoday.com/ct/2007/october/20.26.html.

Jackson, Davil W., Jr., and Raymond W. Turner. *God's Blueprint for Building Marital Intimacy: Transforming a House of Sex into a Home of Intimacy.* Bloomington, IN: Writer's Club, 2000.

Jackson, Robert Max. *Destined for Equality: The Inevitable Rise of Women's Status.* Cambridge, MA: Harvard University Press, 2010.

Jacobs, A. J. *The Year of Living Biblically: One Man's Humble Quest to Follow the Bible as Literally as Possible.* New York: Simon & Schuster, 2008.

Jacobs, John. *All You Need Is Love and Other Lies about Marriage.* New York: HarperCollins, 2004.

James, E. L. *Fifty Shades of Grey: Book One of the Fifty Shades Trilogy.* New York: Vintage, 2012.

John Paul II, Pope. *The Theology of the Body: Human Love in the Divine Plan.* Boston: Pauline, 1997.

Johnson, Michael P. "Patriarchal Terrorism and Common Couple Violence: Two Forms of Violence Against Women." *Journal of Marriage and the Family* 5/2 (1995) 283–94.

Johnston, Robert K. *The Christian at Play.* Grand Rapids: Eerdmans, 1983.

Joseph, Rajani. *Marriage as a Covenant Relationship: A Biblical Perspective.* Saarbrücken, Germany: VDM, 2008.

Keller, Tim. *Counterfeit Gods: The Empty Promises of Money, Sex, and Power, and the Only Hope that Matters.* New York: Dutton, 2009.

———. *The Meaning of Marriage: Facing the Complexities of Commitment with the Wisdom of God.* London: Hodder & Stoughton, 2011.

Kelly, Matthew. *The Seven Levels of Intimacy: The Art of Loving and the Joy of Being Loved.* New York: Fireside, 2007.

Kendrick, Stephen, and Alex Kendrick. *The Love Dare.* Nashville: Broadman and Holman, 2008.

Kenrick, D. T., V. Griskevicius, S. L. Neuberg, and M. Schaller. "Renovating the Pyramid of Needs: Contemporary Extensions Built upon Ancient Foundations." *Perspectives on Psychological Science* 5 (2010). Online: http://www.csom.umn.edu/assets/144040.pdf.

Kern, Jan. *Seduced by Sex, Saved by Love: A Journey Out of False Intimacy.* Cincinnati: Standard, 2008.

Kersten, Karen K., and Lawrence K. Kersten. *Marriage and the Family: Studying Close Relationships.* New York: Harper & Row, 1988.

Kostenberger, Andreas J., and David W. Jones. *God, Marriage, and Family: Rebuilding the Biblical Foundation.* 2nd ed. Wheaton, IL: Crossway, 2010.

Kroeger, Catherine Clark, and Nancy Nason-Clark. *No Place for Abuse: Biblical and Practical Resources to Counteract Domestic Violence.* Downers Grove, IL: InterVarsity, 2010.

Kubler-Ross, Elizabeth. *On Death and Dying.* New York: Macmillan, 1969.

Kuehne, Dale S. *Sex and the iWorld: Rethinking Relationships beyond an Age of Individualism.* Grand Rapids: Baker Academic, 2009.

Lasch, Christopher. *The Culture of Narcissism: American Life in an Age of Diminishing Expectations.* New York: Norton, 1979.

———. *Haven in a Heartless World: The Family Besieged.* New York: Basic Books, 1979.

Laurenceau, Jean-Philippe, Lisa Feldman Barrett, and Michael J. Rovine. "The Interpersonal Process Model of Intimacy in Marriage: A Daily-Diary and Multilevel Approach." *Journal of Family Psychology* 19 (2005) 314–23.

Lavenda, Robert H., and Emily A. Schultz. *Anthropology: What Does It Mean to Be Human?* New York: Oxford University Press, 2008.

Lee, Cameron. *Beyond Family Values: A Call to Christian Virtue.* Downers Grove, IL: InterVarsity, 1998.

Lee, John A. "A Typology of Styles of Loving." *Personality and Social Psychology Bulletin* 3 (1977) 173–82.

Leslie, Barri, and Mandy Morgan. "Soulmates, Compatibility, and Intimacy: Allied Discursive Resources in the Struggle for Relationship Satisfaction in the New Millennium." *New Ideas in Psychology* 29 (2011) 10–23.

Lester, Andrew D., and Judith L. Lester. *It Takes Two: The Joy of Intimate Marriage.* Louisville: Westminster John Knox, 1998.

Levant, R. F., and G. R. Brooks. *Men and Sex: New Psychological Perspectives.* Mississauga: Wiley & Sons Canada, 1997.

Levinas, Emmanuel. *Totality and Infinity: An Essay on Exteriority.* Translated by Alphonso Lingis. Pittsburgh: Duquesne University Press, 1969.

Levine, Arthur, and Jeanette S. Cureton. *When Hope and Fear Collide.* San Francisco: Jossey Bass, 1998.

Levy, Ariel. *Female Chauvinist Pigs: Women and the Rise of Raunch Culture*. New York: Free Press, 2005.

Lewis, C. S. *The Four Loves*. London: Fontana, 1960.

Lopata, H. Z. "Friendship: Historical and Theoretical Introduction." In *Friendship in Context*, edited by H. Z. Lopata and D. R. Maines, 1–22. Greenwich, CT: JAI, 1991.

Lukes, Steven. *Individualism*. Oxford: Blackwell, 1984.

Mace, David, and Vera Mace. *The Sacred Fire: Christian Marriage Through the Ages*. Nashville: Abingdon, 1986.

Macionis, John J., and Linda Marie Gerber. *Sociology*. 7th Canadian ed. Toronto: Pearson Canada, 2011.

Maines, Rachel P. *The Technology of Orgasm: "Hysteria", the Vibrator, and Women's Sexual Satisfaction*. Baltimore, MD: Johns Hopkins University Press, 1998.

Maltz, Wendy, "The Maltz Hierarchy of Sexual Interaction." *Sexual Addiction and Compulsivity* 2/1 (1995) 5–18.

Margolis, Jonathan. *O: The Intimate History of the Orgasm*. New York: Arrow, 2005.

Margolis, Maxine L. *True to Her Nature: Changing Advice to American Women*. Chicago: Waveland, 2000.

Marquardt, Elizabeth. *Between Two Worlds: The Inner Lives of Children of Divorce*. New York: Three Rivers, 2006.

Marx, Karl. *The Eighteenth Brumaire of Louis Bonaparte*. 1852. Reprint. New York: International, 1935.

Marx, Karl, and Friedrich Engels. *The German Ideology: Part 1 and Selections from Parts 2 and 3*. Edited by Christopher John Arthur. 1939. Reprint. New York: International, 1970.

Maslow, Abraham H. *Motivation and Personality*. New York: Harper and Row, 1954.

———. "A Theory of Human Motivation," *Psychological Review* 50/4 (1943) 370–96.

Mason, Mike. *The Mystery of Marriage: Meditations on the Miracle*. Sisters, OR: Multnomah, 2001.

Maugans, Jayne E. *Faith Families Then and Now: Examining Judeo-Christian Families' Structures, Roles, and Values*. Victoria: Trafford, 2002.

Max-Neef, Manfred A. *Human Scale Development: Conception, Application and Further Reflections*. New York: Apex, 1991.

McCarthy, John, editor. *The Whole and Divided Self: The Bible and Theological Anthropology*. New York: Crossroad, 1997.

McDaniel, Susan, and Lorne Tepperman. *Close Relations: An Introduction to the Sociology of Families*. 4th ed. Toronto: Pearson Canada, 2011.

McGuire, Meredith B. *Religion: The Social Context*. 5th ed. Chicago: Waveland, 2008.

McMinn, Lisa Graham. *Sexuality and Holy Longing: Embracing Intimacy in a Broken World*. San Francisco: Jossey-Bass, 2004.

Meilaender, Gilbert. "Men and Women—Can We Be Friends?" *First Things* 34 (June/July 1993) 9–14. Online: http://www.firstthings.com/article/2008/09/001-men-and-women-can-we-be-friends-4.

Michener, H. Andrew, John D. Delamater, and Daniel J. Myers. *Social Psychology*. 5th ed. Toronto: Nelson, 2004.

Miles, Carrie A. *The Redemption of Love: Rescuing Marriage and Sexuality from the Economics of a Fallen World*. Grand Rapids: Brazos, 2006.

Miller, Barbara, Penny Van Esterik, and John Van Esterik. *Anthropology*. 4th Canadian ed. Toronto: Pearson Canada, 2010.

Bibliography

Mills, Charles Wright. *The Sociological Imagination*. New York: Oxford University Press, 1959.

Mintz, Sidney W. *Sweetness and Power: The Place of Sugar in World History*. New York: Viking, 1985.

Moore, Russell D. "Pat Robertson Repudiates the Gospel." *Christianity Today*, September 15, 2011. Online: http://www.christianitytoday.com/ct/2011/septemberweb-only/robertson-alzheimers-divorce.html.

Muck, Terry C. "After Selfhood: Constructing the Religious Self in a Post-Self Age." *Journal of the Evangelical Theological Society* 41 (1998) 107–23.

Murray, H.A. *Explorations in Personality*. New York: Oxford University Press, 1938.

Nelson, J. B., and S. P. Longfellow. *Sexuality and the Sacred: Sources for Theological Reflection*. Louisville: Westminster John Knox, 1994.

Nicholi, Armand M. *The Question of God: C.S. Lewis and Sigmund Freud Debate God, Love, Sex, and the Meaning of Life*. Toronto: Free Press, 2003.

Niebuhr, H. Richard. *Christ and Culture*. New York: Harper & Row, 1951.

NIV Couples' Devotional Bible. New rev. ed. Grand Rapids: Zondervan, 2009.

Nock, Steven L., Laura Ann Sanchez, and James D. Wright. *Covenant Marriage: The Movement to Reclaim Tradition in America*. Newark, NJ: Rutgers University Press, 2008.

O'Brien, Susie, and Imre Szeman. *Popular Culture: A User's Guide*. 2nd ed. Toronto: T. Nelson, 2009.

Ogburn, W. F. "The Family and Its Functions." In *Recent Social Trends in the United States*, edited by W. F. Ogburn, 661–708. New York: McGraw-Hill, 1933.

O'Hear, Anthony. "Diana: Queen of Hearts." In *Faking It: Sentimentalization in Modern Society*, edited by Digby C. Anderson and Peter Mullen, 181–90. New York: Penguin, 1998.

Oliver, Gary J., and Carrie E. Oliver. "Marital Anger in Highly Conflicted Couples." *Christian Counselling Today* 12 (2004) 56–58.

Oliver, Mary Anne McPherson. *Conjugal Spirituality*. Kansas City: Sheed & Ward, 1994.

Olthuis, James H. *I Pledge You My Troth: A Christian View of Marriage, Family, Friendship*. New York: Harper & Row, 1975.

———. *Keeping Our Troth: Staying in Love Through the Five Stages of Marriage*. New York: Harper & Row, 1986.

Omoregbe, Joseph. "Is Polygamy Incompatible with Christianity?" *AFER* 21/6 (1979) 363–72.

Oord, Thomas Jay. *Defining Love: A Philosophical, Scientific, and Theological Engagement*. Grand Rapids: Brazos, 2010.

O'Shaughnessy, Michael, and Jane Stadler. *Media and Society*. 5th ed. New York: Oxford University Press, 2012.

Packer, J. I. *Knowing God*. Toronto: Hodder & Stoughton, 1977.

Papp, Lauren M. "Demand-Withdraw Patterns in Marital Conflict in the Home." *Personal Relationships* 16/2 (2009) 285–300.

Paris, Jenell Williams. *The End of Sexual Identity: Why Sex Is Too Important to Define Who We Are*. Downers Grove, IL: InterVarsity, 2011.

Parsons, Talcott. "The American Family: Its Relation to Personality and Social Structure." In *Family, Socialization, and Interaction Process*, edited by Talcott Parsons and Robert F. Bales, 3–33. New York: Free Press, 1955.

Patrick, H., C. R. Knee, A. Canevello, and C. Lonsbary. "The Role of Need Fulfillment in Relationship Functioning and Well-Being: A Self-Determination Theory Perspective." *Journal of Personality and Social Psychology* 92/3 (2007) 434–57.

Perlman, D., and B. Fehr. "The Development of Intimate Relationships." In *Intimate Relationships: Development, Dynamics, and Deterioration*, edited by D. Perlman and S. W. Duck, 13–42. Beverly Hills, CA: Sage, 1987.

Phillips, Adam. *On Flirtation*. Cambridge, MA: Harvard University Press, 2002.

Phillips, Sharon L., and Richard D. Phillips. *Holding Hands, Holding Hearts: Recovering a Biblical View of Christain Dating*. Phillipsburg, NJ: P & R, 2006.

Pierce, Ronald W., Rebecca Merrill Groothuis, and Gordon D. Fee, editors. *Discovering Biblical Equality: Complementarity Without Hierarchy*. 2nd ed. Downers Grove, IL: InterVarsity, 2006.

Piper, John, and Wayne Grudem, editors. *Recovering Biblical Manhood and Womanhood: A Response to Evangelical Feminism*. Westchester, IL: Crossway, 1991.

Pittman, Frank. "Just in Love." *Journal of Marital and Family Therapy* 23 (1997) 309–12.

Pohl, Christine. *Making Room: Recovering Hospitality as a Christian Tradition*. Grand Rapids: Eerdmans, 1999.

Postman, Neil. *Technopoly: The Surrender of Culture to Technology*. New York: Vintage, 1993.

Rader, R. *Breaking Boundaries: Male/Female Friendship in Early Christian Communities*. New York: Paulist, 1983.

Regnerus, Mark D. *Forbidden Fruit: Sex and Religion in the Lives of American Teenagers*. New York: Oxford University Press, 2007.

———. "Sex Economics 101." *Christianity Today*, Februrary 18, 2011, 26–28. Online: http://www.christianitytoday.com/ct/2011/february/sexeconomics.html.

———. "The Case for Early Marriage." *Christianity Today*, July 31, 2009. Online: http://www.christianitytoday.com/ct/2009/august/16.22.html.

Regnerus, Mark, and Jeremy Uecker. *Premarital Sex in America: How Young Americans Meet, Mate, and Think About Marrying*. New York: Oxford University Press, 2011.

Reidmann, Mary Ann, and Agnes Czerwinski Lamanna. *Marriages & Families: Making Choices in a Diverse Society*. 10th ed. Belmont, CA: Thomson/Wadsworth, 2009.

Rilke, Rainer Maria. *Rilke on Love and Other Difficulties*. Edited by John Mood. New York: Norton, 1975.

Ripley, Jennifer S. "Current Issues in Christian Marriage." *Journal of Psychology and Theology* 31/3 (2003) 175–78.

Ritzer, George. *Sociological Theory*. 8th ed. New York: McGraw-Hill Ryerson, 2010.

Rolheiser, Ron. "Ultimately, We All Sleep By Ourselves." *Catholic Herald*, July 24, 1992. Online: http://archive.catholicherald.co.uk/article/24th-july-1992/10/ultimately-we-all-sleep-by-ourselves.

Rosenau, Douglas E. *A Celebration of Sex: A Guide for Enjoying God's Gift of Married Sexual Pleasure*. Nashville: T. Nelson, 2002.

Rotundo, E. Anthony. *American Manhood: Transformations in Masculinity from the Revolution to the Modern Era*. New York: Basic Books, 1993.

Rubin, Lillian. *Intimate Strangers: Men and Women Together*. New York: Harper & Row, 1983.

Rubin, Zick. *Liking and Loving: An Invitation to Social Psychology*. Boston: Holt, Rinehart & Winston, 1973.

Sanford, Keith. "Perceived Threat and Perceived Neglect: Couples' Underlying Concerns During Conflict." *Psychological Assessment* 22/2 (2010) 288–97.

Santorum, Rick. *It Takes a Family: Conservatism and the Common Good.* Chicago: University of Chicago Press, 2005.

Sapadin, L. A. "Friendship and Gender: Perspectives of Professional Men and Women." *Journal of Social and Personal Relationships* 5 (1988) 65–81.

Scanzoni, Letha D., and John Scanzoni. *Men, Women, and Change: A Sociology of Marriage and Family.* 3rd ed. New York: McGraw-Hill, 1988.

Schaeffer, Edith. *What Is a Family?* New York: Revell, 1975.

Schaeffer, Frank. *Crazy for God: How I Grew Up as One of the Elect, Helped Found the Religious Right, and Lived to Take All (or Almost All) of It Back.* New York: Carroll & Graf, 2007.

———. *Portofino.* New York: Carroll & Graf, 1992.

Segell, Michael. *Standup Guy: Manhood After Feminism.* New York: Villard, 1999.

Sheldon, Charles Monroe. *In His Steps: What Would Jesus Do?* Nashville: Broadman, 1896.

———. *In His Steps Today. What Would Jesus Do in Solving the Problems of Present Political, Economic and Social Life?* New York: Revell, 1921.

Sheler, Jeffery L. *Prophet of Purpose: The Life of Rick Warren.* New York: Doubleday, 2009.

Shumway, David R. *Modern Love: Romance, Intimacy, and the Marriage Crisis.* New York: New York University Press, 2003.

Simmel, Georg. "The Philosophy of Money." In *Social Theory: Roots and Branches*, edited by Peter Kivisto, 130–36. 1907. Reprint. New York: Oxford University Press, 2008.

Singer, Irving. *The Nature of Love.* Vol. 2, *Courtly and Romantic.* Cambridge, MA: MIT Press, 2009.

Smalley, Gary, and John Trent. *Love Is a Decision.* Nashville: T. Nelson, 2001.

Smedes, Lewis B. *Sex for Christians: The Limits and Liberties of Sexual Living.* Rev. ed. Grand Rapids: Eerdmans, 1994.

Smit, Laura. *Loves Me, Loves Me Not: The Ethics of Unrequited Love.* Grand Rapids: Baker Academic, 2005.

Smith, Christian. *The Bible Made Impossible: Why Biblicism Is Not a Truly Evangelical Reading of Scripture.* Grand Rapids: Brazos, 2011.

———. *Moral, Believing Animals: Human Personhood and Culture.* Toronto: Oxford University Press, 2003.

———. *What Is a Person? Rethinking Humanity, Social Life, and the Moral Good from the Person Up.* Chicago: University of Chicago Press, 2010.

Spencer, Aida Besancon, Steve Tracy, and Celestia Tracy. *Marriage at the Crossroads: Couples in Conversation about Discipleship, Gender Roles, Decision-Making, and Intimacy.* Downers Grove, IL: InterVarsity, 2009.

Stafford, Tim. "Can This Institution Be Saved?" *Christianity Today*, November 1, 2004, 52–59. Online: http://www.christianitytoday.com/ct/2004/november/26.52.html.

———. "Imperfect Instrument: World Vision's Founder Led a Tragic and Inspiring Life." *Christianity Today*, February 24, 2005. Online: http://www.christianitytoday.com/ct/2005/march/19.56.html.

Sternberg, R. J. "A Triangular Theory of Love." *Psychological Review* 93 (1986) 119–35.

Stone, Gregory P. "Appearance and the Self: A Slightly Revised Version." In *Social Psychology through Symbolic Interaction*, edited by Gregory P. Stone and Harvey A. Farberman, 141–62. 2nd ed. New York: Macmillian, 1986.

Storey, John. *Cultural Theory and Popular Culture: An Introduction*. 4th ed. Toronto: Pearson Prentice Hall, 2006.

Storkey, Elaine. *The Search for Intimacy*. Grand Rapids: Eerdmans, 1995.

Tannen, Deborah. 1998. "You Just Don't Understand: Women and Men in Conversation." In *Seeing Ourselves: Classic, Contemporary, and Cross-Cultural Readings in Sociology*, edited by J. J. Macionis and N. V. Benokraitis, 110–15. 4th ed. Toronto: Prentice Hall, 1998.

Telushkin, Joseph. *Words that Hurt, Words that Heal: How to Choose Words Wisely and Well*. New York: W. Morrow, 1996.

Tennov, Dorothy. *Love and Limerence: The Experience of Being in Love*. 2nd ed. New York: Stein and Day, 2005.

The Open Bible: New American Standard Version. Nashville: T. Nelson, 1979.

"The Top 50 Books that Have Shaped Evangelicals." *Christianity Today*, October 6, 2006. Online: http://www.christianitytoday.com/ct/2006/october/23.51.html.

Thomas, Gary L. *Sacred Marriage: What If God Designed Marriage to Mak Us Holy More than to Make Us Happy?*. Grand Rapids: Zondervan, 2000.

Toennies, Ferdinand. *Community and Society*. 1887. Reprint. New York: Harper & Row, 1963.

Tolstoy, Leo. *Anna Karenina*. Translated by Richard Pevear and Larissa Volokhonsky. 1877. Reprint. New York: Penguin, 2002.

Trible, Phyllis. *Texts of Terror: Literary-Feminist Readings of Biblical Narratives*. Philadelphia: Fortress, 1984.

Tucker, Ruth A. *From Jerusalem to Irian Jaya: A Biographical History of Christian Missions*. 2nd ed. Grand Rapids: Zondervan, 2004.

———. *Guardians of the Great Commission: The Story of Women in Modern Missions*. Grand Rapids: Zondervan, 1988

Turkle, Sherry. *Alone Together: Why We Expect More from Technology and Less from Each Other*. New York: Basic Books, 2011.

Valenti, Jessica. *The Purity Myth: How America's Obsession with Virginity Is Hurting Young Women*. Berkeley, CA: Seal, 2009.

Van Leeuwen, Mary Stewart. *Gender and Grace: Love, Work, and Parenting in a Changing World*. Downers Grove, IL: InterVarsity, 2006.

Vitz, Paul C. *Psychology as Religion: The Cult of Self-Worship*. 2nd ed. Grand Rapids: Eerdmans, 1995.

Wahba, A, and L. Bridgewell. "Maslow Reconsidered: A Review of Research on the Need Hierarchy Theory." *Organizational Behavior and Human Performance* 15 (1976) 212–40.

Wahlberg, Rachel Conrad. *Jesus According to a Woman*. New York: Paulist, 1975.

Waller, W., and R. Hill. *The Family: A Dynamic Interpretation*. New York: Dryden, 1951.

Wallerstein, Judith S., Sandra Blakeslee, and Julia M. Lewis. *The Unexpected Legacy of Divorce: A 25-Year Landmark Study*. New York: Little, Brown, 2000.

Warren, Neil Clark. *Falling in Love for All the Right Reasons: How to Find Your Soul Mate*. Toronto: Center Street, 2005.

Watson, James, Anne Hill, and Ronald Watson. *Dictionary of Media and Communication Studies*. 8th ed. New York: Bloomsbury, 2012.

Webb, William J. *Slaves, Women, and Homosexuals: Exploring the Hermeneutics of Cultural Analysis*. Downers Grove, IL: InterVarsity, 2001.

Weber, Max. *Economy and Society: An Outline of Interpretive Sociology.* Vol. 1. Berkeley: University of California Press, 1978.

———. *The Protestant Ethic and the Spirit of Capitalism.* Translated by Talcott Parsons. 1905. Reprint. New York: Scribner's, 1958.

Weisman, Carl. *Serious Doubts: Why People Marry When They Know It Won't Last.* Charleston: Booksurge, 2009.

Wheat, Ed, and Gaye Wheat. *Intended for Pleasure.* Old Tappan, NJ: Revell, 1981.

White, James M., and David M. Klein. *Family Theories.* 3rd ed. Thousand Oaks, CA: Sage, 2007.

Whitehead, Barbara Dafoe. *The Divorce Culture: Rethinking Our Commitments to Marriage and Family.* New York: Vintage, 1996.

———. *Why There Are No Good Men Left: The Romantic Plight of the New Single Woman.* New York: Broadway, 2002.

Widmer, Eric. "Couples and Their Networks." In *The Blackwell Companion to the Sociology of Families,* edited by Jacqueline Scott, Judith Treas, and Martin Richards, 356–73. Malden, MA: Blackwell, 2007.

Wilcox, W. Bradford. *Soft Patriarchs, New Men: How Christianity Shapes Fathers and Husbands.* Chicago: University of Chicago Press, 2004.

Wilcox, W. Bradford, and Chuck Donovan. "Marriage: Marginalized in the Middle." *Christianity Today,* December 6, 2010. Online: http://www.christianitytoday.com/ct/2010/decemberweb-only/58–11.0.html.

Wilcox, W. Bradford, and Elizabeth Marquardt, editors. *State of Our Unions 2010: When Marriage Disappears: The New Middle America.* New York: Broadway, 2011.

Wilkinson, Bruce H. *A Biblical Portrait of Marriage.* DVD. Atlanta: Walk Thru the Bible Ministries, 1995.

———. *The Prayer of Jabez: Breaking Through to the Blessed Life.* Sisters, OR: Multnomah, 2000.

Wilson, James Q. *The Marriage Problem: How Our Culture Has Weakened Families.* New York: HarperCollins, 2002.

Wilson, Sandra. *Hurt People Hurt People: Hope and Healing for Yourself and Your Relationships.* Grand Rapids: Discovery House, 2001.

Winner, Lauren F. *Girl Meets God: On the Path to a Spiritual Life.* Chapel Hill: Algonquin, 2002.

———. *Real Sex: The Naked Truth about Chastity.* Grand Rapids: Brazos, 2006.

———. *Still: Notes on a Mid-Faith Crisis.* New York: HarperOne, 2012.

Wirzba, Norman, editor. *The Art of the Commonplace: The Agrarian Essays of Wendell Berry.* Berkeley, CA: Counter Point, 2002.

Witte, John. "Consulting a Living Tradition: Christian Heritage of Marriage and Family." *Christian Century* 113/33 (November 13, 1996) 1108–11.

———. *From Sacrament to Contract: Marriage, Religion, and Law in the Western Tradition.* Louisville: John Knox, 1997.

———. "The Meanings of Marriage." *First Things,* October 2002, 30–41. Online: http://www.firstthings.com/article/2007/01/-the-meanings-of-marriage-21.

Witte, John, and Eliza Ellison. *Covenant Marriage in Comparative Perspective.* Grand Rapids: Eerdmans, 2005.

Wolf, Naomi. *The Beauty Myth: How Images of Female Beauty Are Used against Women.* New York: W. Morrow, 1991.

Wright, Bradley R. E. *Christians Are Hate-Filled Hypocrites . . . and Other Lies You've Been Told: A Sociologist Shatters Myths from the Secular and Christian Media.* Minneapolis: Bethany House, 2010.

Wright, N. T. *Scripture and the Authority of God: How to Read the Bible Today.* New York: HarperCollins, 2011.

———. *Simply Christian: Why Christianity Makes Sense.* New York: HarperOne, 2006.

Wright, P. H. "Men's Friendships, Women's Friendships and the Alleged Inferiority of the Latter." *Sex Roles* 8 (1982) 1–20.

———. "Self-Referent Motivation and the Intrinsic Quality of Friendship." *Journal of Social and Personal Relationships* 1 (1984) 115–30.

Yancey, Philip. "Holy Sex." *Christianity Today*, October 1, 2003. Online: http://www.christianitytoday.com/ct/2003/october/3.46.html.

Young, William P. *The Shack.* Newbury Park, CA: Windblown Media, 2008.

Zelizer, Viviana A. *Pricing the Priceless Child: The Changing Social Value of Children.* Princeton, NJ: Princeton University Press, 1994.

Index

Abimelech, 152
Abital, 33
abolition movement, 20
abortion revolution, 180
Abraham, 22, 32, 136
abstinence industry, 135
Abusive Interaction, in the Maltz
    hierarchy, 145
Accommodation of Yielders, 169
acquaintances, 47
The Act of Marriage (LaHaye), 149
acts of service, 108
Adams, 53–54
addiction, to a drug, 2
adolescence, 119
Adonijah, 33
adulterous woman, of wisdom
    literature, 27
"adverse selectivity" process,
    occurring in cohabitation, 182
affection, 101
affective resources, for a spouse, 160
A-frame codependence, 92
agape, 98, 99, 102
aggravation, exploding into anger, 155
agreement, 163–64
AIDS, fear of, 139
alcoholic families, sexual abuse and
    violence in, 156
alienation, rendering a spouse no
    longer fully present, 155
Allender, 128
Allison, Sadie, 146n42
alone together, 120–23, 220

*Alone Together: How Marriage in
    America Is Changing*, 122
*Alone Together: Why We Expect More
    from Technology and Less from
    Each Other*, 122–23
alternative readings, 9
altruistic love, *agape*, 98
ambilineal descent, 47
American life, individualism in, 186
analogies, proving nothing in
    argument, 73
ancient Israel, mate selection in, 31
Anderson, 114
Anderson, Kerby, 58
androcentricity, 17
"angel of the hearth," 69
anger, 155, 171
annulment, arranging, 175
anorgasmia, 144
antecedents, of marital conflict, 155
antiquity, marriage in, 201
"any cause" divorce, interpretation of,
    179n15
Aristotle, 89, 171
arousal, waning of, 98
arranged marriages
    as historical norm, 35
    matchmaker for, 32
    in premodern societies, 31
    social embeddedness of, 46
    subtypes of, 31n2
"as long as we both shall love," 207
Ashley Madison, online social
    networking site, 134
associates, 47

Astor, Lady, 157n13
asymmetrical relationship, of one
    weak spouse and one strong, 92
"at-one-ment," arriving at, 167
attachment, 101, 163
attraction, potential to become
    disorganizing and pathological,
    102
attribution theory, 190
Atwood, Margaret, 95
Augustine, 95, 147, 201
authentic sexual intimacy, 146, 147
authenticity, as central problem of
    selfhood, 118
authority, 158–59
automobile, effect on custom of
    dating, 37
autonomy needs, 84, 89
Avoidance of Withdrawers, 169

balanced relationships, power existing
    in, 160
Balswick and Balswick, 61, 139, 169,
    203, 209
"bar-gain," learning how to, 163
Barrett-Browning, Robert and
    Elizabeth, 138
bashert, ancient Yiddish word
    meaning "destiny," 127
bathroom disputes, 162
Bathsheba, 33, 152
Bauer, Gary, 58
The Beauty Myth (Wolf), 13
behavioral dimension, to love, 96
being human together, 196–200
being need, 81
Bell, Daniel, 134
Bell, Rob, 147n44
Bellah, Robert, 186–87
Berger and Berger, 68
Berry, Wendell, 54, 56, 188
"best practices," of a culture, 212
Bethuel, 32
Bible, teaching about marriage, 5
biblical construct, marriage as, 8
"biblical dating," concept of, 40n18
biblical hermeneutics, 8, 18
biblical imperative, to love, 222

biblical marital commitment, 209
biblical marriage, 210
A Biblical Portrait of Marriage
    (Wilkinson), 14–15
biblical text
    assuming conflict, 217
    not a detailed marriage manual,
        222
    written in the collectivistic cultural
        milieu, 185
biblicism, 9
The Big Kahuna (movie), 100
bilateral descent, 47
biological factors, of sexuality, 139–40
birth control, 148n49
body, surrendering, 2–3
body oneness, 127
book, overview of this, 5–7
Booth, Catherine, 20
Borg, Sonja, 146n42
Bouma-Prediger, Steven, 56
boundedness, of social networks, 53
brain, as largest sex organ, 144
Brennan, Dan, 91
bridegroom Christ, loving his bride
    the church, 113
brothers, in Christ, 60
brother-sister couples, 21
Brueggermann, Walter, 131

Caleb, 24
Caligula, 136n9
call of God, transcending cultures, 11
calling
    defined, 70
    marriage as primary, 62–77
calling mandate, creative tensions in,
    216
"calling" on a young woman, giving
    her parents extensive control, 37
Calvinist doctrine, of election or
    predestination, 118
Calvinists, distinguishing separate
    callings, 70
candy stores, targeting children, 1
canonization, of Princess Diana, 67

capitalist ethos, everything
commodified and disposable,
188
Carey, Dorothy, 76
Carey, William, 76
caring, 101
Carter, Craig, 212
casual dating, 37
Catholicism, "blanket coverage" of,
118
causes, of divorce, 181
*A Celebration of Sex: A Guide to
Enjoying God's Gift of Married
Sexual Pleasure* (Rosenau),
149n51
celebrities, disregard for solemnity of
marriage, 62
celibacy, 23, 136, 201
celibates, including Jesus and Paul, 83
change, as only constant, 49
Chapman, Gary, 108, 109
chastity, excessive focus on, 13
Chesterton, G. K., 100, 147
children
under care and tutelage of same
household, 66
as an economic liability, 52
children of Israel, organized in
patrilocal extended family
households, 58
Chinese woman, covering her feet,
141
choice, conditions of, 181–85
Christ. *See also* Jesus, transformer of
culture, 211
Christ and Culture (Niebuhr), 211–12
Christian antidote, to extreme
emotional bias of romantic love,
96
The Christian at Play (Johnston),
146n41
Christian conceptions of marriage, 27
Christian conflation, of culture and
the biblical text, 218
Christian function, of the family, 73
Christian interventions, 192–94
Christian intimacy industry, 129–30
Christian marriage. *See also* marriage

diversity across cultures, 24
literature and ministries, 108
reclaiming, 211–22
Christian ode, to intimacy, 116
"Christian perfectionism," 66
Christian premarital sexual practices,
135n6
Christian sex ratio, unbalanced, 193
Christian social text, 10
Christian sociologist, proposing
"market solutions" to premarital
sex, 194
Christian surrender, to culture, 5
Christian talking cure, for couples,
129
Christianity
reducing to a matter of morality,
214
role in Western culture at large, 211
Christians
brothers and sisters to each other in
Christ, 74
democratic movement led largely
by, 20
divorce rates for, 176
embracing personal counseling,
129
embracing sexual pleasure, 148
fed and formed by pop psychology,
92
interpreting marriage problems as
personal, 192
mistaking cultural mandates of
marriage as biblical, 213
modern holding beliefs versus
being held by beliefs, 220
more reluctant to accept same-sex
marriage, 65
non-sexual ways to be promiscuous
Gomers, 27
surrendering to seduction of sex,
135
traditionally favored love as
obligation, 186
Christians for Biblical Equality (CBE),
16–17
chronic aggravation, evolving into
low-grade anger, 155

church
  as bride of Christ, 113
  early, 59
  as social agent, 74
Churchill, Winston, 157n13
clans, 33
Clapp, Rodney, 60, 73, 127
Clark, Jeremy, 43n31
cleanliness codes, Jesus violating, 26
"clear and consistent rules for divorce,
  179
cleaving, 199
Clinton, Hillary Rodham, 57
clitoral orgasm, 143
Cocker, Joe, 103
co-creativity stage, of marriage,
  167–68
codes, for marital love, 107
coffee, engrained in Western culture,
  9–10
cognitive constructs
  determinative of sexuality, 144
  shaping Western culture, 133
cognitive resources, for a spouse, 160
cohabitation, 176, 182
cohabitation revolution, 180
Cohen, Leonard, 104, 122
collaboration, affording verbally
  skilled spouse the advantage, 170
Collaboration of Resolvers, 169, 170
collective interpretation, of reality,
  196
collective life, handling challenges
  of, 30
collective symbols, 12n10
collectivist cultures, 79, 82, 99
"colors of love," 98–99
Colton, Helen, 140
Comfort, Alex, 148
commitment
  contingent on condition of personal
   health and happiness, 207
  good in all three types of, 209
  growing slowly and steadily, 97
  much like *agape*, 99
  to a relationship becoming crucial,
   163

  in Sternberg's triangular theory of
   love, 97
  types of overlapping and
   interplaying, 208
  unilateral (one-way), 204
commitment mandate
  creative tensions in, 218
  in marriage, 195–210
commodification, of culture, 129
"communal manhood," 69
communication
  barriers to, 124–26
  in marriage in other cultures, 114
  as primary vehicle of intimacy, 123
communicator, feelings of inadequacy
  as, 125
community
  belonging to, 57
  different senses of, 55
  disembeddedness from, in
   modernity, 216
  divorce as a failure of, 218
  reconstructing, 61
  senses of, 56
  shared identify, 56
  shared interests, 55
Community and Society (Toennies),
  49n7
community pressure, to stay married,
  175
companionate love, 97, 98
companionate marriage, 164, 220
comparison level, between her ratio
  and his ratio, 189
competence, need for, 84
Competition of Winners, 169
complementarian marriage, 162n22
complementarians, 16
complementarity, in peripheral
  aspects, 38
complementary sex, completing us,
  147
complete disclosure, 124
Compromise of Compromisers,
  169n42
concubines, 135
conditional commitment, versus
  unconditional, 204

conflict
  becoming constructive/destructive, 163
  cannot be denied indefinitely, 169
  defined, 161
  degrading and destabilizing a marriage, 157
  descending into spousal abuse, 155
  displacing, 168
  evidence of the intensity of a marriage, 173
  inevitable, 154
  in marriage, 154–73
  methods of denying, 168
  morally neutral, 163
conflict mandate, creative tensions in, 217
conflict resolution, preferable to conflict management, 161
conflict-habituated marriage, as not necessarily unstable, 174
conflict-minimal marriage, not necessarily stable, 174
conjugal family, 48, 60
connectedness, 45–61, 216
connectivity, of social networks, 53
consanguineal family, 48, 60
conscious domination, 158
constructed postmodern self, 118
consumer market-place, language of, 65
consumer marriage, far from covenant marriage, 188
consummate love, as goal of marriage, 97
consumption, viewed as personal right, 188
contraception and abortion revolutions, 180
contract, defined, 203
contract marriage, intimacy of, 130
contractual commitment, of spouses, 207
contractual marriage, 204, 205, 206
control
  internal or external, 190–91
  legitimacy of, 158–61
Coontz, Stephanie, 32, 155

cooperation, replacing the old commonality, 50
core fears, hurts, and motives, demasking, 166
1 Corinthians, instructions on marital sex, 150
corn flakes, designed to reduce sexual desire, 138
correlation, not cause, 181
Council of Biblical Manhood and Womanhood (CBMW), 16
counseling theories, Christian, 85–87
Counter-Enlightenment movement, key component of, 106
couple conflict, leading to common couple violence, 157
couple violence, less gendered and more explosive, 156
Couples' Devotional Bible, 130
courting, 37
courtly or "chivalrous" love, 105
courtship
  dilemma of intimacy versus imaging, 39
  person with least interest having most power, 161
covenant, 203, 206, 207
covenant marriage, 130, 203n12
Covenant Marriage (Chapman), 203n12
covenant of love, 204
covenantal love, colors and contours of, 110
covenantal marriage, 204, 205
The Covenanted Self (Brueggemann), 131
Covington, Dennis and Vicki, 172
Cowen-Fletcher, Jane, 57
Crabb, Larry, 85–87, 92–93, 127
Crazy for God (Guinness), 172n52
creation myths, 12
creative tensions, reflections on, 215–218
critical knowledge, 215n9
critical theory, 128
criticism, 124
Croft, Scott, 40n18

cross-cultural practices, of patriarchal
  terrorism, 156n7
cross-sex friendships, 90–91
Crouch, Andy, 212
"cult of intimacy," 122
cultural adultery, 27, 29
cultural aspects, of a text, 18
cultural assaults, on social institution
  of marriage, 180
cultural belief, in virtues of passions
  of the heart, 31
cultural conceptions of marriage, 212
cultural construct, marriage as, 8
cultural conventions, surrendering, 5
cultural demands, of marriage, 113
cultural ideals, dysfunctional, 28
cultural infatuation, with romantic
  love, 108
cultural knowledge, 11
cultural mandates
  contemplating effects of, 213
  defined, 13
  generated and justified within a
    cultural context, 63
cultural mandates of marriage
  ancient, 21–23
  ancient and contemporary, 5–6
  contemporary, 23–25
  re-examining thoroughly, 218
  shaping Christian marriage, 8
  tensions between rival conceptions
    of, 215
cultural methods, of deciding who
  should marry, 30
cultural myths, 12–13
cultural norms, 12, 112, 135
cultural obligations, fulfilling, 72
cultural romanticism, emphases of,
  66, 106
cultural sexual scripts, 140, 141
cultural turn, to physical pleasure, 148
cultural values, 11, 220
culture
  Christianity and, 211–12
  components of, 11–12, 12n10
  defined, 11, 196
  of divorce, 207
  as greatest human creation, 21

making kinship feel natural, 47
modern, 19–21
shaping theology and psychology,
  93
simple surrender to, 29
teaching about marriage, 5
as a "text" to be "read," 9
using God's word to preach, 21
culture industry, 126–30
Culture Making (Crouch), 212n4
culture war, over family values, 64
cyberspace communities, 55

dating
  Christian critique of, 43
  defined, 37
  kissing goodbye, 42–44
  twentieth-centry invention of
    Western society, 40
David, 33, 33n4, 89, 126, 152
Davis, Rebecca, 129n58
Days of Glory, Seasons of Night
  (Dunker), 75
death, 3
declarations, negative and positive, 74
deficiency need, 81
deinstitutionalization, of marriage,
  180
demand-withdraw pattern, 116, 170
democratic movement, led largely by
  Christians, 20
demographic factors, related to
  divorce, 183
denial, warding off emotional pain,
  168
dependence, 160
  frames of, 92–93
depression, 169
Derrida, Jacques, 100
Descartes' *ergo sum*, "I think,
  therefore I am," 133
descent, determination of, 47
descriptions
  versus prescriptions, 63
  suggesting prescriptions, 215
descriptive fact, 63
desertion, as recourse for uncoupling,
  175

desires
  compared to goals, 85
  desiring desire, 142
dessert specialty shops, targeting
    adults, 1
developmental stage theory, of
    marriage in Western culture,
    164–69
devotionals, on intimacy, 130
Diana, Princess, 67
differentiation, characteristic of
    modern society, 50
digital technology, architect of our
    intimacies, 123
Dion, Celine, 103
disappointments, with intimacy, 116
disciples
  having all things in common, 60
  Jesus emotional attachment to,
    89–90
  losing biological families, 72
disclosure-responsiveness exchange,
    failure of, 116
disembeddedness, from community
    in modernity, 216
disembodied spirituality, compared to
    sexuality, 147
disengagement, 86
displacement, by a spouse, 155
dispositional attributions, 190
dissolution, marital, 174–94
dissolution mandate, creative tensions
    in, 218
distance, as opposite of intimacy, 117
diversity
  across cultures of Christian
    marriage, 24
  normalization of, 55
divine "wholly other," relationship
    with, 199
The Division of Labor in Society
    (Durkheim), 49n7
divorce
  analysis of, 187–88
  became available for all, 175
  Bohannan's six stations of, 176–77
  categorizing factors of, 181–84

consequence of human brokenness
    and depravity, 178
constituting a failure of some sort,
    178
culture of, 173
debates about biblical permissibility
    and grounds of, 180
effects of, 177
personal and community failure,
    218
personal failure of character, 192
reasons for, 177
redefined as an individual
    experience, 187
valid reasons for, 179
*Divorce and Remarriage: Four
    Christian Views*, 179
The Divorce Culture (Whitehead,
    Barbara Dafoe), 187
divorce rates, recent leveling off and
    even decline of, 175
divorce revolution, 180
Dobson, James, 58, 152–53
Dole, Bob, 57
domestic violence, 156–57, 156n10
dominant reading, 9
domination, 145, 158, 158n14
Doyle, Laura, 14
The Dr. Phil Show, 114
drive theory, Hull's, 83

Eagles (band), 103
early church, 59
economic consumption, families as
    units of, 51
economic production, families as
    units of, 51
economic resources, for a spouse, 160
economism, 190, 194
economy, developing some kind of
    an, 197
egalitarians, 17, 18
Eglah, 33
"ego virtue," of fidelity, 119
eHarmony.com, 39n15
eighteenth century in Europe,
    bawdiest century of all, 142

ejaculation, draining men of "vital
    fluids," 138
electromechanical vibrators, 143
Eliot, T. S., 129
Ellul, Jacques, 221n24
"emotion rules," of every social
    situation, 96
emotional adultery, 27n50, 91
emotional closeness, definitive of
    intimacy, 119
emotional dimension, to love, 96
emotional dovetailing, between
    spouses, 166
emotional engagement, women
    seeking intimacy through, 125
emotional fornication, 91
emotional incest, 91
emotional infidelity, 91
emotional love languages, 109
emotional needs, of husbands and
    wives, 86–87
emotional neglect or abuse, Christian
    couples most likely to claim, 182
emotional primacy in marriage,
    nowhere to be found in biblical
    text, 91
emotions, nurturing above all else, 66
empowerment, concept of, 158
empty-shell marriage
    intimacy absent, 121
    power and conflict seldom issues,
        164
    reasonable coexistence with
        minimum pain of, 166
    relabeled as pragmatic marriage,
        122
enamored, with romance and
    sentiment, 95
endogamy, 33, 34
engagement, 37
enjoyment, 101
entertainment industry, as an example
    of culture industry, 128
Ephesians, on anger, 171
epithumia, translated as lust or desire,
    99
equal partner marriage, 164–65

equitable relationship, in marriage,
    189
ERG theory, Alderfer's, 83–84
Erikson, intimacy for, 119
eros
    no promise of communion, 115
    as passionate love, 98
erotic re-creational co-experience,
    146
Esau, 32
essence
    of being human, 199
    of a marriage, 195
esteem, need for, 81
ethnicity, divorce varying by, 183
evangelical royalty, marital conflict
    among, 172
evangelicalism, psychological
    captivity of, 79
evangelicals
    gender hierarchy persisting among,
        18
    holding to perspective of marital
        decline, 221
    Hollywood portrayals of, 100
    splitting into two camps on
        question of gender, 16
Evans, Rachel Held, 19n28
evolution of the self, 118
exchange relationships, character of,
    160
exchange theory, 189–90
Existence needs, 83
existential loneliness, after sexual
    intercourse, 147
exogamy, 33, 34
expressive divorce, 187
expressive individualism, 186
extended family, 48
extended family system, to a nuclear
    family system, 51
external constraints on Western
    marriage, 175
external situational factors, 191
externalities, of marriage, 79
extrinsic marriage, 121, 122, 164

Facinelli, Peter, 100

factors of divorce, categorizing,
181–84
"fainting rooms," 143
faithful presence, theology of, 209n16
*Falling in Love for All the Right
Reasons: How to Find Your Soul
Mate* (Warren), 38n15
false martyrdom, 86
familism, idolatry of, 71
family
as a Christian calling or vocation,
70
consequence of his coming to
divide, 72
defined, 200n7
focused on nurturing personal
relationship, 51
idolization of, 70–71
Jesus' redefinition of, 72
as just another component of life,
51
living by and living with, 77
major focus of life, 68
minimum components
constituting, 48
not embedded in community as
meaningless, 56
not essential to the Christian life,
71
sacrificing for kingdom building,
74
in a separate social institution, 50
standard sociological functions
of, 73
family of God, meaning of, 59
family system, transmitting culture to
the next generation, 197
family unit, as a whole, 46
family values, 64–66
Fankl, Viktor, 82
*Fanny Hill, or the Memoires of a
Woman of Pleasure* (Cleland),
142n32
father-son pairings, in the Old
Testament, 32–33
fatuous love, 97
feelings, nurturing above all else, 66
female body, ideal, 140n24

*Female Chauvinist Pigs: Women
and the Rise of Raunch Culture*
(Levy), 144
female circumcision, 23n39
female genital mutilation, 156n7
female orgasm, admitting existence
of, 143
female private indulgence, friendship
as, 90
female sexuality, tracing recent course
of, 142
female submission, 16, 18–19
females. *See* women
feminine mystique, 67
femininity, 68, 86
feminization, of Christianity, 104
fictive kin, 47–48
fictive marriages, 48n6
Fiddler on the Roof, 36, 176n3
fidelity, perverted beyond
redemption, 188
Fifty Shades of Grey, 144n37
*Find a Husband After 35: Using What
I Learned at Harvard Business
School* (Greenwald), 42n26
Fireproof (film), 24, 108, 109
first family
distinguished from second family,
74
primary allegiance to, 77
Fishburn, Janet, 71
Five Love Languages (Chapman), 108
"flesh," biblical construct of, 133
fog, of romantic love, 44
folk tales, 12
foot binding, 156n7
Forbidden Fruit (Regnerus), 135n6
Foreigner (band), 103
forms of expression, 12n10
The Four Loves (Lewis), 99
Frankfurt School of social research,
128
freedom, for marriage to become
useful, 219
Freud, Anna, 134n5
Freud, Sigmund, 134, 143n35

Freudian psychoanalytic
revolution, sexualized human
unconsciousness, 134
Friedan, Betty, 67
friends, 47
"friends with benefits," 176
friendship
dating expression of, 37
defined, 91n41
men and women practicing
differently, 90
in the past compared to modern, 90
supplanting family as alternative to
spouses, 89
transformation of the notion of, 90
voluntary by definition, 91
friendship love
between a man and a woman, 91
storge, 98
front porch, to the back seat, 36–38
fulfillment, greater urgency and value
than obedience, 92
fuller ways forward, 218–19
fundamental attribution error, 191n50

Gabor, Zsa Zsa, 184n32
Gaede, 214
Galen, 143
game love, *ludus*, 98
Gardella, Peter, 148
gated communities, 55
gay rights revolution, 180
gender
as a case study, 11
described, 13–15
issue of, 28
gender egalitarianism, 20
gender hierarchy
in all human cultures and history,
15–16
among evangelicals, 18
in biblical culture, 18
gender norms, creating an imbalance
of power, 125
gender reconciliation, moving to, 91
gender roles, differentiated and
hierarchical, 68

gender roles and stereotypes,
redefined as male and female
needs, 87
gender-based violence, systemic, 155
gendering, of primal needs or
longings, 86
genitals, sex associated with, 132
Gibran, Kahlil, 131n67
gift, giving agreement as, 163–64
Gilder, George, 42
*Girl Meets God: On the Path to a
Spiritual Life* (Winner), 177
Girls Gone Wild, 144
goals, compared to desires, 85
God
breaking the heart of, 75–77
calling Christian spouses to
interdependency, 92
covenanted with earth and with
specific persons, 203
disapproval of divorce, 178
discerning the will of, 5
as intelligent designer, 12
intending sex to be primarily
person centered and relationship
driven, 151
in intimate relationship witnin the
Trinity, 113
marriage clearly not dictated in
detail directly by God, 203
preoccupation with knowing, 92
requiring only love, 131
seeking to know equally in return,
113
teaching the first human beings,
199
godly wife, chapter in Proverbs, 22
godparents, 47
going steady, 37
Golden Rule, living out authentically,
190
"good provider," 69
goods and services, producing, 196
gospel, 26
Gouge, William, 137
Graham, Billy, 164, 172
Graham, James, 195
Graham, Ruth, 164, 172

Graham, Sylvester, 138

Graham Wafer, 138

Greek art and sculpture, smaller penis more sexually appealing, 140

Greenwald, 42n26

Gregory the Great, Pope, 136

Groves, Ernest, 138

growth, struggle for, 166

Growth needs, 84

G-spot, 143, 143n36

Guernsey, Dennis, 114

Guinness, Os, 172n52

Gungor, Mark, 15

Gushee, David, 180

"habits of the heart," 64–65

Habits of the Heart (Bellah and colleagues), 186

Haggith, 33

"Hall of Faith," Hebrews 11, 35

halo effect, of beauty, 99

"hanging out," in group activities, 37–38

happy marriages, each happy in its own way, 155

Harley, Willard, 86

Harris, Joshua, 42

hasty conclusion, fallacy of, 178

haves, hidden together in private fortresses, 55

head covering, for women, 18

head-complement marriage, 164

healthy relationships, healing selves, 208

heart

    family as a matter of, 66–68

    following as a moral virtue or cultural mandate, 66

    passionate powers of, 133

Hebrews

    core of being located in loins and wombs, 133

    very positive view of sex, 135

hedonism, 209

Hegel, 130

heterosexual males or females, sexual arousal in socially conditioned ways, 139

H-frame independence, self-reliance and self-sufficiency, 92

Hiebert, Paul, 26

hierarchy, of the meanings of sex, 144–147

higher education, people with, having lower divorce rates, 183

higher income, avoiding financial stresses, 183

Hillingdon, Lady, 138

His Needs, Her Needs: Building an Affair-Proof Marriage (Harley), 86

historical stages of marriage, Witte's, 200–203

historical-cultural analysis, of Western society, 28

Hochschild, Arlie, 96

holy sexual longing, for completion, 147

holy terror, of marriage, 154

holy trinity, of marriage, 132

home

    involving relationships of trust, 57

    primary function of, 69

home alone, as oxymoron, 57

homelessness, concept of, 56–57

honesty, 124

honor killings, 156n7

Horney, Karen, 106

Hosea, 27

hospitality, as core value and norm, 58

hostility rituals, between two conflict-habituated individuals, 164

"household of faith," 59n34

households, 33, 48, 58, 66

Hugo, Victor, 127

human(s)

    constructing and maintaining social institutions, 197

    enculturated beings, 189–190

    essence of being, 199

    responsible creatures, 199

    self-conscious creatures, 199

    sexually socialized, 139

    social creatures, 199

    symbol-using creatures, 199

human and divine love, romantic similarities of, 104
human behavior, driven by meaning, 144
human consciousness, of self, 117
human cultures, variants of, 2
human female, creation of, 199
human needs, 80, 81, 82
human sexuality, not simply either a male or female package, 139
human social life, 210
Humphries, Kris, 175n2
Hunter, James Davison, 209n16
husband and wife, defying dictates of a patriarchal society, 162n22
husbands
    discouraged from talking much with women, 25
    emotional needs of, 87
    greater importance placed on self-disclosure by, 116
    traditionally had more power, 159
hydrotherapy, gushing water massage, 143
hyperindividuation, 55
hyper-sentimentalization, 67
hysteria, women treated for, 142–43
"hysterical paroxysm," 143

I Gave Dating a Chance: A Biblical Perspective to Balance the Extremes (Clark), 43n31
I Kissed Dating Goodbye: A New Attitude Toward Relationships and Romance (Harris), 42–43
"I Want to Know What Love Is" (song), 103
iconic new men, 17–18
ideal culture, undermining real culture, 28
idealization, of marriage and family, 67
idealizing, something, 67
ideational periods, 134
identity, 119, 120
ideologies, 12n10
idolatry, something or someone other than God, 71

idolization, of the family, 70–71
illegitimacy revolution, 180
illumination, sense of, 213
imaging operative, in courtship, 166
immanence, of God, 113
Impersonal Interaction, in the Maltz hierarchy, 145
impression management, goal of, 39
In His Steps: What Would Jesus Do? (Sheldon), 25n46
inadequacy, as a person, 125
incest taboo, imposing, 21
individual rights, language of, 65
individualism
    cultural context of the new, 118
    culture of, quick to blame the individual, 177
    defining contemporary Western culture, 79
    of late modernity, 54–55
    origins of, 186n35
    undermining marriage since the Enlightenment, 186
individualistic marriage, 220
Industrial Revolution, 52, 65
inequitable relationship, in marriage, 189
infallibility of the Bible, insistence on, 9
infanticide, 156n7
infatuation, 97, 101
Infinite Other, God as, 131
inflexibility, producing pathos, 209
informal engagement, 37
initial covenant, 204
Innocent Ecstasy: How Christianity Gave America an Ethic of Sexual Pleasure (Gardella), 148
institution of marriage. *See* social institution of marriage
institutional differentiation, modernity characterized by, 51
institutional marriage, 220
institutionalized individualization, 55
institutions, family as coordinator of inputs from other socializing, 51
Instone-Brewer, David, 179
intelligence, spouses matched in, 160

intelligent designer, God as, 12
intended domination, 158
Intended for Pleasure (Wheat), 149
intercourse. *See* sexual intercourse
intergenerational transmission, to
    children of divorced parents, 182
internalities, of marriage, 79
Internet, searching on, 38
interpersonal attachment, love
    producing, 96
interpersonal communion, 147
interpersonal conflict
    arising from discrepant values, 162
    based on issues, 161
    inevitable, 171
    potential for, 166
    power and, 164
interpersonal pathologies,
    perpetuating, 39
interpersonal power
    concepts clustering around, 158
    conflict and, 164
    derived from personal resources,
        dependency, and interest, 161
    smacking of bullying, 158
    unavoidable, 171
interpersonal problem, resolving, 161
interpersonal process model, 116
interpersonal relationships, evaluated
    in terms of costs and rewards,
    189
interpersonal surrender, as
    psychological pathology, 4
interpretive knowledge, 215n9
intersex, humans with some
    combination of male and female
    physical characteristics, 139
interventions, Christian, 192–94
intimacy
    described, 101
    as detailed knowledge of a close
        relation, 115
    distinct from sex, 115
    embedded in communal
        assumptions of
        environmentalism, 127
    failing, reversing into its opposite,
        117

as greater relational achievement,
    117
growing slowly and steadily, 97
as "knowing that I am not alone in
    the universe," 116
as knowledge of the depth of being,
    115
marriage and, 112–31
most associated with the mind, 132
much like *storge*, 99
not found in biblical text with
    reference to marriage, 131
not requiring authenticity of self-
    disclosure, 14
requiring reciprocity, 117
requiring self-disclosure, 117
seeking with God, 113
seven levels of, 115
in Sternberg's triangular theory of
    love, 97
transactional process of self-
    revealing disclosure, 116
transformation of, 118n19
varying from one marriage to
    another, 120
intimacy mandate, creative tensions
    in, 217
intimate, as an adjective, noun, and
    verb, 115
Intimate Allies (Allender and
    Longman), 128
intimate marriage, 121, 164
Intimate Marriage Curriculum Kit,
    221
irreconcilable differences, 183
Isaac, 32, 151, 152
Islamic woman, covering her face, 141
*It Takes a Family: Conservatism and
    the Common Good* (Santorum),
    58
*It Takes a Village and Other Lessons
    Children Teach Us* (Clinton),
    57–58
It Takes a Village (Cowen-Fletcher),
    57
iWorld, 151

Jacob, 32

Janz, Paul, 104
Jesus. *See also* Christ
    celibate, 83
    condemned divorce without valid
        grounds, 179
    endorsed marriage by performing
        first miracle at a wedding, 71
    expressing deepest emotional
        attachment to his disciples,
        89–90
    on family of God, 59
    ignored strongest of social and
        religious norms regarding
        gender, 25–26
    new covenant through, 203
    placing marriage in the service of
        the kingdom, 72
    practiced each style of conflict
        management at different times,
        170
    taught that sexual desire must be
        firmly controlled, 136
    as twelve-year-old not in traveling
        party of friends and relatives, 59
    unmarried, 71
    welcomed women into his traveling
        party, 26
John, declaring that God is *agape*, 99
Johnson, Robert, 146n41
joint heirs, in Christ, 60
Jonathan, soul of bound to David, 89
Joseph, 59
Journal of Psychology and Theology,
    issue on Christian marriage, 193
joy of mutuality, overflowing into
    sharing and caring, 167
The Joy of Sex (Comfort), 148
Judea-Christian creation myth, 12
Julius Caesar, 136n9

Kardashian, Kim, 175n2
Keller, Tim, 113n3
Kellogg, John Harvey, 138
Kendrick, Alex, 24
K-frame dependence, 92
Kierkegaard, Soren, 106
kingdom building, more important
    than marriage building, 73

Kinsey reports, on sexual behavior,
    139
kinship, 46, 53
kinship networks, deteriorated, 52
kinship system, of each culture, 47
knowledge, systems of, 215n9
"knowledge industry," 128
Kubler-Ross, stages of death, 3
Kuehne, Dale, 151

la petite mort, 3
Laban, 32
lack of transparency, about real state
    of marriages, 218–19
LaHaye, Tim and Beverly, 149
language, 108
Laotian woman, covering her breasts,
    141
Latin cultures, *manic*, 99
Laugh Your Way to a Better Marriage
    (Gungor), 15
law of marriage, creating, 180
laws, preventing anarchy and
    preserving social order, 196
Leah, 32
least interest, social principle of, 160
Lee, Cameron, 187–88
Lee, John, 98–99
legalism, 209
legitimacy
    of authority, 159
    of control, 158–61
Les Miserables (Hugo), 127
Levinas, Emmanuel, 74
Levy, Ariel, 144
Lewis, C. S., 90, 99, 110, 139, 145, 153
liberation, sense of, 213
libido, of our life instinct (eros), 134
"like marries like," 38
liking, 97, 100, 101
limerence, 102
Livingston, David, 76
Livingston, Mary, 76
locus of commitment, as relationship
    itself, 207
locus of control, 190–191
loins, crushing, 133
loneliness, marrying to remedy, 39

Longman, Tremper, 128
long-term relationships, effect on
    romantic love, 107
lose-lose situation, 162
lovable person, loving, 100n9
love
    components of, 96–99
    effects on the lover, 110
    heart of life, 94
    hyper-sentimentalized, 110
    is not, 99–102
    in love with, 95
    marital, 94–111
    metaphors for, 103
    not ensuring intimacy, 113
    not mere attraction, 99
    as obligation, 186
    overuse of the word, 95
    passion of the heart, 110
    personally organizing and
        constructive, 101
    taking individuals beyond
        themselves, 110
    as therapy, 186
    ultimate act not reserved for
        marriage, 88
Love Dare, forty-day, 24, 108
Love Is a Decision, 108
Love Is Something You Do, 96, 108
love languages, universal and
    comprehensive, 108
love mandate, creative tensions in,
    216–217
love songs, popular, 102–5
lover, desiring the Beloved herself,
    153
loving, 100, 101
ludus, game love, 98
lust, 152

Maacah, 33
Maasai, family structure of, 23–24
MacDonald, George, 117
macro-level categories, of divorce
    factors, 181
macro-level factors, of divorce,
    183–84

macro-manipulation, women
    countering with micro, 161
Making Love, in the Maltz hierarchy,
    146
"making love," 132
maladaptive communication pattern,
    116
male myth, of friendship, 90
male power, Christian legitimation
    of, 15
male-centeredness, of a text written
    by and to men, 17
males, sex drive compared to females,
    83
Maltz, Wendy, 144–47
Maltz hierarchy, 145–47, 148, 151
Mama Mia! 176n3
The Managed Heart (Hochschild), 96
mandate, 13
mandates of marriage. *See* cultural
    mandates of marriage
mania, obsessive love, 98
Man's Search for Meaning (Frankl), 82
marital calling, primary for females,
    70
marital commitment, 204
marital conflict
    common areas of, 162
    concerns appearing to underlie all,
        163
    consequences of, 155
    denying as counterproductive, 169
    not entirely preventable by moral
        resolve, 157
marital decline, 220, 221
marital dependence, types of, 92
marital dissolution
    addressing as mostly a personal/
        private trouble, 192
    as personal failure, 174–94
    rates of, 176
    rise of, 185
marital ideals, gaining freedom from
    tyrannical, 219
marital intimacy, Christian embrace
    of, 128
marital love
    equated with intimacy, 112

examples in the Old Testament, 107
expressed in open communication
    and caring, 219
as romantic, 94–111
uniqueness of, 94
marital needs, popularized Christian
    portrayal of, 86
marital partners, selecting, 30–44
marital power, resource theory of, 160
marital power and authority, most
    common measures of, 159
marital quality, 174
marital rape, 145
marital relationship, 207, 221
marital resilience, 220
marital sabotage, 145
marital sex, 136, 145
marital sexual fidelity, 135
marital sexual intercourse, 145
marital sexuality, Christian delight
    in, 149
marital transcendence, not marital
    realization, 219
*Marriable: Taking the Desperate Out of
    Dating* (DiMarcos), 40–42
marriage. *See also* Christian marriage;
    social institution of marriage
adaptable, 220
adding intimacy and attachment,
    47
by arrangement, 31
boot camp for self-transcendence,
    89
by bride capture, 31n1
characterized by love, 94
commitment to relational well-
    being, 208, 209
conducting in a more authentically
    Christian manner, 213
as a couple, 163
covenant versus as a contract, 130
defined, 5, 200n7, 222
diversity across cultures of
    Christian, 24
as duty, 187
envisioned as a dynamic
    relationship between two
    individuals, 208

evolution of, 200–203
evolved from a task and role
    orientation to a companionate
    and intimate relationship, 112
expanding family ties (kin
    relations), 47
formation of, 30
foundational social unit, 8
goal of according to Crabb, 85
governed by voluntary wills and
    preferences of the couple, 202
historical stages of, 200–203
impossible to disembed from
    culture, 221
interpersonal relational dynamics
    of, 79
Jesus' words on, 198
just another state of being human,
    219
limited to life on earth, 72
measure of a successful, 35
for "money" or community assets,
    32
multiple perspectives of, 200
no guarantor of full human need
    fulfillment, 84
not desirable for all followers of
    Jesus, 72
not embedded in community as
    meaningless, 56
not existing in all cultures, 22
object of dating, 41
one way of meeting some human
    needs, 84
overview of Bible passages
    addressing, 73
patriarchal in ancient Israel, 22
person with least interest having
    most power, 161
place of refuge from work, politics,
    and community obligation, 36
primary calling in life, 62–77
primary means of self-realization,
    119
private relationship between two
    individuals, 35
privatization of, 45–46
as resilient, 221

reversing creation, 199
romance and, 106
social institution or class governed
by secular state, 202
supposed to bring personal
happiness, 52
unhappy, 155, 191
value of, 62, 63, 78
as a woman's career, 68
as work, 186
Marriage as a Covenant Relationship
(Joseph), 203n12
*The Marriage Builder: A Blueprint for
Couples and Counselors* (Crabb),
85
Marriage Builders website, 86
marriage counseling, migrating to
professional service sector, 187
marriage counseling industry, 129n58
marriage covenant, in the story of
Hosea and Gomer, 203
The Marriage Crisis (Groves), 138
marriage education programs, for
individuals and couples, 192–93
marriage partners, as *Intimate Allies*,
128
Marriage Partnership magazine, 130
marriage problems, Western
Christians interpreting as
personal, 192
marriage values, rooted in family
values, 64
martyrdom, to maintain a relationship
as pathological, 102
Marx, Groucho, 195
Marx, Karl, 185n34, 219n12
Mary (mother of Jesus), 59, 72
masculine conception, of sexuality,
141n29
masculinity, as a virtual portrait of
significance, 86
Maslow, Abraham, 81, 83
masturbation, 138, 152
matchmaker, for arranged marriages,
32
mate selection, 30–44, 215–16

material culture (technology), shaping
non-material culture (values and
norms), 123
matriarchy, in human history, 14
matrilineal descent, 47
matrilocality, 48
mature covenant, 204
maximum joint profit, gaining, 163
Max-Neef, Manfred, 81–82
McClung, Nellie, 20
McGraw, Phil, 114
McLachlan, Sarah, 3–4
Mead, Margaret, 175
The Meaning of Marriage (Keller),
113n3
men
engaging in a non-relational
sexuality, 141
intent on significance, 86
*Men are from Mars, Women are from
Venus* (Gray), 87n28
*Men are Like Waffles, Women are Like
Spaghetti* (Farrel and Farrel),
87n28
menstruation purity laws, various, 25
meso level, of interpersonal and
institutional power, 158
methodological individualism, 189
M-frame interdependence, mutual
influence and support, 92
Michal, 33n4, 126
daughter of King Saul, 33
micro-level categories, of divorce
factors, 181
middle-class family, idealization of, 52
Midler, Bette, 103
minded behavior, 133
mission, choosing over marriage, 76
mission base, 73, 128
mistrust, contracts driven by, 203
mixed messages, 107–9
mixed-motive conflict, 162
modern culture, 19–21
*Modern Love: Romance, Intimacy, and
the Marriage Crisis* (Shumway),
118–119
modern marriage market, 38–42
modern open marriage, 204

modern societies
  increasingly friendless, 90
  more urban way of life, 49
  placing priority on the individual,
    50
modernism, 118n21
modernity, forced religion to
    disengage from other social
    institutions, 220
modernization, forces of, 49
money and sex, gendered exchange
    of, 38
moral consensus, 49
moral disclosure, types of, 65
moral exhortation, addressed to
    individuals and couples, 192
moral failure, failure to confront, 173
moral horizons, 185–89
moral theology, prescriptive ought
    of, 214
moral value, of virtue, 100
*More Perfect Unions: The American
    Search for Marital Bliss* (Davis),
    129n58
Morgan, Marabel, 122
Moses, 178
Mossholder, Ray, 193n53
mother, Jesus looking after his, 72
Mother Culture, 11–13
mothering, new full-time role of, 52
motivation, for sex, 148
Motivation and Personality (Maslow,
    Abraham), 81n5
Murdoch, Rupert, 130n63
music, probing love for deeper
    meaning, 104
mutual affection, turning into mutual
    antagonism, 154
mutual love, eagerly shares all of life,
    96
mutual need fulfillment, 87–88
mutuality stage, of marriage, 167

Na people, of southwestern China, 21
natural aspects, taken as God-given,
    201
natural institution, 201

nature of marriage, unnatural
    violations of, 201
need fulfillment
  assessing the propriety of, 88
  examining carefully, 82–83
  mandate, 216
  spouse as primary source of, 78–93
needs
  categorized, 80–81
  not met outside of relationship, 85
  shared with non-spousal others, 88
  taxonomy of interrelated and
    interactive, 81–82
negative attachment, to a partner, 39
negative declaration, 74
negative-exchange marriage, 121
negotiated readings, 9
neolocality, 48
network support, limited in various
    ways, 53
neurosis, due to lack of orgasm, 134n5
new members of society, teaching
    values and norms to, 196
New Testament
  codes for marital love, 107
  little attention to marriage, 72–73
  marriage in times of, 22–23
  marriage optional and good, 71
News Corp. media empire, 130n63
nexus, of the gospel and culture, 26
Nicomachean Ethics (Aristotle), 89
Nietzsche, Friedrich, 54
non-basic conflict, versus basic
    conflict, 162
non-living object, meaningful
    relationship with, 206
non-material culture, 12n10
non-moral value, of aesthetics,
    99–100
non-sexual ways, for Christians to be
    promiscuous Gomers, 27
normalization, of diversity, 55
nuclear family, 48, 53, 58
nymphomania, 141n28
O: The Intimate History of Orgasm
    (Margolis), 142n32
obsession, forms of, 135–39
obsessive love, *mania*, 98

O'Hear, Anthony, 67
Old Testament
    allowed divorce for adultery and for
        neglect or abuse, 179
    examples of marital love, 107
    marriage of great importance in, 71
    narratives of rape, brutality,
        murder, human sacrifice, and
        widespread abuse of women in,
        156–157n10
Olthuis, James, 119, 164, 166
"one flesh," 127, 199
oneness, 85, 127
one-night stands, 38
Oord, effort to synthesize perspectives
    of love, 96
The Open Bible (NASB), purposes of
    marriage in, 73
opportunistic marketing, of a hot
    commodity, 129
"opposites attract," 39
oppression, 137
organizational incest, 27n50
orgasm
    admitting existence of female, 143
    clitoral, 143
    neurosis due to lack of, 134n5
    as sweet surrender, 3
    vaginal seated in the clitoris,
        143–144n36
    in women as reproductively
        unnecessary, 149
Origen of Alexandria, 23, 136
original sin, struggle to overcome, 148
other, 130
outward, turning, 219
overlap, of social networks, 53
owner-property marriages, 164
oxytocin, "love hormone," 152

parent and sibling relationships,
    providing relatedness need
    fulfillment, 89
parenting, difference between power
    and authority in, 159
parents
    having respect of their children,
        159

    looking for substitute, 39
    preoccupied with their children, 68
    without respect of their children,
        159
Parsons, Talcott, 53
partner responsiveness, 116
partnership, marriage as, 163
partnership of two, designed from the
    outset to be extrinsic, 128
parts of the body, most sexualized,
    140–41
passion
    definitive of romance, 119
    growing rapidly and then declining,
        97
    much like *eros*, 99
    reversing direction, 31
    in Sternberg's triangular theory of
        love, 97
passionate love, *eros*, 98
"passionate manhood," emergence
    of, 69
passive aggression, retaliating
    indirectly through tactics, 169
passive victim, of a spell cast by the
    other, 101
patriarchal oppression, 13
patriarchal terrorism, 155–56
patriarchy, universal, 14
patrilineal descent, 47
patrilocality, 48
Paul, 59
    celibate, 83
    condemned divorce without valid
        grounds, 179
    exhortation that husbands should
        love their wives, 20, 70, 99, 203
    instructions on marital sex, 150
    on "last days" people, 134
    outraged by standards of sexual
        behavior of the Greco-Roman
        world, 136
    positive things to say about
        marriage, 72
    on women being silent in churches,
        18n27
pederasty, 136n9

"pelvic massage," for female patients, 143

perceived neglect, 163

perceived threat, 163

perils, of mate selection, 40

permissibility of divorce, most recent round of debate about, 178

personal choice, of partners based on love, 35–36

personal development, complicating intimacy, 119

personal explanations for divorce, flowing from demographic and sociocultural factors, 185

personal failure
  divorce as, 185, 192, 218
  marital dissolution as, 174–94

personal lifestyle factors, for divorce, 181–82

personal maturity, demonstrated by styles of conflict management, 170

personal misery, having nothing to do with the marriage, 155

personal need fulfillment, compared to self-fulfillment, 82

personal needs, 79, 80

personal quality of life, prioritized over social order, 185

personal resources, neutralizing and overriding by social statuses and roles, 160

personal/private troubles, distinction from social/public issues, 191

person-based conflict, 162

person-centered, relationship-driven sex, 152

personhood, 133–34n4, 198–99n4

perspectives of marriage, competing, 200

Peter, Paul, and Mary, 110

phenomenological families, 48, 60

pheromones, 152

philia, translated as "brotherly love" of equals, 99

physical abuse, in intact, highly religious homes, 156

physical attractiveness, trigger mechanism for couple formation, 99

physical beauty, almost entirely culturally defined, 99

physical force, threat of, 159

physical forms, of sweet surrender, 2–3

physical intimacy, inadequate euphemism for sex, 115

physical needs, products of universal human nature, 83

physical pleasure, 148, 217

physical resources, for a spouse, 160

physical touch, 108

physiological effect, of love, 96

piano legs, covered with skirts, 137

Pierce, Bob, 75–77

Pierce, Lorraine, 75

pietism, rise of, 66

Pittman, Frank, 106

Plato, 126–127

Playboy magazine, founding of, 139

playing hard to get, 41, 41

pleasure, mutual focus on, 146

"the pleasure principle," 134, 138

Pliny the Elder, 66

politicization, of nearly everything, 57n28

polyandry, 34

polygamous marriages, 34

polygamy, 24n41, 28, 34

polygyny, 34

"poor person's divorce," 175

pop psychology, Christians fed and formed by, 92

Popenoe, David, 180

population, maintaining, 196

pornography industry, 134

Portofino (Schaeffer), 172, 172n51

possessiveness, of romantic love, 107

post-modernism, 118n21

poverty, Tevye's, 36

power, 158, 159, 160, 161n21

power imbalance, between spouses, 155

"Power of Love" (song), 103

power struggle, 164–168

power-dependence theory, 160
A Practical Guide to Finding Intimacy, Passion, and Peace with a Man, 14
premarital abstinence programs, 139
premarital cohabitation. *See* cohabitation
premarital pregnancy, 182
premarital sex, Christian rates of, 176
Premarital Sex in American (Regnerus and Uecker), 135n6
premodern marriages, shift away from, 45
premodern self, 118
premodern societies, 49, 50
premodern world, transition to modern, 49
preoccupation, with fulfillment, 93
prescriptive values, 63, 214
privacy, 50n8, 60
private interpersonal contract, marriage today as, 202
privatization
    of the family, 53
    of marriage, 45–46
    of religion, 45n1
    of self-selected marriages, 46
problem solving, divorce as a method of, 173
procreation, family of, 48
products of mass culture, features of, 128
projection, by a spouse, 155
promiscuity, 152
The Prophet (Gibran), 131n67
prostitutes, part of Greek temple worship, 136n9
prostitution, in Victorian era, 137
The Protestant Ethic and the Spirit of Capitalism (Weber), 211n1
Protestant Reformation, doctrinal basis for accepting the self, 118
Protestant reformers, abandoned celibacy, 137
Protestants, on marriage, 201–202
Proverbs
    as erotic, 136
    on sexual pleasure, 150

warning not to "lust in your heart after her beauty." 152
pseudo-intimacy, implicit in books, 122–23
pseudo-intimate marriage
    A-frame codependent commitment to a merged identity, 121
    perceived options of, 166
    power contested and conflict constant, 164
    preoccupied with togetherness bound by fear, 124
    strongest testament to the power of the cultural mandate, 122
psychological coercion, 145
psychological needs, 83, 93
psychological revolution, 187
psychological substance, inserting into definitions of needs and wants, 80
psychological taxonomy, employing Greek words for love, 98
psychological theory, of intimacy, 116
psychology, transpersonal school of, 82
Psychology as Religion: The Cult of Self-Worship (Vitz), 93
psychosocial development, stages of, 119
psychotherapy, 65, 129, 187
public cultural adultery, 27
public education, 52
public realm, entrance of women into, 37
public sphere, fledgling couples meeting in, 37
"pure relationship," 118n19
Puritans, 65–66, 137
The Purity Myth (Valenti), 13

quality time, 108

race, divorce varying by, 183
Rachel, 32
rapport talk, 125
"real man," one of virtue and responsibility, 69
Real Sex (Winner), 135n6

reality, adequate descriptions of, 214
reasoning powers, of the mind, 133
reasons couples give for divorcing,
     182–83
Rebekah, 32, 43, 151
rebellion, marrying as, 39
rebound, marrying on, 39
receiving gifts, 108
reciprocal negativity, cycles of, 172
*The Redemption of Love: Rescuing
     Marriage and Sexuality from
     the Economics of a Fallen World*
     (Miles), 194
reflexive project, self as, 118
Reformational Calvinist theology,
     211n1
Regnerus, Mark, 120, 193–194
Reich, Wilhelm, 134
relatedness, 82–87
relatedness needs, 84, 89
relating, changed ways of, 167
relational character, of sexuality, 150
relational equity, calculating, 189
relational exchange, social dynamics
     of, 161
relationship
     cooperating for the sake of, 162
     faithful presence in, 209
     only as healthy as its weakest
          member, 208
     renegotiation of, 209
     requiring transcendence of the
          self, 55
     types produced by Sternberg's
          components, 97
relatives, ascribed involuntarily, 46
religion, privatization of, 45n1
religious couples, less likely to
     divorce, 183
religious dissimilarity, increasing risk
     of divorce, 183
Renaissance, most desirable woman
     during, 140
report talk, 125
repression, 137
reproductive technology revolution,
     180
resentments, taking root, 166

residence, setting up, 48
resolvers, 169, 170
resources, giving a spouse power, 160
respect, described, 101
responsible creatures, humans as, 199
resurrection, women first witnesses
     to, 26
Rethinking Christ and Culture
     (Carter), 212n3
Rilke, Rainer, 131
Robertson, Pat, 58, 182n28
Role Fulfillment, in the Maltz
     hierarchy, 146
Rolheiser, Ron, 147n48
Roman Catholic Church, legal control
     of marriage, 201n9
Roman Catholics, on status of
     marriage as a sacrament, 201
romance
     criticizing romance, 109
     marrying out of, 39
     medieval tale of imaginary
          characters, 105
romance stage, of marriage, 166
romantic experience of falling in love,
     110
romantic love
     associated with the heart, 132
     being taken in by, 95
     chivalry in medieval courts, 109
     compared to a dangerous drug, 106
     criterion of marriage, 36
     emotional grip of, 95
     likely to undermine a marriage,
          216–17
     mix of intimacy and passion, 97, 99
     motive for self-selected marriage,
          68
     one immature kind of marital love,
          110
romantic lovers, coming to secretly
     resent each other, 107
romantic movies, 102
Romantic period, of the nineteenth
     century, 106
romanticism, cultural reaction
     to industrialization and
     rationalization, 106

"The Rose" (song), 103
rules or roles, of a marriage, 162
The Rules: Time-Tested Secrets for Capturing the Heart of Mr. Right (Fein and Schneider), 40–41
Ruskin, Effie, 138
Ruskin, John, 138
rWorld, 151

sacrament of matrimony, marriage as, 201
sacraments, or "divine mysteries," 201
sacred institution, marriage as, 198
Sacred Unions, Sacred Passions (Brennan), 91
safety needs, 81
Saint Jerome, on marital sex, 136
Salvation Army, 20
Samaritan woman at the well, 26
Samaritan's Purse, founder of, 75
same-sex marriage, 28, 65, 178
Samoan woman, covering her navel, 141
Santorum, Rick, 58
Sarah, 33
satyriasis, 141n28
Saul, King, 33n4, 126
Schaeffer, Franky, son of Francis and Edith, 171
Schaeffer, Francis and Edith, 172
scientistic knowledge, 215n9
scripture, sex is more about relationship than pleasure, 150
The Search for Intimacy (Storkey), 116
second family, 74, 77
secrecy, theory of, 124
"Secret Garden" (Springsteen), 125n41
secularization, 184
security, of being loved freely and unconditionally, 85
self
    as the agent or practitioner of intimacy, 117
    evolution of, 118
    increasingly problematic nature of, 120

intimacy with the other through, 205
    laid bare, 115–117
    multiple senses of, 4
    opening and owning of, 167
    surrendering, 3–5
self-abdication, *agape* as, 102
self-actualization, 81, 82
self-certainness, 119
self-consciousness, 198, 199
self-determination theory, 84
self-disclosure, 116, 123, 124
self-esteem, 81, 123
self-fulfillment, 81, 205, 207
self-giving love, 97, 98
self-interest, 50, 78
"self-made man," 69
self-reported causes for divorce, 183
self-sacrificial love, *agape* as, 102
self-selected marriage based on love, 43
self-selection, forming couples by, 78
self-transcendence, 82, 219
semiology, academic field of, 9
senior partner-junior partner marriage, 164
sensate periods, emphasizing materialist values, 134
sense of satiation, 183
sense of self, relentlessly morphing, 4
sensual pleasure, obsession with, 151
servile marriage, 197, 197n3
"The Seven Habits of Highly Defective Dating," 43
Seven Levels of Intimacy (Kelly), 115n8
Seventh-Day Adventist, 138
sex
    associated with the genitals, 132
    best understood as a drive or a longing, 83
    in contractual marriage, 205
    disparate motivations for, 148
    essence of, 144
    in marriage, 132–53
    as meaning-rich, 144
    more than sensational, 150
    mystery of, 153

not necessary for individual
survival, 83
not reduceable to mere physical
pleasure, 144
other-centered, meaning-driven,
152
as a physical expression of rage and
hostility, 146
as principally a seal and celebration
of relationship, 153
as procreational, 149–50
reduced primarily to physical
pleasure, 134
as sacramental, 149
science of, 144
sternly controlled by Victorians,
137
thoroughly physical reality, 133
Sex and the City, 144
sex appeal, replaced submission, 138
sex drive, according to Freud, 134
*Sex God: Exploring the Endless
Connections between Sexuality
and Spirituality* (Bell), 147n44
sex industry, of products and services,
134
sex mandate, creative tensions in, 217
sex manuals, 148
sex organs, used as weapons or
targets, 146
sex play, devolving into sex work, 146
sex-driven male, as normal, 141n28
sexes, friendship between, 90
sex-selective abortion, 156n7
sexual abstinence, question of, 13
sexual aggressor, man as, 37
sexual appetite, controlling by diet of
whole-grain flours, 138
sexual arousal, not a purely natural
physical and emotional response,
139
sexual attraction, generating love, 132
sexual behaviors, cross-cultural
variations of, 141
sexual capitalism in marriage,
desolation of, 188
sexual controller, woman as, 37
sexual desire, 137, 153

sexual elevator, 144–48
sexual energy, 134, 144–45
sexual engagement, 115, 125
sexual exchange, in covenantal
marriage, 205
sexual expression, building into
marriage, 23
sexual interaction, 142
sexual intercourse
forcing, 145
as "making love," 132
marital, 145
not stimulating clitoris sufficiently,
143
returning two separated humans to
the "one flesh" of creation, 147
tragedy of, 147
sexual orgasm, as sweet surrender, 3
sexual revolution, 180
sexual scripts, 139–42
sexual union, 147, 188
sexuality
area of sole or exclusive need
fulfillment in marriage, 88
body-centered and pleasure-driven,
152
in contemporary non-Western
cultures, 140
equated with the fall, 136
historical and cross-cultural
comparison, 140
as part of an interactive
developmental process, 139
relational character of, 150
tactical tool to be used prudently,
15
women undersexed and men
oversexed, 141
The Shack (Young), 113n3
Shakespeare, William, 106
shared place, community as, 55
Shaw, George Bernard, 36, 106
Sheldon, Charles, 25n46
shifting gears stage, of marriage,
166–67
sibling relationships, providing
relatedness need fulfillment, 89
sibling units, 21

siblings, 60, 101
"side-by-side" activity, companionship of shared, 90
significance, of having a meaningful impact on another person, 85
Silas, 59
silent treatment, the most painful, 123
similarity, in central aspects, 38
Simmel, Georg, 27n50, 124
sisters, in Christ, 60
situational attributions, 190
situational conflict, 162
situational conflict management, styles of, 169
slavery, economic social structure of, 197
Slaves, Women, and Homosexuals (Webb), 200n7
slippery slope arguments, as fallacious, 178
Smith, Christian, 147n43, 198–99n4
social activism, conservative Christians not embracing, 129n57
social behavior, understanding causes and consequences of, 214
social bonds, in premodernity compared to modernity, 50
"the social construction of reality," 213
social context, script for marriages to adopt to, 45
social contract, marriage as, 202
social control, facilitating, 12
social creatures, humans as, 199
social disestablishment, of marriage, 180
social embeddedness, of arranged marriages, 46
social environment, constructing, 11
social estate, marriage as, 202n10
social exchanges, 49
social forces, 8, 63
social goods, fair exchange with, 38
social history, of systemic power and conflict in marriage, 164
social inequality, categorical forms of, 4

social institution of marriage. *See also* marriage
abandoned by culture, 218
colloquial references to, 195
God's creation of, 198
identifiable forms of, 200–203
traditional commitment of spouses to, 206
social institutions
constructed and maintained by humans, 197
differentiating and specializing, 50
establishing order, 200
necessitated by sin, 198
recently emergent, 197n2
social integration, 50, 184
social learning, process of, 11
social needs, 81
social networking technology, 123
social networks, 53
social pressure, toward conformity, 49
social processes, of any society, 196
social psychological reasons, for marrying, 39
social reality, 213–15
social revolution, cracking pillars of cathedral of marriage, 180
social standing, Protestant form of marriage as, 202
social structural supports, holding a marriage together, 174
social unit, marriage as a separate, 45–61
socially embedded premodern self, 118n18
social/public issue, addressing divorce as, 193
societal and cultural mandates, of marriage, 184
societal factors, effects on marriage, 184
society
core values, 186
defined, 196
sentimentalization of modern, 67
sociocultural factors, 140, 184
sociological imagination, 213, 214
sociology, 214, 215n9

soft drinks, abstaining from, 2
soft patriarchs, 17–18
Solomon, 33
Song of Solomon, 136, 150
Sorokin, Pitrim, 134
sororal polygyny, 34n6
sorrows, drowning in substance
    abuse, 169
soul, perpetual virginity of, 147
soul oneness, 85, 127
soulmates
    ancient notion of, 126–27
    "othering" counterpoint to, 131
    from yokemates to, 117–20
source of behavior, factors of, 190
Spacey, Kevin, 100
specialization, characteristic of
    modern society, 50
spirit oneness, 85, 127
spiritual realities, leading Christians
    to embrace sexual pleasure, 148
spiritual significance, of the modern
    family, 70
spirituality, 131, 199
spousal abuse, not sufficient for
    divorce, 181
spousal all-sufficiency, cultural
    mandate of, 93
spouses
    as best friends, 89
    biblical text calling to love each
        other, 101
    as contributing factors to need
        fulfillment, 88
    depending on each other, 92
    effect of prostituting, 145
    intensely affectionate to one
        another, 68
    loving without being intimate, 131
    not singled out for a special, greater
        love, 94
    part of a church community, 56
    pathologically codependent on
        each other, 208
    preferred style of each, 170
    sending the other out into the
        world beyond the marriage, 167
Springsteen, Bruce, 39, 125

St. Augustine, 95, 147, 201
stability (stable or unstable), 190–191
stage theories, bolder claims than
    typologies, 164
standpoint theory, 79n1
Starbucks, 10
Sternberg, Robert, 96–98, 99
Still: Notes on a Mid-Faith Crisis
    (Winner), 177
Stookey, Paul, 110
storge, friendship love, 98
Storkey, Elaine, 116, 127
stranger, concept of, 124
strangers, hospitality to, 59
Studd, C. T., 76
Studd, Priscilla, 76
"styles of love," 98–99
submission, 4, 29, 158
subordination, 4
sufficient factors, not necessary
    factors, 181n24
suffragette movement, 20
sugar addiction, personal
    consequences of, 2
Sumatran woman, covering her knees,
    141
suppression, 137
surrender
    facilitating inappropriate, 4
    forms of, 1–7
    of one whole category of people to
        another, 4
    of sexuality, 15
    as tactical, 14
The Surrendered Wife (Doyle), 14
survival, 80–82
sweet, yielding to something, 1
"Sweet Surrender" (McLachlan), 3–4
"swinging sixties," bringing free love
    to all, 139
symbolic role, of family, 65
symbol-using creatures, humans as,
    199
The Symposium (Plato), 126–127
systemic conflict, such as patriarchy,
    162

technical manuals, for sex, 146

The Technological Society (Ellul), 221n24
technologies, 12n10
Technology of Orgasm (Maines), 143n34
Technopoly: The Surrender of Culture to Technology (Postman), 12n10
telephone, invention of, 37
Telushkin, Joseph, 126
tensions, as creative and activating, 215
Tenth Commandment, list of property owned by men, 17n21
Tevye, marriages of his daughters, 36
texts, interpreting in a variety of ways, 8
"texts of terror," 156–57n10
theistic evolution, 12
theocracy, God's original form of political governance, 197
theological model of marriage, 113, 203–204
Thonga of Southeast Africa, kissing as revolting, 141
Tim Horton's, 10
time, effects on components of love, 97
Titanic (movie), 104
Tolstoy, Leo, 155
"Total Woman" script, for Christian wives, 122
"Toward a Post-Postmodern Concept of Self" (Hiebert), 118n21
traditional family, reconstructing in the 1950s, 67
traditional marriage
    calling for return to, 193–94
    cultural assault on, 178
    intimacy determined by traditional gender roles, 121
    power unequal, 164
transcultural aspects, of a text, 18
transference, by a spouse, 155
transparency, lack of exacerbating problems of, 218–19
triangular theory of love, 96–98, 99
tribal societies of Southeast Asia, public dress, 141

tribes, 33
Trible, Phyllis, 156–57n10
trust, 49, 117
Turkle, Sherry, 123
tWorld, 151
typology of contemporary marriage, 120–22

ultimate biblical ethic, 19
ultimate commitments, 206–10
uncertainties engulfing marriage, 175
unconscious domination, 158
unequal power, making reciprocal self-disclosure less likely, 125
unhappy marriages, 155, 191
unilateral (one-way) commitment, versus bilateral (two-way), 204
unilineal descent, 47
unintended domination, 158
unmarried man, many options, 69
uterus, Greek word for, 142
utilitarian individualism, 186

vaginal orgasm, seated in the clitoris, 143–44n36
Valenti, Jessica, 13
van Leeuwen, Mary Stewart, 156
veiling practices, in the Muslim world, 141
verbal communication, communicating feelings, 123
Victorian doctors, considered sexual desire in a woman to be pathological, 142
Victorian era, sexually repressed, 137
views, on what God permits in regard to divorce, 179
Violent Interaction, in the Maltz hierarchy, 145–46
virginity, cultural obsession with, 13
virtues, practice of basic Christian, 219
Vitz, Paul, 93
vocational and avocational interests, separate as healthy, 88
voluntary self-disclosure, 116
voluntary union, marriage as, 202
von Goethe, Johann Wolfgang, 106

Walsh, Brian, 56
wants, 80
Warnes, Jennifer, 103
Warren, Neil Clark, 39n15
Warren, Rick and Kay, 167–68, 172
Webb, William, 19
Weber, Max, 158n14
"The Wedding Song," 110
wedlock, 207, 208
Wesley, John, 66
Western cultures
    Christianity, role in, 211
    coffee engrained in, 9–10
    cognitive constructs shaping, 133
    developmental stage theory of
      marriage in, 164–69
    individualism defining
      contemporary, 79
    mandating romance, 99
    mixed messages on value of
      marriage, 62
Western social history, identifiable
    eras of, 105–6
Western woman, covering her breasts
    and genital area, 141
What Is a Person? (Smith), 147n43
"What would Jesus do?," 25–26
Wheat, Ed and Gaye, 149
When Marriage Disappears, 183n31
Whitehead, Barbara Dafoe, 42, 187
whole against the sky, seeing the
    other, 131
*Why There Are No Good Men Left: The
    Romantic Plight of the New Single
    Woman* (Whitehead), 42
widow burning (suttee), 156n7
wife/wives
    battery of as systematic male
      violence, 156
    calling to become pragmatically
      manipulative, 14
    emotional needs of, 86–87
    greater importance placed on
      partner responsiveness, 116
    having multiple, 34
    paramount in the home, 68
    submission, 18, 20

Wild at Heart (Eldredge), 109
Wilde, Oscar, 106
Wilkinson, Bruce, 14–15, 19–20
will of God, discerning, 5
Willard, Frances, 20
Winner, 170
Winner, Lauren, 177
winners, competition of, 169
win-win situation, 162
witch burning, 156n7
withdrawers, 169, 170
Witte, John, 54
Wolf, Naomi, 13
*A Woman's Spiritual Guide to True
    Intimacy with a Man*, 14
women. *See also* human female
    alienated from own bodies and
      obsessed with appearance,
      141–142
    "base, carnal, and licentious"
      (medieval period), 137
    bearing and rearing children, 69
    Christian in disadvantageous
      demographic position, 193
    forced into one extreme role or the
      other, 137
    as fount of all purity (Victorian
      period), 137
    ideal body shape and manner of,
      140
    imbalance of power, 42
    intent on security, 86
    intimacy with own mothers,
      children, and friends, 89
    in Jesus' times, 69
    Jesus treating as persons, 26
    kept uneducated, 18
    needing to be protected, 52
    principal calling to obey God, 72
    rules for, 40–41
    sex drive compared to males, 83
    subordination to men, 13
Women's Christian Temperance
    Movement, 20
women's movement, 20, 157
words, power of, 123
words of affirmation, 108
World Vision, founder of, 75

Worldwide Evangelisation Crusade, 76

Yeats, 147
yielders, 169, 170
yokemates, to soulmates, 117–20
Young, William Paul, 113n3
young adult stage, tension of, 119
younger the age at marriage, higher
    the statistical probability of
    divorce, 182

zero-sum conflict, 162
Zondervan (publisher), misgivings
    about, 130n63

Lightning Source UK Ltd.
Milton Keynes UK
UKOW02f1421041216
289079UK00002B/146/P